THE CAMBRIDGE COMPA

NOZICK'S ANA~~~~~~, ~~~~~~, AND UTOPIA

Robert Nozick's *Anarchy, State, and Utopia* (1974) is recognized as a classic of modern political philosophy. Along with John Rawls's *A Theory of Justice* (1971), it is widely credited with breathing new life into the discipline in the second half of the twentieth century. This *Companion* presents a balanced and comprehensive assessment of Nozick's contribution to political philosophy. In engaging and accessible chapters, the contributors analyze Nozick's ideas from a variety of perspectives and explore relatively neglected areas of the work such as his discussion of anarchism and his theory of utopia. Their detailed and illuminating picture of *Anarchy, State, and Utopia*, its impact and its enduring influence will be invaluable to students and scholars in both political philosophy and political theory.

RALF M. BADER is a Bersoff Assistant Professor and Faculty Fellow in the Philosophy Department at New York University. He is the author of *Robert Nozick* (2010).

JOHN MEADOWCROFT is Lecturer in Public Policy in the Department of Political Economy, King's College London. He is the author of *The Ethics of the Market* (2005), *James M. Buchanan* (2011), and (with Mark Pennington) *Rescuing Social Capital from Social Democracy* (2007).

Continued at the back of the book

The Cambridge Companion to

NOZICK'S
ANARCHY,
STATE, AND
UTOPIA

Edited by

Ralf M. Bader
New York University

and

John Meadowcroft
King's College London

CAMBRIDGE
UNIVERSITY PRESS

University Printing House, Cambridge CB2 8BS, United Kingdom

Published in the United States of America by Cambridge University Press, New York

Cambridge University Press is part of the University of Cambridge.

It furthers the University's mission by disseminating knowledge in the pursuit of education, learning and research at the highest international levels of excellence.

www.cambridge.org
Information on this title: www.cambridge.org/9780521197762

First published 2011
3rd printing 2013

Printed in the United Kingdom by Clays, St Ives plc.

A catalogue record for this publication is available from the British Library

Library of Congress Cataloguing in Publication data
The Cambridge companion to Nozick's *Anarchy, state, and utopia* /
    [edited by] Ralf M. Bader, John Meadowcroft.
    p.   cm. – (Cambridge companions to philosophy)
    Includes bibliographical references and index.
    ISBN 978-0-521-19776-2 (hardback) – ISBN 978-0-521-12002-9
    (paperback)
    1. Nozick, Robert. Anarchy, state, and utopia.   2. Nozick,
    Robert–Political and social views.   3. State, The.   4. Anarchism.
    5. Utopias.   6. Political science–Philosophy.   I. Bader, Ralf M.
    II. Meadowcroft, John, 1971–   III. Title.   IV. Series.
    JC571.N683C36 2011
    320.101–dc23
    2011019268

ISBN 978-0-521-19776-2 Hardback
ISBN 978-0-521-12002-9 Paperback

CONTENTS

CONTRIBUTORS

RICHARD J. ARNESON is Distinguished Professor of Philosophy at the University of California at San Diego, where he has taught since 1973, and a Co-director of the Institute for Law and Philosophy at the School of Law, University of San Diego. He has been visiting professor at the University of California, Davis and at Yale University, as well as a visiting fellow at the Research School of Social Science, Australian National University. He has published widely in ethics and political philosophy.

RALF M. BADER is a Bersoff Assistant Professor/Faculty Fellow in the Department of Philosophy at New York University. His research focuses on contemporary metaphysics and Kant scholarship, as well as on moral and political philosophy. He is the author of *Robert Nozick* (2010).

FRED FELDMAN is Professor of Philosophy at the University of Massachusetts at Amherst, where he has been teaching since 1969. He is the author of numerous books, including *Doing the Best We Can* (1986), *Confrontations with the Reaper* (1992), *Utilitarianism, Hedonism, and Desert* (Cambridge University Press, 1997), *Pleasure and the Good Life* (2004), and *What Is This Thing Called Happiness?* (2010).

BARBARA FRIED is the William W. and Gertrude H. Saunders Professor of Law at Stanford Law School. She has written extensively on questions of distributive justice, in the areas of tax policy, property theory, and political theory. She is the author of an

ix

intellectual history of the progressive era law and economics, entitled *The Progressive Assault on Laissez-Faire: Robert Hale and the First Law and Economics Movement* (1998).

GERALD GAUS is the James E. Rogers Professor of Philosophy at the University of Arizona. He is the author of *On Philosophy, Politics and Economics* (2008), *Contemporary Theories of Liberalism: Public Reason as a Post-Enlightenment Project* (2003), and *Justificatory Liberalism: an Essay on Epistemology and Political Theory* (1996), among other books. His book *The Order of Public Reason* has been published by Cambridge University Press. He is co-editor of *Politics, Philosophy, and Economics*.

CHANDRAN KUKATHAS is Chair in Political Theory in the Department of Government at the London School of Economics. Influential contributions include his books *The Liberal Archipelago: A Theory of Diversity and Freedom* (2003), *Rawls: A Theory of Justice and Its Critics* (with Philip Pettit, 1990) and *Hayek and Modern Liberalism* (1989) and his articles on the concepts of cultural rights, multiculturalism, and diversity. Kukathas has visited and lectured at many academic institutions across the world and in 2003 was awarded the Centenary Medal for services to Australian society through the study of social and political theory.

ERIC MACK is Professor of Philosophy at Tulane University, where he is also a member of the faculty of the Murphy Institute of Political Economy. He has been a Visiting Fellow in Political Philosophy at Harvard University and a Visiting Research Scholar at the Social Philosophy and Policy Center at Bowling Green State University. He specializes in social and political philosophy, ethics, and the philosophy of law. He is the author of *John Locke* (2009).

JOHN MEADOWCROFT is Lecturer in Public Policy in the Department of Political Economy at King's College London. He is the author of *The Ethics of the Market* (2005) and *James M. Buchanan* (2011), and co-author of *Rescuing Social Capital from Social Democracy* (2007). Since 2004 he has been a deputy editor and book review editor of the journal *Economic Affairs*. He is also series editor of the *Major Conservative and Libertarian Thinkers* series, published from 2009 to 2011.

MICHAEL OTSUKA is Professor of Philosophy at University College London. Before moving to London, Otsuka taught at UCLA and the University of Colorado. He is the author of *Libertarianism without Inequality* (2003) and has published widely on equality, left-libertarianism, and the morality of harming and saving from harm.

DAVID SCHMIDTZ is Kendrick Professor of Philosophy and joint Professor of Economics at the University of Arizona. He is author of *The Limits of Government* (1991), *Rational Choice and Moral Agency* (1995), *Elements of Justice* (Cambridge University Press, 2006), *Person, Polis, Planet* (2008), co-author of *Social Welfare and Individual Responsibility* (Cambridge University Press, 1998), and *A Brief History of Liberty* (2010), and editor of a volume on Robert Nozick, as well as co-editor of *Environmental Ethics: What Really Matters, What Really Works*.

PETER VALLENTYNE is Florence G. Kline Chair in Philosophy at the University of Missouri. He is editor of *Contractarianism and Rational Choice* (Cambridge University Press, 1991) and of a six-volume series on *Equality and Justice* (2003), as well as co-editor of *Left-Libertarianism and its Critics* (2000) and *The Origins of Left-Libertarianism* (2000). His research focuses on the role of liberty, security, equality, and prosperity in the theory of justice, as well as on libertarianism, egalitarianism, and consequentialism.

NOTE ON CITATION

Unless otherwise indicated, all citations refer to Robert Nozick's *Anarchy, State, and Utopia* (New York, 1974).

Introduction

Robert Nozick's *Anarchy, State, and Utopia* (1974) is recognized as a classic of modern political philosophy. In tandem with John Rawls's *A Theory of Justice* (1971), it is widely credited with breathing new life into political philosophy in the second half of the twentieth century. It effectively moved libertarianism from a relatively unimportant subset of political philosophy to the center of the discipline.

Anarchy, State, and Utopia (*ASU*) was written whilst Nozick was a fellow at the Center for the Advanced Study in Behavioral Sciences in Stanford during the academic year of 1971–1972. It constitutes the combination of three separate projects that Nozick was working on at that time. Part I is based on a talk concerned with how a state would arise out of the state of nature that Nozick presented to a student group at Stanford, whilst also incorporating some of the ideas developed in his 1971 paper "On the Randian Argument." Part II primarily results from his engagement with John Rawls's theory of justice, which led to the formulation of the entitlement theory of justice, much of which Nozick developed whilst co-teaching a course on capitalism and socialism at Harvard with Michael Walzer. Part III, in turn, derives from Nozick's contribution to a panel on utopia at a meeting of the American Philosophical Association. Although Nozick initially wanted to work on the problem of free will whilst at Stanford, he instead ended up combining these three projects, yielding *ASU*.

ASU almost instantly received acclaim and fame, winning the National Book Award in 1975. Whilst well respected, widely praised and much discussed, the theory Nozick propounds therein is almost universally rejected, even by those who agree with many of his substantive conclusions. Most discussions are of a critical nature, trying to respond to Nozick's objections to end-state and patterned conceptions of justice, in particular his famous Wilt Chamberlain argument, rather than attempts to develop further and defend the project outlined by Nozick. In addition, there are a number of examples, arguments, and discussions put forward by Nozick in *ASU* that have had a significant impact on philosophy that are separable from Nozick's primary concern of providing a case for the minimal state, most notably Nozick's discussion of the experience machine, which has generated a vast secondary literature on its own.

Nozick never returned to political philosophy in a systematic manner. With the exception of brief and occasional discussions in *Philosophical Explanations* as well as in *The Examined Life*, Nozick almost exclusively focused his attention on other philosophical problems. Rather than trying to defend and develop further the ideas set out in *ASU*, he wanted to tackle new problems and engage with different questions. As he famously said: "I did not want to spend my life writing 'The Son of Anarchy, State, and Utopia,' 'The Return of the Son of ...,' etc. I had other philosophical questions to think about" (Nozick: 1997, p. 2). Whilst not returning to these issues, he nonetheless made a number of remarks that have been taken to indicate a rejection of the theory propounded in *ASU*. Most notably, in *The Examined Life* Nozick said: "The libertarian position I once propounded now seems to me seriously inadequate, in part because it did not fully knit the humane considerations and joint cooperative activities it left room for more closely into its fabric. It neglected the symbolic importance of an official political concern with issues or problems" (Nozick: 1989, pp. 286–287). Although he became critical of certain aspects of his earlier theory, he retained most of his libertarian commitments as is evidenced by his discussion in *Invariances* (2001) and as he explicitly stated in an interview towards the end of his life: "What I was really saying in *The Examined Life* was that I was no longer as hardcore a libertarian as I had been before. But the rumors of my deviation (or apostasy!) from libertarianism were much exaggerated. I think [*Invariances*] makes clear the extent to which I still am within the general framework of libertarianism, especially the ethics chapter and its section on the 'Core Principle of Ethics'."

Thirty-five years after the original publication of the book, it is an opportune time to step back and re-evaluate the content of *ASU* as well as examine the way in which it has helped to shape political philosophy up to the present day. Such a re-evaluation allows, in particular, an assessment of those aspects of Nozick's work that have been relatively neglected as well as an examination of the extent to which a unified and coherent theory is to be found in *ASU*. The former is particularly important given the extent to which the secondary literature is skewed toward the critique of Rawls and egalitarian theories of justice contained in the second part of the book, whilst largely ignoring the fascinating discussions of anarchism and utopia to be found in the first and third part, respectively. The latter is pressing, given that most commentators focus on particular parts of the book and treat it primarily as a "neat" critique of Rawls's theory of justice, rather than considering it as a whole. Moreover, given that the book resulted from the combination of three projects Nozick happened to be working on, rather than from the systematic development of a single research project, there is a suspicion that the book is an assemblage of disparate, though connected, projects, rather than a unified account that is derived from a well-defined starting-point.

This collection makes good these lacunae by providing a comprehensive treatment of the whole of Nozick's work, allowing for a re-engagement with Nozick's work and encouraging greater focus on *ASU* in its entirety. The essays are organized around four parts: (1) Nozick's moral framework; (2) his critique of anarchism; (3) the entitlement theory and the critique of patterned as well as end-state accounts of justice; and (4) the framework for utopia.

MORALITY

In Chapter 1 Richard J. Arneson examines Nozick's argument for the existence of absolute side constraints. Nozick suggests that a commitment to absolute side constraints follows from the rejection of a "utilitarianism of rights" and then argues that Lockean libertarian rights provide the most plausible basis for the content of these constraints. Arneson rejects the claim that there are absolute side constraints. The existence of absolute side constraints is equated with complete self-ownership, which Arneson argues to be problematic since it precludes enforceable positive duties to others, as well as enforceable duties to oneself. Rather than adopting absolute side constraints, Arneson argues that Nozick's arguments at best support a moderate view. In particular, he claims that it is possible to develop a hybrid theory that includes both end-state and side-constraint considerations without ending up with absolute constraints. According to Arneson, this can be done by incorporating principles that govern the ways in which the end-state and side-constraint components of the theory interact as well as the ways in which they can be weighed up against each other. Arneson concludes that Nozick has failed to develop a convincing argument for his claim that the fundamental enforceable moral requirements binding all of us consist entirely of side constraints with the content of Lockean libertarian rights.

Michael Otsuka's contribution (Chapter 2) also focuses on Nozick's theory of side constraints that prohibit the sacrifice of one person for the benefit of others. Otsuka focuses on "the irrationality objection" to such constraints: that if what matters is the avoidance of constraint violation, then this should rationally lead to an argument for the minimization of constraint violation, but this would seem to be prohibited within Nozick's theory by his rejection of a "utilitarianism of rights." In other words, the prohibition of the violation of any individual's libertarian right of self-ownership would seem to permit even greater harms to take place, such as if the lives of five people in the path of a falling boulder could be saved if a sixth person were pushed in front of it, thus changing its direction. Otsuka argues that Nozick fails to provide a basis for believing that side constraints are rational in the face of the claim that they would not necessarily minimize constraint violation. In particular, Otsuka examines whether the rationality of side constraints can be defended by recasting them within complex goal-directed structures. He considers agent-relative rather than agent-neutral goals, as well as temporally specific agent-relative goals rather than temporally neutral agent-relative goals. While the former account faces straightforward counter-examples, the latter proposal is implausible and unmotivated since it relies on drawing morally arbitrary distinctions. Otsuka then argues that providing a moral status rationale for constraints is much more promising than attempting to recast side constraints within a goal-directed structure. The idea underlying the moral status rationale is that persons have an elevated moral status that ensures that they ought not be treated merely as means. Otsuka points out that merely appealing to the distinctness of persons is not sufficient for establishing constraints, as can be seen from the fact that the distinctness of animals does not generate analogous constraints. Nozick attempts to bridge this gap by connecting side constraints to the notion of a meaningful life. Yet this connection cannot be based on the idea that the possibility of leading a meaningful life is to be promoted since one would then not end up with constraints. Instead, the connection is to be based on the idea that the possibility of leading such a life is to be respected. This strategy, however, is subject to the problem that the increased inviolability of a being leads to a reduction in saveability, by which Otsuka means that fewer things can be done to beings of the same type to save it.

In the third chapter Fred Feldman provides a detailed examination of Nozick's famous thought experiment involving an experience machine that would enable a person to experience anything that one wished – the experiences would not be real, but they would seem real to the person attached to the machine. Feldman identifies four different targets which the experience machine example might be thought to be an attempt to undermine (1) utilitarianism, (2) ethical hedonism, (3) mental state theories of welfare, and (4) psychological hedonism. Each of these interpretations is rejected on the grounds that no persuasive argument can be devised to establish the falsity of any of these possible target theories on the basis of the claim that a person would not choose a life in the experience machine. Moreover, all of these interpretations lack adequate textual support. In particular, Feldman argues that drawing conclusions from the thought experiment is problematic since this either relies on problematic claims about how what we would choose is connected to what really has value or needs to appeal to problematic idealizations. For instance, from the fact that someone would not choose to plug into an experience machine, it does not follow that life in the experience machine is less valuable than living a normal life. This would only follow if the person were rational, welfare selfish, and "axiologically insightful," yet whether such a person would plug in is something that can be doubted by a hedonist. In an appendix Feldman mentions a fifth alternative interpretation, according to which the experience machine is concerned with what has intrinsic value, the idea being that this thought experiment is meant to make us reflect on whether we consider experiences to be the only features of our lives that have intrinsic value or whether there are other things that matter as well. Feldman claims that this interpretation, whilst interesting, is at best suggested by what Nozick says but lacks solid textual support.

ANARCHY

In Chapter 4 Eric Mack provides a critique of Nozick's response to the challenge put forward by the individualist anarchist who would deny Nozick's claim to have shown in Part 1 of *ASU* that a state can come into being without infringing anyone's rights. After pointing out that Nozick is not warranted in inferring the existence of procedural rights from the wrongness of using risky procedures, he goes on to argue that the defense of the minimal state on the grounds provided by Nozick is unstable. This is because the principle of compensation to which Nozick appeals leads to an attenuation of rights. In particular, the compensation principle has the effect that (in the absence of special conditions) a right amounts to nothing more than a claim to receive due compensation for transgressing the boundary defined by the right. Mack then appeals to this attenuation of rights to put forward an extrapolated response to the anarchist. This extrapolated response is based on the idea that protective services are not standard marketable goods that can be provided by voluntary mechanisms but are special insofar as they are public goods that would not be provided or would be under-funded due to widespread attempts at free-riding resulting from their non-excludable nature. This forms the basis for an argument in favor of the mandatory purchasing of protection services, leading to a minimal taxing state. Yet, the attenuation of rights, which represents a shift from rights as claims protected by property rules to being merely protected by liability rules, would undermine principled anti-paternalism. This is because it would justify not only the mandatory purchasing of protection services but also justify taxation for the provision of other public goods, leading to the mutual advantage state. Mack then provides a response to the anarchist that only allows some forced exchanges, namely those that protect people from rights violations more extensive than the rights violations involved in the forced exchanges. This response leads to the minimal taxing state but does not end up with the mutual advantage state.

In his chapter Gerald Gaus focuses on the role of invisible-hand theorizing and the project of explanatory political philosophy that Nozick pursues in his attempt to show that a minimal state can arise without violating any rights. He examines what role such explanations can play by assessing what Nozick's argument would have established had it been successful. Gaus argues that invisible-hand accounts provide particularly informative explanations of emergent properties via filtering and equilibrium processes. This explains how invisible-hand accounts can be important for explaining how certain systems or features are maintained and preserved even if they did not arise via the processes identified by the account. Gaus points out that the invisible-hand account that Nozick develops to respond to the anarchist's challenge attempts to provide a justification of the state by incorporating moral filters into the processes giving rise to the emergent property, thereby ensuring that the resulting state arises without there being intentional rights violations. This then suggests that the state is not intrinsically immoral. Gaus argues further that ultra-minimal states are morally justified in using coercion to enforce compliance with laws, showing that "a legitimate political order is an emergent property for all populations of Lockeans," thereby answering the question what the properties of a just state are. Moreover, it not only shows that such states are morally legitimate but also that they are justified insofar as everyone will be better off than in the state of nature in terms of having rights to life, liberty, and property protected.

JUSTICE

Peter Vallentyne (Chapter 6) examines Nozick's libertarian theory of justice. He argues that, according to Nozick, justice is concerned with respecting rights, which is understood as not infringing or violating duties owed to individuals. While Nozick seems to reject the claim that rights are necessarily enforceable, it seems that justice is restricted to respecting enforceable rights, whereby Nozick is appealing to a near-absolute choice-protecting conception of rights grounded in the capacity for autonomous choice. These rights in particular take the form of an entitlement theory specified

in terms of principles of justice in acquisition, transfer, and rectification. Vallentyne supplements the account by adding principles
regarding prevention of injustice as well as principles regarding initial rights, in particular self-ownership rights. He then argues that
Nozick's famous Wilt Chamberlain example is ineffectual against
weak patterns as well as against starting-gate theories that specify a
patterned initial distribution but that appeal to a procedural understanding of the transfer principles. Moreover, he argues that the Wilt
Chamberlain example presupposes absolute rights, an implausible
commitment that can be avoided by combining a purely procedural
theory of justice with property rights that have limited content.

In Chapter 7 John Meadowcroft explores and evaluates Nozick's
critique of Rawls. The importance attached to *ASU* in contemporary
political philosophy owes a great deal to the relationship between
ASU and John Rawls's *A Theory of Justice*. These two books are
often said to have framed the contemporary debate about the nature
of justice by representing the two fundamental opposing views of
what constitutes justice in the distribution of income and wealth.
In *ASU* Nozick pays generous tribute to the brilliance of Rawls's
philosophical construction, but he also sets out a fierce critique of
Rawls's work. Meadowcroft shows that at the center of this critique
is the entitlement theory of justice, which Nozick proposes as an
alternative conception of justice to that advocated by Rawls. The
success or otherwise of Nozick's critique of Rawls is highly contested. Meadowcroft argues that Nozick's critique of Rawls is more
telling than is commonly assumed: Nozick successfully shows that
the concept of entitlement must play some part in any theory of
justice, that the maintenance of any preferred pattern of distribution must involve continuous interference in people's lives that will
violate their rights, and that Rawls's theory of justice is an artifact
of the assumptions built into his philosophical construction of the
original position.

David Schmidtz's contribution focuses on Part II of *ASU*, examining Nozick's account of justice and its relation to Rawls's theory.
Schmidtz emphasizes that Nozick's critique of patterns, in particular the Wilt Chamberlain example, applies only to strong patterns
and that it is possible to devise weak patterns that are sensitive to
both history as well as to patterns and that are compatible with liberty and do not require constant interference with everyday life. He

then focuses on Nozick's entitlement theory, discussing the principles of acquisition, transfer, and rectification. Schmidtz points out that while appropriation diminishes the stock of what can be originally appropriated, it need not reduce the stock of what can be owned but on the contrary generally leads to the creation of vast amounts of resources. Moreover, he notes that the key component of Nozick's theory is the idea that a thoroughly voluntary transfer is a thoroughly just transfer, and that while many past injustices cannot be rectified, conforming to the voluntariness standard ensures at the least that no new injustices are introduced. Finally, he considers the issue of luck or moral arbitrariness, distinguishing between a benign version to be identified with randomness and a problematic version amounting to capriciousness, noting that the natural lottery belongs to the benign variety.

In Chapter 9 Barbara Fried argues that no coherent theory of property rights is to be found in *ASU*. While Part I is broadly utilitarian in that property rights are protected by liability rules and thus are to be understood in welfarist terms, Part II contains a Lockean libertarian understanding of property rights that considers them as being protected by property rules. Finally, Part III only imposes minimal constraints that do not go beyond ensuring that a minimal possibility of exit be preserved, insofar as opting out must be possible at the national level even though it need not be possible at the local level despite the fact that there is a limited range of communities and that there might not be any community catering to a particular person's preferences. Fried argues that Nozick's failure to come up with a coherent theory is symptomatic of a set of general problems that deontologists and rights theorists face when it comes to applying abstract rules or rights. While they can deal with clear cases in a straightforward manner, they quickly run into trouble when more complicated cases are considered, in particular cases involving risk. In order to provide a plausible account of cases involving risk, they need to appeal to other principles, in particular to welfarist principles, thereby undermining the project that they set out to pursue. For instance, dealing with the risky enforcement procedures of independents requires Nozick to downgrade the right to self-defense from being protected by a property rule to being protected by a liability rule, thereby allowing the dominant protection agency to prohibit risky activities as long as adequate compensation is provided. Once Nozick extends this reasoning to all cases of risky actions in which it would be too costly to obtain consent as well as to cases in which the transactions costs involved in getting prior agreement are higher than the costs of the compensation system, he ends up with an account that is strongly utilitarian or welfarist in character.

UTOPIA

Ralf M. Bader (Chapter 10) provides an analysis of Nozick's possible-worlds model of utopia. He identifies and examines critically the following three arguments in favor of the minimal state: (1) the minimal state is the real-world analogue of the possible-worlds model and can hence be considered to be inspiring; (2) the minimal state is the common ground of all possible utopian conceptions and can hence be universally endorsed; and (3) the minimal state is the best or at least a very good means for approximating or achieving utopia. Each of these arguments is found to be problematic and unable to yield the conclusions that Nozick intended to establish. Nonetheless, Bader argues that interesting results can be established on the basis of these utopian considerations, in particular the result that the minimal state is the maximal institutional structure that is in principle compatible with the complete satisfaction of the maximal non-arbitrary set of preferences that are in principle co-satisfiable, as well as the corollary that in utopia any state will exert at most the functions of a minimal state.

In the final chapter of the collection Chandran Kukathas provides a critique of Nozick's argument that the minimal state is a framework for utopia. In particular, he criticizes the argument that the minimal state functions as a filter device that allows us or helps us to identify and realize utopia. Nozick claims that the vast complexity of life implies that we cannot design utopia but instead have to rely on filter devices and that the framework serves as such a filter that eliminates inappropriate alternatives, insofar as it allows there to be many different communities, some of which will flourish while others will be modified or abandoned. Kukathas questions what role the minimal state plays in this process of trial and error, of experimenting and imitating, pointing out that such a process could take place without a state in an anarchical situation. Moreover, he argues that the state constrains rather than enables the pursuit of utopian visions. Utopia consists of many utopias, of a vast array of diverse communities, yet the nature of the state consists in getting the many to live as one and thereby essentially restricts the pursuit of utopian aspirations. The state imposes standards that essentially limit the ways in which people can pursue their ends. This means that the state is the problem and not the solution and that utopia can only be achieved outside the state.

The contributions to this collection considered as a whole thus suggest that Nozick's main legacy consists in a large number of insightful suggestions, ideas, and arguments, as well as a range of powerful criticisms of alternative views. While these ideas and arguments broadly cohere and characterize an identifiable libertarian project and world view, no complete unified theory emerges from the text. The significant effect on shaping political philosophy over the course of the last thirty-five years is thus to be explained primarily in terms of the way in which *ASU* has challenged mainstream conceptions of justice, in particular by means of the Wilt Chamberlain example, while much of its continuing appeal is due to Nozick's vivid examples and insightful suggestions as well as his playful rhetoric and engaging tone. In many respects, *ASU* is a book that raises more questions than it answers, a book that primarily challenges other accounts rather than providing a complete theory of its own. Nonetheless, it provides the outlines and general structure of a distinctive libertarian political philosophy that is based on rights considered as side constraints and has at its core an entitlement theory of justice. No one can fail to benefit from reading *ASU*, even though no one will come away from it with a fully worked out political philosophy. In short, it identifies a project rather than completes it. As Nozick said in *ASU*: "There is room for words on subjects other than last words" (p. xii).

Part I Morality

1 Side constraints, Lockean individual rights, and the moral basis of libertarianism

The brilliant discussion in Chapter 3 of Robert Nozick's *Anarchy, State, and Utopia* (*ASU*) is vitiated by an illicit slide between "some" and "all" or, better, between "to some extent" and "entirely." In this chapter Nozick discusses the moral theory background to his Lockean libertarian doctrine of individual moral rights. He seeks to show that structural features of the account of moral requirements and permissions that most of us accept turn out to be reasons also to accept the more controversial Lockean libertarianism.[1]

The brilliant part of the discussion describes the structure of a non-consequentialist deontological moral theory that denies that each person ought always to do whatever would produce the impartially best outcome, even if the idea of the best outcome is interpreted as the greatest overall fulfillment of individual moral rights ranked by their moral importance. In this connection Nozick introduces the idea of a "side constraint" and of a morality that consists of side constraints, in whole or in part. This discussion advances our understanding of moral theory. We are all in Nozick's debt for this advance even if at the end of the day the case for accepting a consequentialist theory proves compelling.[2]

Here is the confusion. Nozick tends to suppose that if there are constraints on what we may do, these constraints may never legitimately be overridden. From the fact that there are some side constraints that limit the permissible uses of a person to advance one's goals it does not follow that any such side constraint is absolute, exceptionless, and may never be overridden by any other moral considerations come what may. Nozick does not completely ignore this possibility but repeatedly he writes as though a consideration he adduces that at most provides some support for the claim that "there are constraints" also fully justifies the claim that "there are absolute constraints." Partly because the moderate position on rights and side constraints is shunted to the side in his discussion, and not confronted, what he says puts no pressure whatsoever on someone inclined to a moderate side-constraint view to shift to the more radical side-constraint absolutism.

This confusion is linked to another. This comes out clearly when Nozick observes: "Side constraints upon action reflect the underlying Kantian principle that individuals are ends and not merely means; they may not be sacrificed or used for the achieving of other ends without their consent" (pp. 30–31). However, the idea that an individual is not to be treated merely as a means is most plausibly read as the thought that an individual ought to be treated only according to principles which she has good and sufficient reason to accept. The Kantian thought is that we should respect the rational agency capacity in all individuals and this requires acting toward them in ways, and only in ways, to which as fully rational agents they would consent. The difference between treating hypothetical rational consent and actual consent as a strict moral constraint on how one ought to treat others is momentous. Nozick just assumes that given a background in which people are not interacting and none is harming anyone in ways that count as libertarian rights violations, forcing someone to act as one wills (who has not consented to be so treated) is immediately and obviously morally wrong. But once one has in mind the possibility that my refusal actually to consent to what you propose may reflect grotesque stupidity on my part or my horrible failure to show due consideration for myself or for other persons or both things together, Nozick's assumption looks to be flatly wrong.

1.1 A NON-CONSEQUENTIALIST MORALITY OF SIDE CONSTRAINTS AND OPTIONS

The insightful part of Nozick's discussion nowadays sounds boringly familiar. This impression is testimony to how thoroughly his analytical points have become accepted knowledge. Others had surveyed this same conceptual territory, but Nozick's treatment adds clarity. He notes that our common-sense morality has a non-consequentialist structure, the core of which is that one is not permitted always to do whatever would produce the impartially calculated best outcome, even if the idea of the best outcome is interpreted as the greatest overall fulfillment of individual moral rights ranked by their importance. This latter interpretation would be suitable if moral rights were correctly understood just as claims that society ought to ensure are honored. However, this is not our ordinary common-sense understanding of individual moral rights. A right is an agent-relative side constraint on action and not a goal to be promoted. A side constraint is to be interpreted as follows: in deciding which of the available options for action one should pursue at any given time, one should eliminate from consideration those options that would involve one's violating any individual's moral rights. One then is morally at liberty to choose any of the remaining options and act in that way, whether or not doing so would lead to the best outcome one could achieve, according to the appropriate standard of outcome assessment. For example, if an individual has the right not to be assaulted, then in deciding what to do one should eliminate from consideration any action options available for choice that would involve one's assaulting that individual. As Nozick puts it, the imperative of rights tells each of us "Don't [you] violate anyone's rights!" not "Act in such a way that rights fulfillment overall is maximized!" In another terminology, individual moral rights and any other moral side constraints there are issue in agent-relative reasons – meaning that any adequate indication of the reason will contain an ineliminable reference to the agent.[3]

A side-constraint view might be conjoined to a moral doctrine that requires people to promote good outcomes. The duty to promote good outcomes might compete with side constraints and sometimes override them. The duty might also be subordinated to side constraints, so that the duty to promote the good never requires one to violate any side constraint. In accepting the duty to promote the good, either in partnership with side constraints or in subordination to them, we might also accept that the duty to promote the good is qualified by a personal prerogative that allows one to pursue one's own favored aims, to some extent, even when forgoing this personal pursuit would enable one better to promote the impartial good. Nozick takes a simple and in a way elegant line here. He affirms no binding moral requirement of any sort to promote what is good by one's actions. One might commit oneself by making a contract or promise or the equivalent to another person, and then the other person has a right that one carry through this commitment. Apart from these commitments that always stem from voluntary undertakings, according to Nozick one is morally free always to choose any act available for choice that is not ruled out as ineligible by conflict with an applicable side constraint. In one's conduct one must conform to the side constraints that bear on one's choice; beyond that, all available acts are morally open for choice. They are moral options.[4]

Nozick continues his discussion in Chapter 3 of *ASU* with a characteristically virtuoso wide-ranging performance. In a short space he raises a host of issues that arise in considering a morality of side constraints and options, including what we owe to animals, what characteristics a being must have to qualify as a person with all the rights that go with that status, and so on. His discussion also contains brilliant asides that so far as I can see have no bearing at all on the issues under discussion. Of these, the most well known is his short, trenchant discussion of the question, whether anything matters or should matter to us beyond the quality of experience we have.

1.2 FROM SIDE CONSTRAINTS TO LIBERTARIAN RIGHTS

Facing this cornucopia of achievements to praise in the chapter, one is disappointed to find that the main line of argument from the side-constraint idea to the more controversial Lockean libertarian doctrine is pretty meager.[5] It is odd to find such poverty alongside such wealth. The objections I develop in this essay barely need stating; they virtually leap at the reader from Nozick's text.

For our purposes the claim that the content of morality consists in a set of Lockean libertarian individual moral rights may be interpreted as follows.

1. Each person has a moral right to act in whatever way she chooses with whatever she legitimately owns so long as she does not thereby impinge on others so as to cause them harm or frustrate some interest of theirs in certain specified ways (force, fraud, theft, physically harming another person or her property, breach of contract, or threatening to do any of the previously mentioned items on this list).

2. Each person has a right that others not act in ways that impinge on her in any of these certain specified ways.

3. Each person legitimately fully owns herself. No one has any initial property rights in any other person.

4. Each person can acquire full ownership over unowned material resources (pieces of the Earth) by staking out a claim to them, so long as her claiming ownership and maintaining ownership leaves others no worse off than they would have been under a system under which these resources remain unowned and freely available for use by anyone.

5. The ownership rights that individuals have over themselves and acquire over material resources can be transferred to other persons in whole or in part by gift or contract (or abandoned so they revert to unowned status).

That fundamental individual moral rights have the particular content Nozick assigns to them is one controversial feature of this doctrine. A more general controversial feature is that the fundamental moral rights of individuals are all of them negative rights not to be harmed or aggressed upon in certain ways and none of them positive rights to be aided by others in any way. A related controversial feature is that the fundamental moral requirements that limit what any individual may permissibly do are all side constraints or limits as opposed to moral goals to be promoted. Still another controversial feature is that these side constraints are absolute and exceptionless. They are rules that admit of no exceptions and must always be followed and are never overridden by any other moral considerations that bear on the choice of action.

The claim that it is controversial that a proposed set of moral rights holds absolutely and without exception is not crystal clear. Exceptions to a rule could be incorporated into the rule, and the question then arises, is the revised rule exceptionless? If not, reiterate the process. One might think that in principle, some exceptionless rule always underlies any rule allowing exceptions, even if we lack epistemic access to it. Even if the legitimate exceptions are uncodifiable, one might suppose one can amend the rule by adding that it holds unless certain specified factors, in particular circumstances, generate reasons that outweigh it. A set of side constraints may not be composable: respecting one constraint in some circumstances might require violating another constraint. So a complete statement of the side-constraint morality includes priority rules specifying which side constraints trump others in the various possible circumstances in which they can conflict. At any rate, it is plausible to hold that at the fundamental level, the correct moral principles must hold universally and necessarily. So if the project is to conceive fundamental principles as assertions of individual rights, why is it controversial to claim these moral rights hold without exception and are not overrideable?

The problem is that negative rights not to be harmed or interfered with in certain ways as Nozick conceives of them are to hold come what may, whatever the consequences of abiding by them in any possible circumstances. For any Nozickian right of this sort, the consequences of conformity to this rule can be bad, sometimes extremely bad, and quite possibly horrendously bad. Nozick is adamant that side constraints in the form of Lockean rights do not incorporate any relaxation of their requirements on conduct in view of the consequences that respecting them would generate. In a wily footnote, Nozick acknowledges a difficulty lying in wait: "The question of whether these side constraints are absolute, or whether they may be violated in order to avoid catastrophic moral horror, and if the latter, what the resulting structure might look like, is one I hope largely to avoid" (p. 30 fn.). Many adherents of non-consequentialist morality would contend that the problem arises in non-catastrophic scenarios. They hold that individuals have rights, but any such right gives way when the consequences of not violating it are excessively bad.

1.3 THE DENIAL OF INTERPERSONAL COMPARISONS OF GOOD

Nozick presents several arguments and hints of arguments in support of the general idea that morality has a side-constraint structure and the more specific claim that this side-constraint morality consists in a set of individual moral rights with a Lockean libertarian shape. One argument appeals to doubts about whether the idea of summing gains and losses across persons to determine the overall social benefit from alternative actions and policies is even coherent, let alone plausible. Nozick asks: "But why may one not violate persons for the greater social good?" He notes that we do not regard it as morally problematic if a person balances costs and benefits within her own life, accepting a smaller loss now to avoid a larger loss later. Nozick continues:

Why not, *similarly*, hold that some persons have to bear costs that benefit other persons more, for the sake of the overall social good? But there is no *social entity* with a good that undergoes some sacrifice for its own good. There are only individual people, different individual people, with their own individual lives. Using one of these people for the benefit of others, uses him and benefits the others. Nothing more. (pp. 32–33)

Of course, one who supposes it makes sense to sum benefits and losses across persons need not hold that there is some collective entity that benefits when overall benefits are increased. The claim is just that, for example, when violating Smith's right to his extra shirt button brings it about that Smith suffers slight inconvenience and Jones and Black are cured of dread diseases and enabled to enjoy many extra years of good life, the wellbeing loss that accrues to Smith is far less than the wellbeing gains that Jones and Black gain.

This leaves it open for Nozick to deny that interpersonal comparisons of wellbeing are well-defined even if there are examples in which aggregation of wellbeing gains and losses across persons appears intuitively plausible. Common-sense intuitions in this matter might be wrong. Notice that Nozick's opponent need not insist on full comparability – a scale of wellbeing that enables one to determine, for any combinations of gains and losses of any types of goods and bads across any number of people, that it is always metaphysically determinate or epistemically determinable what exact wellbeing total would result. Partial comparability, in this context, will do. Nozick is claiming that side constraints may never be overridden on the ground that doing so would produce sufficiently greater overall good to justify the override, because greater overall good can never be determined. This claim falls to the ground if sometimes, it can be determined that violating a side constraint would bring about a sufficiently large boost in overall wellbeing (or avoidance of loss) to justify the violation.

Defenders of Nozick's position could dig in their heels and deny that one can make any sense of the idea of interpersonal comparisons of wellbeing. This strategy is possible, but carries costs. The premises to which one must appeal to justify skepticism about the coherence of commensurability of the good might also tend to undermine the side-constraint advocate's non-skepticism about the existence, nature, and justification of individual rights and other moral constraints. If we screw up our epistemic standards to the point where we cannot say whether a life with ample friendship, love, pleasure, meaningful work, achievement, genuine empirical knowledge of the world and the causal forces that operate within it, and wisdom concerning practical affairs is better or worse than a life that lacks all these things, what makes us think that any claims about what moral rights people have are going to withstand critical scrutiny?[6] For a start, how does the Nozickian determine that some rights violations are more serious than others, and so merit greater punishment, and justify greater imposition of harm on those who are in the process of carrying out some rights violation, in order to prevent their success?

I.4 THE ROOT IDEA AND SELF-OWNERSHIP

Nozick writes: "The moral side constraints upon what we may do, I claim, reflect the fact of our separate existences ... There is no justified sacrifice of some of us for others. This root idea, namely, that there are different individuals with separate lives and so no one may be sacrificed for others, underlies the existence of moral side constraints" (p. 33) and also leads to a specifically libertarian understanding of the content of side constraints.

There are several ideas here. One is that interpersonal comparisons of good are impossible. Nozick is also committed to the idea that interpersonal comparisons of rights fulfillment are impossible, so that one can never justify, for example, violating Jones's right by taking an extra shirt button he owns in order to prevent Alicia from being raped on the ground that the right of Jones that would be violated is less important or less morally weighty than the right of Alicia that would be violated if we refrain from violating Jones's right.[7]

Another suggestion in the passage does not depend on any sort of skepticism about interpersonal comparisons of good or right. Suppose we can weigh different people's goods and rights and correctly determine what outcome of those we might reach would be morally best. This information, even if we can obtain it, is morally irrelevant for determining the content of people's moral rights and corresponding duties (the content of a side-constraint morality). Each person has her own life to lead, separate from others, and so no sacrifice of one in order to benefit others can be warranted.

Let us grant that each person has her own life to lead, and that each human individual's life has a unity over time from start to finish that distinguishes it sharply from any other individual's life. (In my view, the basis of his unity is the spatio-temporal continuity of a single live, functioning brain.[8]) These truths are compatible with many opposed moralities besides libertarianism – utilitarianism, liberal egalitarianism, and egoism, to name three. So maybe the crucial claim inherent in what Nozick calls the libertarian "root idea" is that no one may permissibly impose sacrifice on one person, not even to benefit others. This still cannot be quite right. The libertarian norm forbids *harmless* aggression against or interference with another along with the harmful variety. Nor can the crucial idea be that impositions that involve intrapersonal compensation can be acceptable, whereas impositions that involve interpersonal compensation cannot be. Nozick does not endorse the idea that it is morally permissible to violate a person's moral rights whenever one follows that by fully compensating the individual for the injury. Moreover, as Nozick emphasizes, the basic moral rights ascribed to each individual by libertarian doctrine include a right against paternalistic interference – restriction of an individual's liberty against her will for her own good. Paternalism so understood always includes a promise of intrapersonal compensation that more than outweighs the cost to the individual of the restriction of her liberty. The individual in Nozick's view, being sovereign over her own life, has an absolute, exceptionless right against such interference regardless of the benefit to herself that is part of the paternalistic package.

If the assertions in the previous paragraph are on the right track, then the root idea around which Nozick's argument for side-constraint morality and libertarian morality pivots cannot be just the claim that individuals have separate lives and none may permissibly be sacrificed for others. A better candidate for this pivotal role is self-ownership – the claim that each human adult person initially has full ownership rights over herself and no one initially has any property rights in any other person.[9] Owning oneself (including one's body), one is free to do with oneself whatever one chooses so long as one does not harm others in certain ways. Like any property rights, property rights in oneself are fully transferable and waivable by individual voluntary consent. What one owns, one may use and abuse and destroy as one chooses.

The self-ownership idea needs further elaboration. Even as just adumbrated, the idea appears to be deeply flawed (see Arneson: 2010). That prior to voluntary transfer of rights no one has any ownership rights in any other person means that there are no enforceable duties of solidarity to aid those in need. That rights in oneself are all fully alienable and waivable means there are no enforceable duties to oneself. This thought jars against the conviction that possessing rational agency capacity and having a life to live gives one dignity and entails a duty to make something worthwhile of the (except in rare, tragic cases) valuable opportunity to live a life. This duty rules out suicide and destruction of one's rational agency capacities for no good reason as morally impermissible.[10] The idea that someone's voluntary consent to a transaction, however unreasonable the consent, just so long as it passes a threshold of voluntariness, licenses one to do to that person whatever she has consented to, however grotesquely bad, makes a fetish of actual voluntary consent and grossly exaggerates its moral importance.

The phrase "the fact of our separate existences" may suggest a picture of people living autarchically on land they cultivate, no one being dependent on others or vulnerable to others, except that each would suffer if others were physically aggressive toward them. But suppose our separate existences are frequently intertwined, as in this scenario. We find ourselves in a large pit, being preyed on by a wild beast. If we all stand and fight together, we can defeat the threatening predator. Each of us would improve our own chances to live and live well if all of us joined the effort to fight against the beast, and each of us benefits roughly equally from reductions in risk of suffering predation. A common defense effort is organized, but some fight and some shirk, and the shirkers benefit from the efforts of the fighters just as much as fighters themselves do. Plus, the shirkers do not put themselves at risk as fighters do. If a fair scheme is in place for providing public goods that assigns to everyone duties to contribute and that brings about a roughly fair distribution of benefits and burdens if each person does his or her assigned part, then the shirkers can appeal to Nozick's self-ownership norm to insist that there is no enforceable duty to contribute one's share to fair schemes for provision of public goods in circumstances like those described, which as a matter of fact are ubiquitous in modern life. The right of self-ownership includes the moral right to be a free rider.[11]

Nozick might respond that individuals surely have rights to live as they choose, and there is no nonarbitrary way of singling out any of the infinite number of positions between full self-ownership and no self-ownership as morally special. Individuals cannot be deemed to have no self-ownership, so they must have full self-ownership.

In reply: first, if it is morally arbitrary at what point one cuts into a line, declaring that acts that are permissible when located on one side of the line are impermissible when they lie on the other side, the moral arbitrariness of cutting here rather than there is not lessened by selecting one of the extreme end points of the line as the point at which to make the cut. *Ex hypothesi* the end points are just points on the line, the same as any other points, and enjoy no special moral status. Also, the particular end point of the line that Nozick singles out as uniquely morally privileged appears from a variety of plausible moral perspectives to be uniquely indefensible. Self-ownership is not an especially appealing abstraction, and when one examines its implications, no hidden allure is revealed. Finally, I deny the assumption that no middle-of-the-road position could correctly reflect the balance of opposed moral reasons.

Imagine that someone is about to commence savagely beating a helpless small child with the intent of murdering him or her. There is every reason to believe this enterprise will be successful: the child will suffer horrible pain and then die a victim of wrongful homicide. Apart from the bad luck of falling victim to this murderous assault, the child would have a long life, well worth living. The parents of the child can see what is happening, but by sheer bad luck are so placed that they can do nothing to block the impending murder. As it happens, I am in a position to act, at some cost and risk to myself, to prevent the assault and save the child's life. I have my own life to lead, however, and I am engrossed on fiddling with my stamp collection. I prefer to keep working on my stamp collection and allow the murder to proceed. This is a morally nasty attitude, Nozick can agree. However, Nozick's position is that "individuals are ends and not merely means: they may not be sacrificed or used for the achieving of other ends without their consent. Individuals are inviolable" (p. 31). The child has no right to my assistance in preventing his murder. Moreover, it would be a violation of my Lockean rights, and thus morally wrong, for anyone to threaten or coerce me or attack me in order to induce me to act to save the child, no matter how slight the cost or risk to myself of my doing so. Lockean rights are trumps in moral discourse: in conflict with any other moral consideration, rights by themselves entirely determine what is morally permissible, forbidden, and required. This is the idea that persons are inviolable.

The example illustrates the point that in the Lockean perspective, persons, though inviolable, are entirely ignorable (see Lippert-Rasmussen: 1996). The fact that you are in peril and I could help you never by itself gives you any moral right to my assistance, no matter how grave your peril and no matter how slight the cost I must bear to render the assistance.

Someone might object to my use of hypothetical examples to argue against Nozick's conception of the moral rights that individuals possess. The ground of the objection is that my examples are far-fetched, extreme possibilities. In practice the administration of a Lockean rights regime would work out tolerably well for people.[12]

The objection reflects a basic misunderstanding of Nozick's position. Nozick is not proposing Lockean natural rights as a policy proposal to be assessed by its overall likely effects. He is making a proposal as to what we owe one another as a matter of fundamental moral principle. At this level of argument, a single counterexample to a principle defeats a proposed principle. If the principle yields recommendations in any possible situation that after reflection we find we cannot accept, the principle must be rejected.

However, any argument by counterexample is subject to evaluation by wide reflective equilibrium methods. In the present state of moral theory, any candidate moral principle is likely to have counterintuitive implications in some possible situations. Most people's considered judgments taken together are inconsistent, they cannot all be true together, and some doubtless reflect prejudice and reactions that would not withstand ideally extended critical deliberation. In this context, any candidate moral theory or set of principles is likely to offend common-sense judgment in one way or another. The moral principles that we should provisionally accept are those that taken as a whole best match our considered moral judgments after critical deliberation. If our current moral inclinations are latently inconsistent, no such match will be perfect, so no single anomaly defeats a proposed principle. The argument against Nozick's conception of Lockean moral rights has to be that it massively offends deep-seated moral convictions that further critical reflection only entrenches and that some available rival moral view does better on this score.

The idea that Lockean rights are trumps in reasoning about what one morally ought to do is a crucial point. An alternative view might interpret moral rights just as the Lockean does but hold that other moral considerations can oppose and sometimes outweigh rights. This type of view need not endorse the implications of Lockean rights with respect to the entire absence of enforceable duties to aid those in peril or to promote the aggregate fulfillment of moral rights (weighted by their moral importance) that I have been at pains to highlight.

1.5 NOZICK'S MAIN ARGUMENT

Nozick's main suggested argument in support of the Lockean libertarian conception of rights turns on his claim that side constraints set absolute, exceptionless requirements on individual conduct. The idea is that the root idea that individuals have separate lives to lead and no one may be sacrificed for others is the best explanation for the fact that there are absolute side constraints. Given our conviction that there are absolute side constraints, an inference to the best explanation of this fact supports the root idea, and this root idea in turn implies the specific Lockean libertarian conception of rights as side constraints. Since we are talking about moral explanations, the claim is this: what justifies the claim that morality has a side-constraint structure also justifies the claim that the content of these side constraints is the set of Lockean libertarian rights.

The argument then goes as follows:

1. There are morally binding, absolute, exceptionless side constraints.

2. The best justification of the moral claim that there are morally binding, absolute, exceptionless side constraints is that

individuals have separate lives to lead and no one may be sacrificed for others.

3. The best justification of a true moral claim is itself true.
4. It is true that individuals have separate lives to lead and no one may be sacrificed for others.
5. From the truth that individuals have separate lives to lead and no one may be sacrificed for others and further uncontroversially true premises it deductively follows that individuals have moral rights according to the Lockean libertarian conception of individual moral rights.

This argument goes awry with premise 1. Even if the rest of the argument were unimpeachable, the starting point is not one we should accept. Nozick is then engaged in something akin to a transcendental deduction of a non-fact. He is seeking the conditions that must hold if there are absolute side constraints, but it is not sensible to accept that there are any such entities, so even if the Nozickian root idea were uniquely and ideally suited for the role of justifying the existence of absolute rights, that is not a reason for anyone to accept the root idea and with it the Lockean conception of individual rights.

Suppose that contrary to my insistence, there do exist absolute, exceptionless moral side constraints. Would Nozick's root idea be the best explanation of this moral fact? (Compare the question: If it were morally acceptable to torture animals for fun, what would be the best justification of this fact?) This is an interesting question, but not one this essay pursues. I will simply note that this essay has tried to show that Nozick's root idea, fully articulated, amounts to self-ownership, and there are good reasons to reject self-ownership, quite independently of the issue, whether or not there are absolute, exceptionless side constraints.

The denial that there are absolute, exceptionless rules might sound overly dogmatic. If there are fundamental moral principles, they will hold necessarily and universally. They will be absolute, exceptionless moral rules. So one might hold.

I want to set this issue aside. Let us just assume – what I suppose is anyway true – that there are fundamental principles that hold universally, necessarily, and without being conditioned on any empirical facts. It still remains implausible to hold that there are absolute, exceptionless moral rules of the type the Lockean libertarian upholds. Such rules identify a type of act by some putatively wrong-making feature it possesses and say no act of that type is ever morally permissible, whatever the consequences in particular circumstances of refraining from doing an act of that type. Prominent examples of such codes include the biblical Ten Commandments and the standard set of Lockean individual moral rights. Such codes might be regarded as practical rough guidelines for ordinary choices rather than as fundamental moral principles. They might be more plausible in the former role, but Nozick insists that they should function in the latter role. But consider, for example, the norm that one has a right not to be physically assaulted. Some assaults are very minor inconveniences, and some assaults do an enormous amount of good, so a blanket exceptionless prohibition is unreasonably rigid. A sensible non-consequentialist morality is not one that pays no heed to consequences. This means that any remotely plausible statement of a set of rights intended to form a set of fundamental moral principles would have to include qualifications to the individual rights specifying what to do in the case of conflict of rights and qualification in the form of a beneficence principle and a weighting principle that determines when a right should give way in virtue of the fact that the consequences of upholding it would be excessively bad.

Nozick writes as though he is supposing that either morality has "an end-state maximizing structure" or there are absolute side constraints. He comments: "The stronger the force of an end-state maximizing view, the more powerful must be the root idea capable of resisting it that underlies the existence of moral side constraints" (p. 33). If there are these opposed moral forces as Nozick suggests, one wonders why he does not consider that perhaps the truth of the matter is a resultant of these forces – a hybrid moral view that combines side constraints and moral goals. The fundamental moral principles would affirm both and include rules that balance the two factors and assign the proper weights to each. The side constraints so understood would not be absolute and exceptionless, but would this matter? Nozick must be assuming this balancing project faces insuperable obstacles, but he does not say what these might be.

One obstacle stares us in the face. Perhaps there is no morally nonarbitrary way of balancing these disparate moral elements that hybrid views combine. If side constraints are non-absolute and admit exceptions, the question immediately arises, how does one decide in a principled way under what circumstances exceptions should be made? If no satisfactory answer to this question is forthcoming, my dismissive response to Nozickian absolutism will have been ill-advised.

My answer leans heavily on work on this topic by Judith Thomson (cf. Thomson: 1990, ch. 6). She notes that rights vary enormously in their importance. If one's moral rights include property rights, then I certainly have a property right over the extra button on the shirt I am now wearing. The shirt is my property, and the extra button is part of the shirt. But surely it is implausible in the extreme to suppose that there are no circumstances in which it would be morally right all things considered for someone to act against my property right in the button by taking it without my express or implied permission. Moreover, although types of rights can be important or unimportant – the right to free speech is important – for purposes of determining when it is morally permissible to act against someone's particular right, what matters is the importance of this particular token of that type of right. Adapting a suggestion made by Thomson, I propose that what is decisive is how much in total non-right-holders would lose, if the right is respected, compared with how much in total the right-holder would lose, if the right is not respected. In Thomson's words: "It is permissible to infringe a claim if and only if infringing it would be sufficiently much better for those for whom infringing it would be good than not infringing it would be for the claim holder" (Thomson: 1990, p. 153).[13]

She qualifies this suggestion by what she calls the High-Threshold thesis. This says that it is permissible to act against a right only if there is a single non-right-holder for whom it would be sufficiently good that the right is not respected, given the harm that the right-holder would suffer in that case, to justify the infringement of the right. In other words, the High-Threshold thesis rules out the possibility that small gains to each of many non-right-holders if the right in question is not respected might add up to a sufficiently great amount of good to outweigh even a large harm that would be suffered by the right-holder if the right is not respected. We are not permitted to add up gains and losses to many people in this way, to determine if acting against or infringing a right in particular circumstances is permissible. Instead what is called for is pairwise comparison: compare what the right-holder would lose if the right is not respected, with what each non-right-holder would lose if the right is respected, in turn.[14]

One might worry that one needs to modify the Thomson account by some personal responsibility factor. Suppose that if you infringe my right not to be assaulted by inflicting a slight cut on my finger, I will respond to this incident with culpable recklessness or carelessness, with the result that I get gangrene in my finger and my arm must be amputated to save my life. Suppose that if you infringe my right by inflicting this (what should be a trivial) cut, you can thereby bring about great gains for non-right-holders, that sufficiently outweigh the loss I would have suffered from the cut if I had responded with anything close to reasonable prudence. This should qualify as a case of permissible infringement, even if I end up dead.

I accept the Thomson framework for determining under what circumstances it is morally permissible to act against (infringe) someone's moral right. I alter the account only by dropping the High-Threshold thesis. This surely must be done. Consider a case in which one would have to infringe Smith's right not to have his arm broken in order to prevent some large number of people from suffering a fate just a tiny bit less bad than the bad that accrues to Smith if his arm is broken. Surely there is some number of lesser harms that would accrue to many people if Smith's right is not infringed that outweighs the harm that accrues to Smith if his right not to have his arm broken is infringed sufficiently to justify acting against the right – breaking Smith's arm. At least, this must be so if moral rights can ever be overridden for any reason. As the number of suffering non-right-holders increases in this example, the case for acting against the right becomes increasingly weighty. Thomson's High-Threshold thesis oddly would have it that if one individual non-right-holder would stand to suffer a harm that is just barely insufficient to justify acting against Smith's right, then no number of additional right-holders suffering that same nearly sufficient harm could tip the moral scales, no matter what, but on the other hand if we discovered we had been wrong in our initial assessment and the sole non-right-holder in the example would stand to lose just a tiny jot more if Smith's right is not infringed, Smith's right does give way. This is unacceptable.

If it is morally acceptable to add up benefits and losses that would fall on the ensemble of people who would be affected if we refrain from acting against someone's right or do act against it, we then end up accepting Aggregation. This is the claim that for any moral right or claim possessed by one individual, however morally important or stringent the right, it may be overridden if sufficiently greater harm would accrue to non-right-holders in the aggregate, and for any harm however tiny that might accrue to a non-right-holder, the right in question may be overridden if each of sufficiently many non-right-holders would suffer that tiny harm if one does not act against the right. Aggregation is in a way a strong claim, which many are inclined to reject.[15] In another way it is a very weak claim, since it says nothing about the correct trade-off ratios that determine when any given right would be morally overridden in any given circumstances. These could be very steep indeed, consistent with Aggregation.

So what are these trade-off ratios? The skeptical worry still obtrudes. However, as I see it, this is simply another case in which one follows reflective equilibrium methods, surveying a wide range of cases and considering moral principles that match one's general and particular intuitions until one finds a stable match after ideal reflection. If one accepts any plural values at any place in one's theories of the right and the good, and also insists that when plural values conflict, there is sometimes a correct weighting that determines what one morally ought to do when all things are considered, then one must accept the legitimacy in principle of seeking to discover proper weights by reflective equilibrium methods. There is no special problem here about deciding on the stringency of moral rights; this is just another case of plural values to be balanced. Nozick faces an issue of this kind in Chapter 4 of *ASU*, where he acknowledges that there are plural, independent, weighty moral factors that together determine when it is permissible to act against a right provided compensation is paid to the right-holder and when it is impermissible to inflict this combination of rights violation plus compensation on an individual.[16]

1.6 RATIONAL AGENCY CAPACITY AND MEANINGFUL LIFE

Nozick thoughtfully addresses the question of what traits a being must possess to be morally considerable, and further, to qualify as a person with moral rights. He focuses on moral limits on how we may treat higher animals, so does not explicitly consider the conditions for the lowest moral status. His view is roughly that insofar as an animal possesses some but not all of the traits necessary for personhood, the animal is owed moral consideration, the amount varying with the extent to which the being comes close to personhood status. Regarding personhood, he affirms possession of rational agency capacity as the necessary and sufficient condition for this status. He stresses that rational agency capacity, to be a credible criterion for personhood, has to be interpreted as including capacity for formulating and pursuing long-terms plans: a person is "a being able to formulate long-term plans for its life, able to consider and decide on the basis of abstract considerations or principles it formulates to itself and hence not merely the plaything of immediate stimuli, a being that limits its own behavior in accordance with some principles or picture it has of what an appropriate life is for itself and others, and so on" (p. 49). Rational agency capacity so understood includes affective and volitional as well as cognitive capacity. The volitional capacity in question includes a capacity for second-order volition. Possession of rational agency capacity at some threshold level or beyond endows one with the moral status of person.

Nozick suggests that inquiring into the necessary and sufficient conditions for personhood will generate a further argument in support of the claim that the moral rights that persons have and the moral constraints by which they are bound are exactly the rights and constraints specified in the Lockean libertarian conception. Once we see clearly what it takes to be a person we will understand why persons are inviolable, with inviolability cashed out in terms of possessing absolute, exceptionless Lockean moral rights.

Nozick's development of this suggestion is sketchy. He suggests that a being with the capacity for rational agency capacity in his expansive sense is a being with a capacity for meaningful life. "A person's shaping his life in accordance with some overall plan is his way of giving meaning to his life; only a being with the capacity so to shape his life can have or strive for meaningful life" (p. 50).

I cannot make anything of this suggestion. A life might be meaningful in that a reasonable impartial observer would rate it as meaningful. Alternatively, one might hold that an individual life is meaningful only if the individual herself finds meaning in her life and subjectively affirms her life to be meaningful. The latter strikes me as unpromising: suppose Alessandra is a great athlete, has enjoyed stable rich friendships, has run a successful business, written excellent novels, and so on, but oddly believes that only being an astronaut or a religious visionary could make one's life meaningful and views her own life as meaningless because it falls short of that standard. Al, on the other hand, has stumbled through life in a deadening alcoholic stupor but believes his life is deeply meaningful. The former suggestion is best interpreted as follows: the more one's life includes genuinely worthwhile goods, with accurate appreciation being one of those goods, the more meaningful one's life. The good life is one type of meaningful life. Another is an admirable life, which involves doing what is morally right, in ways that significantly benefit others, but at the cost of leaving one's own life mainly bereft of good. Nozick suggests that shaping one's life according to some overall plan constitutes one's life as meaningful, but surely a person could drift from day to day but still make great decisions each day in response to that day's opportunities, which by luck turn out to be wonderful. This life would fail to be meaningful by Nozick's test, which looks to be too narrowly drawn in light of the example.[17] One might say a meaningful life is one that could have been shaped by a reasonable person planning his or her life, even if in fact it was not so shaped.

However exactly we interpret the idea of a meaningful life and whatever importance we assign it, I see no connection between meaningfulness and Lockean constraints. Is one's life meaningful just to the extent that one respects Lockean constraints and does not suffer violation of one's Lockean rights? Consider Sam, who upon reaching adulthood falls off a cliff and dies. He overestimates his agility, perhaps, or underestimates the slipperiness of the rocks, or perhaps is moved by an immature romantic ideal of dying young in the face of natural peril, even if the peril is self-imposed. He is not a skilled climber doing what he loves most in life, he is unathletic and acting on a whim. Were he to suffer a paternalistic restraint before venturing on the fatal jaunt, he would, let us assume, grow more mature and lead a choice-worthy life. Or consider Bea, who lives in dire poverty, and is never able to exercise her capacity for ambition formation. She just races on a treadmill to survive and dies young. If she were provided with a small sum of capital by means of redistributive taxation in violation of people's Lockean rights, she would have escaped from the grinding treadmill of poverty, gone to school, developed her abilities, lived well. Or, for that matter, consider Tony, who engages in youthful transgressions, including violations of people's Lockean rights, but the rights violations he inflicts are not serious, and anyway he repents, and goes on to lead an enviable, upright life.

1.7 CONCLUSION

Nozick hints at several arguments supporting his claim that the fundamental enforceable moral requirements binding all of us consist entirely of side constraints with the content of Lockean libertarian rights. I have argued that none of these hints can be developed into an argument for this claim that is successful or even close to successful.

NOTES

1. On John Locke's views, as opposed to "Lockean" libertarianism, see Simmons: 1992. For a Locke-inspired left-wing version of libertarianism, see Otsuka: 2003.

2. A major element in any plausible defense of act consequentialism is the discussion of distinct levels of moral thinking in Hare: 1981, chs. 2 and 3. Another major element in the case for act consequentialism is the baroque complexity that defenders of non-consequentialist moral theory are driven to ascribe to the moral principles they uphold. See Kagan: 1989. See also Kamm: 2006. For the record, I myself uphold act consequentialism. In this essay I argue that if we had to choose between a morality of moderate, limited side constraints and a Nozickian morality of absolute, exceptionless side constraints consisting of Lockean libertarian rights, we would come closer to the truth by embracing moderation.

3. The terminology of agent-relative versus agent-neutral reasons does not appear in Nozick's discussion, but the idea is implicit in what he does say. Thomas Nagel introduces the terms in Nagel: 1987, pp. 152–153.

4. Some caution is needed in stating this point. Nozick does not deny that an action that one has a moral right to perform can be criticizable from various moral perspectives. I have the right to drink all of the lemonade, since it is my property, but still it might be nasty on my part not to share it with my thirsty brother. The key Lockean libertarian claim is that rights are trumps in the sense that other types of moral

considerations do not limit or expand the rights one has and one must always respect everyone's moral rights in any decision problem one faces regardless of how non-rights considerations might bear on the situation.

5. Here I echo the verdict of Thomas Nagel in his review of *ASU*, "Libertarianism without Foundations" (Nagel: 1981).

6. The question posed in the text is an open question, not a rhetorical question. See, for example, Fleurbaey: 2008 for a sophisticated attempt to elaborate a theory of justice while eschewing interpersonal comparisons of welfare. He is working in the economics tradition of "fairness theory" as developed by Hal Varian and others.

7. On this issue, see Sen: 1982.

8. This physical criterion of personal identity is elaborated and criticized in Parfit: 1984, Part II. Its foremost recent defender is Bernard Williams.

9. Of course, self-ownership can hardly be a rock-bottom premise in an argument for libertarian rights. Self-ownership presupposes the importance of the moral distinction between doing and allowing, the idea that each person has certain moral rights not to be harmed or interfered with in certain ways, and so on. A deontological morality is a cloth that weaves together many threads, many notions. Lockean libertarianism is one version of deontological morality, and is itself a combination of distinct moral ideas. We should not take too seriously Nozick's offhand suggestion that there is a single "root idea" that justifies both the side constraint form of morality and its libertarian content.

10. For elaboration, see Arneson: 2005b.

11. See Nozick's brief discussion of this topic in *ASU*, pp. 90–95. This discussion has given rise to much commentary. A. John Simmons broadly defends Nozick's line of thought in Simmons: 1979, ch. 5, and in "Fair Play and Political Obligation: Twenty Years Later," in Simmons: 2001. I argue for some claims asserted in this paragraph in my "Doubting and Defending the Principle of Fairness." See also Arneson: 1982.

12. Nothing in the text tells against the possibility of defending something close to Lockean libertarian rights as policies on the ground that implementing them will produce better consequences than any feasible alternative policies would produce. Such a position is utterly different from the natural moral rights position that Nozick defends. This broadly consequentialist approach to the defense of Lockean libertarianism is pursued by Epstein: 1995 and by Schmidtz: 2006.

13. In this formulation the gain to non-right-holders is to be interpreted as net gain: if five non-right-holders lose if Smith's right is respected,

but six other non-right-holders would gain, the total gain to non-right-holders of infringing this right is what the five would gain minus what the six would lose. In this formulation *infringing* a right is acting so that the right is not fulfilled; an infringement of a right that is morally wrong all things considered is a *violation* of a right. The terminology allows that some infringements might not be violations.

14. One might worry that cashing out the force of a right in terms of how much good and harm are gained and lost if the right is respected or not gives no moral weight to the anti-paternalism in a doctrine of moral rights. Suppose it would not harm Arneson at all to deprive him of liberty to make some important life choice such as whether to say Yes or No to a marriage proposal. Left to his own devices, he will make the wrong choice, and if constrained, he will be better off. Here the right not to be deprived of liberty to make important life choices for oneself seems to become weightless, against the letter and spirit of a Lockean doctrine of rights. So let us interpret "harm" and "benefit" here loosely, so that one who is deprived of personal liberty for pater-nalistic reasons does suffer harm and is made badly off just in virtue of being treated paternalistically. We leave it to case by case judgment how strong a presumption against paternalism is thereby established.

15. For criticism of Aggregation, see Scanlon: 1998, ch. 5.

16. For interpretation and criticism of Nozick's Chapter 4 arguments, see Arneson: 2005a.

17. Shaping one's life in accordance with some overall plan looks to be neither necessary nor sufficient for achieving a meaningful life. The text gives an example in which the overall shaping is not necessary, but it is not sufficient either: consider the example of the person who arranges his life with the aim of counting the blades of grass on court-house lawns, over and over.

2 Are deontological constraints irrational?

2.1 DOING EVIL THAT GOOD WILL COME OF IT

Most deontologists find bedrock in the Pauline doctrine that it is morally objectionable to do evil in order that good will come of it.[1] Uncontroversially, this doctrine condemns the killing of an innocent person simply in order to maximize the sum total of happiness. It rules out the conscription of a worker to his or her certain death in order to repair a fault that is interfering with the live broadcast of a World Cup match that a billion spectators have been enjoying.[2] It rules out such sacrifice even if it would maximize the sum total of everyone's happiness. An act utilitarian, by contrast, would require the sacrifice of the one whenever this latter condition obtains, since such a utilitarian is committed to the view that one ought always to act so as to bring about the greatest sum total of happiness.[3]

An act utilitarian might, however, consistently hold that a large number of rather insignificant pleasures, such as that which a spectator derives from witnessing men in shorts running around and kicking a ball, is never sufficient to justify the infliction of a great harm on a single individual.[4] He might take such a position without abandoning utilitarianism by denying that the sum total of such minor pleasures could ever be sufficiently great to outweigh the harm of death to the one. Under the inspiration of John Stuart Mill, a utilitarian might draw a more general distinction between serious and trivial harms and pleasures and maintain that no amount of a trivial pleasure could ever amount to a sum of happiness that is greater than the disutility of a serious harm.[5]

Even such an act utilitarian would, however, be committed to the claim that if one could prevent a number of people from suffering a harm of a given type by means of inflicting an equally great harm on a single individual, one ought to do so. If, for example, one could save five from being killed by means of killing a sixth, then the act utilitarian would maintain that one ought to kill the sixth. Suppose, for example, that a boulder dislodged by an earthquake is rolling toward five persons at the bottom of a hill. You see that it will crush and kill them unless you push a sixth person into the pathway of the oncoming boulder, whereupon it will crush and kill this sixth person and then come to a gentle halt before it picks up enough speed to crush the five. An act utilitarian, it would seem, is committed to the claim that in such a scenario, you are morally required to push this one person into the boulder's path.

Not all act *consequentialists*, however, are committed to this claim, where an act consequentialist is someone who maintains that one is obliged to perform that action which does the most good. Act utilitarianism can be understood as a particular species of the genus of act consequentialism. An act utilitarian agrees with all other act consequentialists that one is obliged to perform that action which does the most good, but he holds to a particular and rather narrow conception of the good as consisting of nothing other than happiness. Other act consequentialists might, however, endorse a more expansive conception of the good that consists of more than happiness.

Such an act consequentialist could reject the claim that one ought to push the individual into the path of the oncoming boulder. There is conceptual space for him to maintain that what would happen to each of the five is not really as bad as what would happen to the sixth. In that case, the five will be killed if you do nothing. But they will not be *unjustly* killed. Rather, they will be killed as the result of natural causes. Naturally rolling boulders cannot commit injustices or infringe the rights of individuals. If, however, you kill the sixth, you will unjustly kill him in violation of his right not to be killed. Hence it could be argued that the fate that would befall each of the five if they are killed is not, all things considered, just as bad as the fate that would befall the sixth if he is killed. Either five will be killed, but not unjustly so, or a sixth will be unjustly killed. Even if the unjust killing of someone is no greater a harm to the person than the accidental killing of an individual, it might nevertheless be a worse thing, given a richer conception of good and bad than the utilitarian acknowledges.

Suppose, however, that the boulder is rolling toward the five because it was set on its downward course by a morally responsible sadist who has dislodged it with explosives in order to kill the five. Here, if you do nothing, this person will unjustly kill the five. This is a case in which you are faced with the following dilemma: either the right of five not to be killed will be infringed or the right of one not to be killed will be infringed. If you do nothing, you will allow the rights of five to be infringed. If, however, you push the one into the oncoming path of the boulder, you will infringe the very same right of the sixth. An act consequentialist appears to be driven to the conclusion that you are morally obliged to push this person into the pathway of the boulder. A deontologist, by contrast, would insist that it is impermissible for you to infringe the right of one innocent person as a means to prevent the same type of rights of five other innocent persons from being infringed. Such infringement of the right of the one runs contrary to the Pauline doctrine that I mentioned at the outset.[6]

2.2 THE IRRATIONALITY OBJECTION TO DEONTOLOGICAL CONSTRAINTS

However intuitive it might seem that one ought not push the person into the path of the boulder even to prevent the unjust killing of the five, one might object that such deontological constraints against the infringement of rights are simply irrational. Robert Nozick was, it appears, the first to formulate the irrationality objection to such constraints. He presents this objection in the opening pages of Chapter 3 of *Anarchy, State, and Utopia* (*ASU*):

Isn't it *irrational* to accept a [deontological] constraint C, rather than a view that directs minimizing the violations of C? ... If nonviolation of C is so important, shouldn't that be the goal? How can a concern for the non-violation of C lead to the refusal to violate C even when this would prevent other more extensive violations of C? What is the rationale for placing the nonviolation of rights as a [deontological] constraint upon action instead of including it solely as a goal of one's actions? (p. 30)

If, however, the non-violation of C is one's goal, then it appears that one ought to push the person into the path of the boulder on the following grounds that Samuel Scheffler has articulated: "if one accepts the desirability of a certain goal being achieved, and if one has a choice between two options, one of which is certain to accomplish the goal better than the other, then it is, *ceteris paribus*, rational to choose the former over the latter" (Scheffler: 1985, p. 414).

Much of the literature on deontological constraints since the publication of *ASU* can be characterized as an attempt either to overcome or to vindicate the irrationality objection. In this chapter, I shall assess the success of deontologists in responding to this objection. Nozick is himself a deontologist, and much of the remainder of Chapter 3 of *ASU* is a sketch of an implicit response to this objection. Before turning to a reconstruction of Nozick's own line of resistance, I shall consider a line of response that Nozick rejects.

2.3 THE AGENT-RELATIVE GOAL AS A RESPONSE TO THE IRRATIONALITY OBJECTION

This line of response is to argue that deontological constraints are not irrational because they can in fact be shown to be consistent with the maximal realization of a morally significant goal. This goal is not the act consequentialist's goal of maximizing the good, where the good is understood to be *agent-neutral* – that is, the same for all agents. It is conceded that deontological constraints will fail to maximize a non-rigged agent-neutral goal.[7] Nevertheless, it is claimed that deontological constraints serve a morally significant *agent-relative* goal – that is, one that is personal to each agent rather than being shared by all.

2.3.1 The temporally neutral agent-relative goal

Scheffler notes that deontologists might appeal to the distinction between what one does and what one allows others to do to try to defend constraints against the charge of irrationality by showing that they can be rendered compatible with goal-maximizing rationality in the following way (see Scheffler: 1985, p. 415). Constraints could be conceived as assigning "each person the agent-relative goal of not violating any restrictions himself," rather than the agent-neutral goal of minimizing the "overall non-occurrence of such violations" by all persons. If the deontologist can make the agent-relative goal of minimizing one's own constraint violations over one's own lifetime consistent with constraints that enforce the Pauline doctrine, then he will have provided at least a partial defense of constraints that shows them not to be in conflict with maximizing rationality. As noted above, this would not amount to a reconciliation of deontological constraints with act consequentialism, since consequentialists are committed to an agent-neutral good and therefore an agent-neutral goal. It would, however, be a reconciliation of deontological constraints with goal-maximizing rationality more generally construed.

Nozick contemplates such a reconciliation. "One might think," he writes,

that each person could distinguish in his goal between *his* violating rights and someone else's doing it. Give the former infinite (negative) weight in his goal, and no amount of stopping others from violating rights can outweigh his violating someone's rights. In addition to a component of a goal receiving infinite weight, indexical expressions also appear, for example, "*my* doing something." (p. 29 fn.)

Nozick (p. 29 fn.) rejects such a reconciliation as "gimmicky." His objection appears to be that this move is gimmicky because it is the artificial creation of a goal that is tailored to the deontologist's prescriptions. By contrast, Nozick maintains that "an interesting maximization structure involves the maximization of some function that was not devised especially for that (type of) occasion" (Nozick: 1981, p. 733 n. 71).

This objection to the positing of an agent-relative goal of minimizing one's own constraint violations appears, however, to sell this goal short. This is because the positing of such a goal can be motivated by considerations above and beyond the task of finding a goal that the deontologist can fully realize. In his critique of utilitarianism, for example, Bernard Williams powerfully advances the view that one has a special responsibility for actions that flow from one's agency that one does not have for the actions of others. Such special responsibility might provide independent motivation for the positing of an agent-relative goal of minimizing one's own constraints violations (see Williams: 1973, pp. 93–100).

Even if, however, we take this goal seriously rather than dismissing it as gimmicky, it can be shown that this agent-relative goal of minimizing one's own constraint violations over one's lifetime cannot be rendered fully consistent with the Pauline doctrine. Recall that it follows from the Pauline doctrine, under standard interpretation, that you ought not kill one innocent person when the killing of the one is a means to prevent five other innocent persons from being killed. Notice that this doctrine does not require that the greater evil that you may not prevent by doing evil be caused by someone *other than yourself.* Nor should it, according to Pauline deontologists, who will insist, not only that you may not kill one as a means to prevent another from killing more, but also that you may not kill one as a means to prevent *yourself* from killing more.[8] The Pauline doctrine constrains your pursuit of both the agent-neutral goal of minimizing the bad that people do and the agent-relative goal of minimizing the bad that you do. Hence a defense of the unconstrained pursuit of the agent-relative goal appears to serve the purposes of the Pauline deontologist just as poorly as does a defense of the unconstrained pursuit of the agent-neutral goal.

In order to test the soundness of the Pauline deontological claim that you may not violate one person's right as a means of preventing *yourself* from violating more rights, consider the following case which is a variation on the case I introduced in the final paragraph of section 2.1. Suppose that *you* are the sadist who has dislodged the boulder with explosives in order to kill the five at the bottom of a hill. As you watch the boulder roll down the hill, you realize that there is now only one way to prevent yourself from violating the rights of the five not to be killed: the pushing of a sixth person on to the pathway of the boulder, which will result in its coming to a halt after crushing and killing him before it gains enough momentum to run over the five.[9]

Should you violate the right of the one not to be killed as a means to prevent yourself from violating the same rights of the five?[10] Deontologists who adhere to the Pauline doctrine would insist that it should be as clear that you may not kill the one here as it would be in our earlier case in which you are presented with the opportunity to kill one to prevent somebody else from killing five. As far as the present case under consideration is concerned, a deontologist would, of course, note that you should not have dislodged the boulder in the first place. But a deontologist would also insist that your having done wrong in the past cannot cause deontological constraints on your behavior to lapse in the present.

2.3.2 *The temporally specific agent-relative goal*

A deontologist who would like to reconcile constraints with goal-maximizing rationality might concede that the Pauline doctrine is incompatible with a temporally neutral, agent-relative goal. In the light of this difficulty, she might search for a temporally *specific* agent-relative goal that is compatible with deontological constraints.[11] Let us consider, for example, the temporally specific goals of minimizing one's violations at each point in time during one's life (as opposed to the temporally neutral goal of minimizing one's violations over a lifetime).

One will be challenged to find actual cases in which pursuit of this temporally specific, agent-relative goal is inconsistent with the Pauline teaching. This is because one will encounter the following difficulty in coming up with cases in which you must use the violation of a constraint at a given point in time as a means of preventing yourself from violating more constraints at that same point in time. The means–ends relation is typically one in which the means cause the end. Yet a cause, at least of one physical event by another, is normally temporally prior to its effect.

There are, however, cases in which a harm serves as a means of realizing another harm or a benefit, where the realized harm or benefit occurs at the same instant as the harm that realizes this result. You might, for example, want the crown prince and heir to the throne to become the king because you want to benefit the crown prince. If you kill the king at noon, then you will, at that very instant, benefit the crown prince by making him king at noon. (As the saying goes, "The king is dead. Long live the king!")[12] You will also, at that very instant, harm the king. Moreover, your killing the king at noon is the cause of the crown prince's becoming king at that same instant in time. Here what is caused – a change in a person's status from crown prince to king – is a normative rather than a physical transformation. Normative change need not take any time in the manner of a physical process such as the movement of one physical particle that causes the movement of another.

We might try to construct cases involving changes in normative states in which your violating a constraint of a specific type at a given point in time serves as a means of realizing the non-violation of a greater number of constraints of roughly the same type and seriousness at that very same point in time. Consider the following not so unrealistic example. You simultaneously promised each of five siblings not to let their sixth sibling know that his spouse is cheating on him. At the same time, you promised this sixth sibling not to spare him the truth.[13] Let us suppose that these six promises are equally weighty and stringent. The sixth sibling begins to suspect that his wife is having an affair with X. He asks you: "Do you know whether my wife is having an affair with X?" If you do not lie, then he will know that you know. If, for example, you say "yes I know that she is" or "I've promised not to say," then he'll know. Even if you pause and say nothing, he will be able to infer, from this silence, that his wife is having an affair. Unless you lie, you will therefore have broken your promise to the five by letting their sibling know of his wife's infidelity. If, however, you convincingly lie by saying "I'm sure that she isn't" or "No, I don't know," then you will have broken your promise to him. It is arguable that such a promise-breaking would make it the case, at that very instant, that you have not broken your promises to the five.

In the end, though, it does not matter whether this is a genuine case in which *the violation of one constraint at a given point in time serves as a means of ensuring that you not violate more such constraints that you would otherwise have violated at that same point in time.* It does not even matter whether we can construct *any* realistic case of this italicized type. It does not matter because surely this type of case is conceivable even if we can be sure that we would never actually encounter such a case. Moreover, reflection on cases of this type, whether real or imagined, should lead the deontologist to reject the temporally specific, agent-relative goal for the following two reasons. First, the violation of the one constraint in such a case would straightforwardly be condemned by the Pauline doctrine that one not do evil that good will come of it. Second, the deontologist believes that it is impermissible for you to violate one constraint now as a means of preventing yourself from violating more such constraints later and he cannot sensibly think that there is a moral distinction to be made between such a violation and a violation now that is a means of preventing yourself from violating more constraints now. Surely he would not want to affirm moral principles that imply that it is impermissible for you to violate a constraint now as a means of preventing yourself from violating more constraints one millisecond from now, but that it is permissible for you to violate one constraint now as a means of preventing yourself from violating more constraints now.

The difference between now and a moment from now does not appear to have sufficient moral significance to justify pursuit of this temporally specific version of the agent-relative goal. In this respect, the temporally specific agent-relative goal is less well motivated than the temporally neutral agent-relative goal. With respect to the latter goal, one can grant the prima facie moral significance of the distinction between what one does during the course of one's life versus what another person does during the course of his life. It is reasonable to maintain that one has special responsibility for what one does during one's lifetime as opposed to what anyone else does during his lifetime. It is much less reasonable to maintain, by contrast, that one has special responsibility for what one does now as opposed to what one did or will do at any other point in one's life, however close in time to the present.

In this section, I have argued that the deontologist opposes the maximal satisfaction of the agent-relative goal, on two natural spellings out of that goal, thereby lending support to the view that one cannot reconcile deontology with goal-maximizing rationality by making the deontological constraints serve a non-rigged morally compelling agent-relative goal.

2.4 THE MORAL STATUS RATIONALE FOR DEONTOLOGICAL CONSTRAINTS

Rather than trying to show that deontological constraints realize a morally significant goal, Nozick attempts to counter the irrationality objection by showing that such constraints have a compelling rationale. He maintains that deontological constraints reflect the "underlying Kantian principle that individuals are ends and not merely means; they may not be sacrificed or used for the achieving of other ends without their consent. Individuals are inviolable" (pp. 30–31). I take Nozick to be saying the following. Because persons are ends in themselves, they are worthy of such high respect that they may not be sacrificed for the good of others without their consent, which would be to treat them as a mere means. Treating us as beings who enjoy the moral protection of deontological constraints shows the appropriately high degree of respect for persons. Constraints are therefore justified because they reflect our elevated moral status as persons who are inviolable insofar as it is impermissible to sacrifice any one of us in order to realize the greater good of minimizing the violation of constraints. I shall call this the *moral status rationale* for constraints.

Frances Kamm has cultivated this core insight and transformed it into an extended justification of deontological constraints that offers the most fruitful development of Nozick's somewhat inchoate, sketchy, and cryptic rationale for deontological constraints that I have quoted and elaborated in the previous paragraph (see Kamm: 1996, ch. 10).[14] In particular, Kamm draws attention to the fact that on the deontological view a human being who enjoys the protection of a right against, for example, murder or torture may *never* be sacrificed for the greater good, not even to prevent more murders or torture. On a view that calls for the minimization of the violation of constraints, by contrast, we may *sometimes* permissibly be sacrificed for the greater good. An innocent person *may* be murdered or tortured in order to prevent more murders or torture. Such permission appears to indicate a lesser moral status than one would enjoy if one were wholly morally immune from such sacrifice. Here is how Thomas Nagel represents Kamm's point:

[R]ules, by which murder and torture are *always* wrong, confer a certain status on persons which they do not have in a moral or legal system in which murder and torture are regarded merely as great evils – so that sometimes it may be permissible to commit them in order to prevent even more of the same. Faced with the question whether to murder one to save five from murder, one may be convinced that fewer people will be murdered if one does it; but one would thereby be accepting the principle that anyone is legitimately murderable, given the right circumstances. This is a subtle but definite alteration for the worse in *everyone's* moral status. Whereas if one refuses, one is saying that all murders are illegitimate, including of course the five that one will have refused to prevent. (Nagel: 1991, p. 148)

Kamm would, I think, depart from Nagel's formulation of her view in one respect. She would deny that moral rules that take the form of deontological constraints *confer* moral status on persons. Rather, she would maintain that such rules accurately *reflect* the moral status that persons independently possess. This elevated moral status of persons does not depend on whether it is reflected in the rules of any moral system that people actually accept.

2.4.1 The separateness of persons

The following question now arises: What are the grounds for Nozick's belief that we must be treated with such a high degree of respect, that we may not be treated merely as means? Nozick says that the "root idea, namely, that there are different individuals with separate lives and so no one may be sacrificed for others, under-lies the existence of moral ... constraints" (p. 33). He elaborates this view as follows:

> [W]hy may not one violate persons for the greater social good? Individually, we each sometimes choose to undergo some pain or sacrifice for a greater benefit or to avoid a greater harm: we go to the dentist to avoid worse suffering later; we do some unpleasant work for its results; some persons diet to improve their health or looks; some save money to support themselves when they are older. In each case, some cost is borne for the sake of the greater overall good. Why not, *similarly*, hold that some persons have to bear some costs that benefit other persons more, for the sake of the overall social good? But there ... are only individual people, different individual people, with their own individual lives. Using one of these people for the benefit of others, uses him and benefits the others. Nothing more ... To use a person in this way does not sufficiently respect and take account of the fact that he is a separate person, that his is the only life he has. *He* does not get some overbalancing good from his sacrifice, and no one is entitled to force this upon him. (pp. 32–33)[15]

Nozick is right that sacrificing one human being for the benefit of another is morally problematic in a way in which my making a sacrifice now in order that I may reap benefits later is not. It is much harder to justify such sacrifice of one human being for another than it is to justify sacrifices within the life of a single human being. But the mere fact that we are distinct beings, each with his or her own life to lead, does not seem to be sufficient to establish our status as inviolable beings. Note that it would arguably be permissible, in some circumstances, to kill a small number of deer in a given overpopulated stretch of wilderness in order to spare a greater number from death by starvation in the next generation, even though it would not be permissible, in analogous circumstances, to kill a minority of human beings in a given overpopulated society in order to spare a greater number from death by starvation in the next generation. Yet a deer is, just as much as a human being, a distinct being, with its own life to lead. A deer that is killed for the sake of other deer does not gain any overbalancing good as compensation for its sacrifice. In order to establish our status as inviolable beings, we need therefore to do more than affirm the distinctness of persons. We also need to explain why these distinct persons, as compared with other distinct beings such as deer, are worthy of such high respect and hence ought to be treated as inviolable rather than ever as mere means that may be sacrificed for the greater good.

2.4.2 Constraints and the capacity to lead a meaningful life

Nozick offers such an explanation in a section of Chapter 3 of *ASU* entitled "What Are Constraints Based Upon?". There he says that persons must possess some property or trait by virtue of which they are entitled to the respect of inviolable beings rather than treatment as mere means. According to him, this property is *a capacity to shape one's life in accordance with an overall plan that one chooses to accept*. According to Nozick, this capacity is morally significant because "only a being with the capacity to so shape his life can have or strive for meaningful life" (p. 50).

Nozick's attempt to ground deontological constraints in this fashion attracted early and influential criticism that built upon observations such as the following by Samuel Scheffler:

Nozick *believes* that the moral basis of rights has to do with the capacity to live a meaningful life … [But if] the capacity to live a meaningful life is a uniquely valuable characteristic, and if we say that beings with this characteristic have *rights*, in virtue of which there are constraints on the way others must behave, then presumably the function of the rights is to safeguard the ability of beings with this valuable characteristic to *develop* it. To say that this valuable capacity to live a meaningful life is the *basis* of rights, is presumably to suggest that the moral protections and guarantees which rights assign to people may be understood as jealous of people's ability to actually *live* meaningful lives. (Scheffler: 1976, pp. 69–70)[16]

Scheffler maintains, however, that certain positive rights to assistance that are incompatible with such constraints would better "protect and guarantee the valuable capacity to live a meaningful life" (Scheffler: 1976, p. 70) than would the deontological constraints that Nozick affirms. Here Scheffler is concerned to argue that anti-libertarian positive rights to the distributable goods that the welfare state provides are implications of Nozick's rationale for deontological constraints. But the considerations to which Scheffler appeals also lend support to the claim that Nozick's rationale implies a permission to violate the deontological constraints of a small number against being harmed in a manner that deprives them of their abilities to lead meaningful lives in order thereby to prevent many others from suffering the same type of harm. For more people would be able "to actually *live* meaningful lives" if such constraints were violated rather than respected.

In *ASU*, Nozick anticipates this line of objection. He writes:

Why are there constraints on how we may treat beings shaping their lives [in accordance with some overall plan]? Are certain modes of treatment incompatible with their having meaningful lives? And even if so, why not destroy meaningful lives? Or, why not replace "happiness" with "meaningfulness" within utilitarian theory, and maximize the total "meaningfulness" score of the persons of the world? Or does the notion of meaningfulness of a life enter into ethics in a different fashion? (p. 50)

In order to rebut this line of objection, the last question stands in need of an affirmative answer.

To provide such an answer on Nozick's behalf, one might point out, as Scanlon and Parfit recently have, that *promoting* that thing is not the only appropriate response to something of value (see Scanlon: 1998, ch. 2 and Parfit: 2011, section 34). *Respecting* that thing is an appropriate response in the case of some such things. As an illustration of the latter, Parfit invokes Immanuel Kant's approach to moral status or standing: "Kant means that all rational beings have a kind of value that is to be respected, since these beings ought to be treated only in certain ways. This value is a kind of *status*, or what Herman calls 'moral standing'" (Parfit: 2011, p. 243). Similarly, Kamm writes that the value of "the high degree of inviolability of persons ... is not a consequentialist value that we promote by bringing about something through action or omission. The value already resides *in* persons and we act in the light of it" (Kamm: 2007, p. 29).

Another way to put this point is that we should understand the value of our high moral status as something that is respected by deontological constraints rather than something that is to be promoted through constraint-minimizing violations. As Warren Quinn explains:

The value that lies at the heart of my argument [for deontological rights not to be harmed] – the appropriateness of morality's recognizing us as independent beings – is in the first instance a virtue of the moral design *itself*. The fittingness of this recognition is not a goal of action, and therefore not something that we could be tempted to serve by violating or infringing anybody's rights ... It is not that we think it fitting to ascribe rights because we think it a good thing that rights be respected. Rather we think respect for rights a good thing precisely because we think people actually have them. (Quinn: 1989, p. 312)

2.4.3 Does greater inviolability reflect a higher moral status?

The moral status rationale for deontological constraints is premised upon the claim that human beings to whom deontological constraints apply have a higher moral status, which these constraints reflect, than beings such as deer that are less inviolable. This claim has been subjected to the following powerful line of criticism. Shelly Kagan has argued that the greater inviolability of those who enjoy the moral immunity provided by deontological constraints is a double-edged sword: it is bought at the expense of a lesser "saveability" (see Kagan: 1991, pp. 919–920).[17] The greater the inviolability of a being, the greater its moral status insofar as less may be done to it (without its consent) for the sake of the greater good of other beings of the same type. But the greater the inviolability of a being, the less may be done to other beings of the same type in order to *save* it from being violated. Saveability, like inviolability, is surely an important indicator of moral status. Consider an example of an emperor who is so revered that it is permissible to engage in the human sacrifice of many to save his life. Surely this high degree of saveability would constitute a mark of a very high moral status. For the moral status rationale for constraints to succeed, one must therefore show that the greater moral status that our greater inviolability reflects in comparison with the lesser inviolability of deer (and other animals) more than outweighs the apparently lesser moral status that our lesser saveability reflects in comparison with the greater saveability of these same animals.[18]

Kamm attempts to do so when she writes:

to say that their status would go down if they were violable (in certain ways) even if they were more saveable is to claim that the properties that underlie one's inviolability are more important than those that give rise to any other significance one has. Might it be to claim that having a rational will, whose consent we must seek when interfering with what a person has independently of imposition on us, will give a person higher status than being a complex, feeling creature who cares about whether it lives or dies? (Kamm: 1996, pp. 276–277)

The suggestion here is that we should identify the property of persons that grounds their inviolability, and also identify the property of persons that grounds their saveability, and then compare the relative significance of these properties. The former property is, Kamm suggests, the possession of rational, autonomous agency, whereas the latter is the possession of desires to persist rather than perish. Perhaps it will be possible to argue that the former property is more morally important than the latter.

Even if, however, this can be done, Kamm notes that the following problem for the moral status rationale of constraints would remain: "But what if it is only a question of the saveability of individuals whose rational wills are being interfered with?" (Kamm: 1996, p. 277). The challenge raised here is that the property of rational, autonomous agency would appear to provide compelling grounds for a permission to be saved as well as for constraints against interference when the interference in question from which one might be saved is interference with one's rational will. Kamm replies (1996, p. 277) that a permission to interfere with the rational will of a person in order to prevent comparable interference with the rational wills of more persons would amount to the denial of "a high degree of personal sovereignty" and also of the significance of "the existence of separate persons with rational wills" that grounds such sovereignty.

But why isn't the extent of one's personal sovereignty, and the significance of the grounding property of rational, autonomous agency, also a function of the extent to which it is permissible to save one from interference with one's rational will – that is, a function of one's saveability?

Other things equal, the permissibility of others rushing in to prevent interference with a person's rational will appears to be a mark of the significance of that grounding property. If, for example, it were permissible for the police to put on their sirens and speed to the scene of an individual whose rational will is being interfered with by a kidnapping torturer, whereas such would not be permissible in order to prevent a petty act of shoplifting, that would be an indication of the greater significance of rights of non-interference with rational agency than of rights over certain material possessions.

The extent to which people are permitted to protect their rational agency against interference also appears, other things equal, to mark the extent of that personal sovereignty itself. Another way of putting this point is that the extent of someone's personal sovereignty is greater not only to the extent to which one's rights against interference with one's rational agency are greater but also to the extent that people's rights to enforce these rights against interference are greater. Even if the extent of someone's personal sovereignty is not a function of the rights of *others* to enforce his rights against interference, it at least appears to be a function of his *own* rights to enforce his rights against interference. Imagine, for example, that all morally innocent agents have absolute rights against interference with their rational wills, but nobody has any enforcement rights over these rights against interference whatsoever. We do not even possess enforcement rights against such interference where the enforcement would involve only thwarting the wills of morally responsible agents who are interfering with our agency and not also the harming of innocent bystanders. It would not, therefore, be permissible for a victim of aggression even gently to push away a morally responsible aggressor even if that were necessary and sufficient to prevent him from interfering with this person's rational agency by killing him. By virtue of our powerlessness, morally speaking, to protect our personal sovereignty, we would, in this scenario, arguably possess a lesser degree of personal sovereignty than we would possess if we had the right to thwart the wills of morally responsible aggressors to a much greater extent in order to prevent them from interfering with our rational agency.

Why, then, should not the right to enforce our rights against interference in a manner that involves the harming of innocent bystanders also constitute an increase, in one dimension, of the extent of our personal sovereignty? Granted, there would be a decrease, in another dimension, of our personal sovereignty, as our rights against interference would be diminished if such enforcement were permitted.[19] There is, moreover, a case for rights against interference taking some precedence over enforcement rights when the two come into conflict. Take, for example, the clash between one's right not to be killed and an enforcement right to kill one innocent bystander in order to enforce one's right not to be killed. It seems that the right not to be killed makes a greater contribution to our personal sovereignty than the enforcement right over that right, other things equal. But what if other things are not equal? Suppose that each of us had an enforcement right to non-lethally maim one innocent bystander in order to prevent oneself from being killed by somebody else. Why would not our personal sovereignty be greater, all things considered, if such means of protecting ourselves against interference were morally protected?

It is not clear that a defender of the moral status rationale can provide a convincing answer to this question. It would not, for example, be open to such a defender to claim that, as a conceptual matter, one's personal sovereignty simply involves the extent of one's rights against interference and is nothing to do with one's rights to enforce these rights. For if one were to advance that claim, then one would simply be identifying personal sovereignty with inviolability. But then it would become empty to claim that greater inviolability is a mark of higher moral status because such greater inviolability correlates with more extensive personal sovereignty. This would be empty, since the claim that greater inviolability correlates with more extensive personal sovereignty would amount to the claim that greater inviolability correlates with greater inviolability, which could not provide an explanation of the claim that greater inviolability is a mark of higher moral status.

2.5 THE SIGNIFICANCE OF MERE MEANS VERSUS ENDS IN THEMSELVES

I shall conclude with a few words on the Kantian distinction that Nozick draws between beings that are ends in themselves and those that are mere means. Recall that deontological constraints provide much greater moral protection against being harmfully used as a means than they do against merely foreseen harm. Moreover, anyone who opposes the killing of someone as a means to prevent more people from being killed by, for example, pushing one into the path of the boulder rolling downhill must explain why it is, by contrast, permissible to divert such a boulder along a path where it will merely foreseeably kill one in order to prevent it from running over and killing the greater number towards which it is now headed.[20] Insofar as an individual's degree of inviolability is concerned, these two ways in which one's rights against interference might be violated seem to be roughly on a par. Why, then, do we enjoy so relatively little moral protection against being the victim of merely foreseen killings? Is it because there remains room for other creatures, real or imaginary, who stand above us in the great chain of being and possess a higher moral status than ours? Nozick famously entertains the possibility of creatures with a higher moral status than our own. Perhaps their higher moral status is reflected in an inviolability that is greater than that of human beings insofar as they may not be foreseeably harmed as well as not being harmed as a means (see *ASU*, pp. 45–47).[21] The problem with this particular proposal is that it does not appear that much more rational or otherwise exalted creatures than human beings would, vis-à-vis one another, be more inviolable in this regard. It does not appear, for example, that it would be impermissible to divert a boulder away from five and toward one such exalted creature.[22] Perhaps, then, rather than such a multi-layered hierarchy of differences in moral status, there is a simpler and starker division between those beings that are ends in themselves and those that may be treated as mere means, where anyone who exceeds – or perhaps who belongs to a species of beings whose normal members exceed – a threshold of rational agency gains entry into the kingdom of ends and the correlative right to treatment as an end in itself rather than as a mere means, the latter of which is precisely the sort of treatment that deontological constraints are meant to exclude.[23]

NOTES

I presented a version of this paper at a conference at King's College London in January 2010 and should like to thank the participants for their comments.

I also thank Ralf Bader, Peter Graham, Thomas Porter, Alex Voorhoeve, and Ralph Wedgwood for their comments.

1. Named after St. Paul, who says: "And not rather, (as we be slanderously reported, and as some affirm that we say,) Let us do evil, that good may come?" Romans 3:8.

2. This is a modified version of a case of T. M. Scanlon's (cf. Scanlon: 1998, p. 235).

3. More precisely: the greatest sum total of *net* happiness (happiness minus unhappiness).

4. For the purposes of this chapter, a person suffers a harm whenever he suffers a non-trivial reduction in his welfare (or "utility") in comparison with the welfare he would otherwise have enjoyed.

5. See John Stuart Mill's discussion of "higher" and "lower" pleasures in Mill: 1867, ch. 2.

6. Note that this doctrine only condemns the doing of evil as a *means*. It does not condemn the doing of evil whenever so doing is necessary if you are to prevent a greater evil. Imagine that the only way to prevent the boulder from rolling over and crushing the five is to divert it from its path but on to a different pathway down which it will eventually roll over and kill one other person instead. Such redirecting of the boulder would not be ruled out by the Pauline doctrine, since here the killing of the one is merely a foreseen consequence of, rather than a *means* to, the prevention of the killing of the five. For classic discussions of cases akin to this one involving diversion towards the lesser number, see Foot: 1967 and Thomson: 1985.

7. It is, according to Nozick, always possible to posit a rigged goal that a moral theory fully realizes, since it is always "possible to define an artificial real-valued function whose maximization mirrors the judgments about impermissibility of the view; simply define a function f taking actions as argument values, such that $f(A) = 0$ if and only if according to the moral view in question, A is morally impermissible, and $f(A) = 1$ when according to that moral view, A is permissible. That moral view then can be said to mandate the maximization of f" (Nozick: 1981, p. 733 n. 71).

8. Two such deontologists are Frances Kamm: 1996 and Richard Brook: 1991.

9. This type of case and variations have been extensively discussed by Kamm: 1996, ch. 9. There Kamm notes that Alan Zaitchik: 1977 is the first of whom she is aware to discuss "cases in which the person who needs to act is the person who tried to kill."

10. It is of course true that whatever you do in these bizarre circumstances, you will be blameworthy for having killed, since you are morally responsible for, and could have avoided, getting into this dilemma in the first place.

11. This strategy of reconciliation of goal and constraint has been suggested by Brook: 1991, Kamm: 1996, ch. 9, and Montmarquet: 1985.

12. Nancy (Ann) Davis: 1984 employs such an example to make a different point. She credits Derek Parfit as her source for the example.

13. Perhaps you made these promises in emails that you sent to, and which were received by, the six simultaneously.

14. In an interview, Kamm describes Nozick's inspiration for her own work as follows: "[When I was a graduate student] I took an ethics course with Bob Nozick at Harvard – and that's what did it, because I found what he was doing *really* interesting. You know, about one-and-a-half years before he died, Nozick gave a talk in my ethics colloquium at NYU, where I was teaching at the time. And when I introduced him, I said that for the last twenty years I had been finishing the term paper for his class" (Voorhoeve: 2009, p. 18).

15. Compare Rawls's critique of classical utilitarianism in Rawls: 1971, section 5.

16. See also Nagel: 1981 for a somewhat related line of criticism.

17. See also Kasper Lippert-Rasmussen: 1996.

18. Here I am assuming that these magnitudes of inviolability and saveability are expressed in terms of ratios of the number of beings that one would need to be able to save from harm of a given type before it would be permissible to inflict harm of a given type on a being *of the same type*. I leave to one side measures of the relative moral status of different beings that take account of what one may do to beings of one type for the sake of beings of *another* type – for example, whether one may kill one or more deer in order to save a single human being from being killed.

19. Enforcement rights against morally responsible agents would arguably not involve a decrease in this dimension, as it is plausible to maintain that they have already partially forfeited their personal sovereignty by interfering with the sovereignty of others.

20. See n. 6 plus the main text of section 2.1.

21. Here I set to one side the "saveability" objection to such a claim that was discussed in the previous section.

22. See Otsuka: 1997, pp. 204–205.

23. This is not to say that animals that fall below the threshold may be treated as nothing more than tools or other instrumental means to the

maximization of the good. We would also need to draw a distinction between at least some such animals and mere objects. Nozick does so when he rejects the slogan "utilitarianism for animals, Kantianism for people" on grounds that animals are worthier of a higher moral status than utilitarian treatment even if not as high a status as that of persons (see pp. 35–42).

3   What we learn from the experience machine

3.1   A LITTLE PASSAGE WITH A BIG IMPACT

Nozick discusses the experience machine in a little (four paragraph) section of Chapter 3 of *Anarchy, State, and Utopia* (*ASU*).[1] The section seems to be a mere speculative digression from Nozick's main line of argument, and yet it has come to be perhaps the most widely discussed passage of the book. It has been reprinted and paraphrased and discussed thousands of times. Yet it seems to me that the passage is a bit of a mystery – perhaps it functions as a kind of Rorschach test for readers. Different readers apparently find different arguments in Nozick's remarks. It may seem that the various interpretations tell us more about the interests of the readers than about the argument that Nozick actually presented.

In section 3.2 I outline the context in which the controversial passage appears. What I say in this part may come as a surprise to anyone whose knowledge of the passage derives entirely from seeing it only as a selection in an anthology, isolated from its original context. After sketching the contents of the passage in section 3.3, I go on in section 3.4 to explain and evaluate some versions of one fairly popular interpretation of the argument. Under these interpretations, the argument is taken to be an attack on utilitarianism. I claim that every one of these interpretations is implausible. According to a much more popular style of interpretation, Nozick's argument was intended to refute ethical hedonism (or perhaps the entire class of "mental state" theories of welfare). In section 3.5 I present several versions of the argument so understood. I go on to explain why I think every such version of the argument fails. A few commentators have supposed that Nozick was attacking some form of psychological hedonism. I discuss their views in section 3.6. Finally, in section 3.7, I summarize my views on all the arguments that are discussed in the chapter. In a short appendix I offer – briefly and tentatively – a somewhat different argument that is merely suggested by Nozick's remarks.

3.2 THE CONTEXT

Nozick's project in the first sections of *ASU* is straightforwardly at the heart of political philosophy: he is trying to show how the existence of a state could be justified. He is trying to do this by starting with a description of a certain anarchic situation. In this situation, people have certain inviolable moral rights – fundamentally the right not to be attacked or killed and the right not to have their possessions stolen. He imagines that voluntary "protective associations" might spring up in this state of nature. People might get together for mutual protection, each one pledging to the others that if they are attacked, he will come to their aid. This might be a good idea. But such protective agencies would not be states; they would just be voluntary associations of individuals who have banded together for one fundamental purpose: mutual protection.

It is possible that a "dominant protective agency" would arise in some area. This one would be the most powerful in its geographical region. It would have the power to protect its members (for a fee) and could insist on various concessions from members. But even such a thing would not be a state. One crucial factor is voluntariness. Suppose some individual is residing in the domain of a protective agency. Suppose he chooses to fend for himself, and thus not to make use of the agency's services. Then the agency cannot force him to join. It is voluntary after all. Furthermore, it is under no obligation to protect the interests of non-members living within its domain. Such an agency could not claim any monopoly on the determination of who can use force and when they can use it. The agency would have no power to say, for example, that other groups living within its domain cannot form independent militias. A state, on the other hand, apparently would be able to do these things.

The Nightwatchman State (or Minimal State) goes well beyond this sort of dominant protective agency. It does offer protection to everyone in its domain. If some cannot pay for this protection, it provides tax-funded vouchers. Thus, it takes money from some members so as to pay the costs involved in defending others. It thus appears to be redistributive.[2] It compels some people to pay for benefits to be enjoyed by others. This is a state, though of course a minimal one.

Nozick claims that there is a form of state-like arrangement that is intermediate between the dominant protective agency and the minimal state. He calls this the "ultraminimal state." Unlike the mere protective agency, the ultraminimal state does claim a monopoly on the use of force. It prohibits the formation of other protective agencies (such as the Mafia, or the KKK) within its domain. However, unlike a full-blown Nightwatchman State, it does not provide services to those who do not join or cannot pay. It is still a "private" association. Nor does it provide any other services to members. It takes money from members and provides protection (but nothing else) to members.

Nozick wonders whether an advocate of the ultraminimal state might be open to charges of inconsistency. What could justify minimal redistribution for protective services but not for anything else? The advocate of such a state seems to think that there is something especially important about the protection of members' rights not to be harmed; but at the same time he seems to think it is acceptable to violate these rights when exacting payments from members to set up a system to protect the rights of others. So he advocates the violation of the rights of some in order to protect certain of the rights of others. Is this coherent?

This is the context in which Nozick starts talking about the utilitarianism of rights. He sees two options: the non-violation of rights might be taken as a goal. In this case, it would be permissible to violate some rights if that were required in order to ensure that rights as a whole would be minimally violated. On the other hand, the non-violation of rights might be taken as a constraint. In this case, the violation of someone's rights would be forbidden even if as a result many others would have their rights violated.

If a proponent of the ultraminimal state takes non-violation of rights to be the goal, with violations of such rights to be minimized as the utilitarianism of rights would suggest, he is in a bind. For in this case he is taking the non-violation of rights as a goal; and he is willing to adopt any means necessary to achieve this goal – even if it involves violating someone's rights. This may seem to be an incoherent conception. But on the other hand, if he accepts a side constraints view, there is no inconsistency. For in this case he does not advocate violating anyone's rights for the purpose of defending the rights of others.

This leads Nozick to a discussion of the question whether the side constraints view should be understood to include a constraint against violating the rights of animals as well as those of humans. And this leads him into a somewhat unexpected discussion of vegetarianism. And this leads him into an even more unexpected discussion of something like the non-identity problem (later discussed more directly by Parfit). And all this leads him to a consideration of a surprising moral principle: "utilitarianism for animals; Kantianism for people." Nozick sketches this principle as follows:

UA/KP: (1) Maximize the total happiness of all living beings; (2) place stringent side constraints on what one may do to human beings. (p. 39)

UA/KP does not include a constraint against violating the rights of animals. It would be permissible to violate their rights if that were required in order to maximize happiness overall.

Nozick mentions "a thicket of questions" about utilitarianism for animals. Some of these are reminiscent of questions that were subsequently made famous by Parfit (1984) (though of course Parfit did not restrict himself to consideration of non-human animals). For example, does the theory imply that there is a duty to increase the number of animals even when each animal is less happy just so long as the total amount of happiness is increased? (This is the Repugnant Conclusion.) Would it be morally permissible for someone to kill off everyone else if that made him ecstatic – after all, the average level of happiness would thereby be maximized? (This is the Ten Little Indians Case or perhaps the Utility Monster Case.) Is it OK to kill one person provided that you immediately replace him with another person who is slightly happier? (This is the Non-Identity Problem.)

Those are all tough nuts for the utilitarian to crack. They raise serious questions about utilitarianism for people. However, it remains possible that utilitarianism for animals would be acceptable. And this at last leads to the discussion of the experience machine. If there were such a machine, would we choose to plug in? It seems to be a digression within a digression within a digression. Nozick strongly suggests (p. 45) that he is discussing it for one main reason: we need to know what matters for people in addition to their mere experiences, and we need to know whether this thing (whatever it may turn out to be) also matters for animals, and so long as we have not answered these questions, we "cannot reasonably claim that only the felt experiences of animals limit what we may do to them" (p. 45).

There follows the famous passage.

3.3 THE PASSAGE ITSELF

The section entitled "The Experience Machine" consists of only four paragraphs. The thought experiment described in the first three paragraphs is nowadays familiar to virtually all philosophers. I will provide only a reminder. The reader is encouraged to reread the passage itself.

In the first paragraph (pp. 42–43) Nozick briefly describes the machine. He says it would "give you any experience you desired." He mentions the experiences of writing a great novel, making a friend, or reading an interesting book. "All the time you would be floating in a tank, with electrodes attached to your brain."[3] He then asks: "*Should* you plug into this machine for life ...?" (p. 42, emphasis added). He then describes how you could emerge from the tank after two years and pick a new set of experiences that you could enjoy upon your return to the tank. Then he asks: "*Would* you plug in?" (p. 43, emphasis added).

In the second paragraph (p. 43) Nozick mentions two things that matter to us in addition to our experiences: "First, we want to do certain things, and not just have the experience of doing them." Second, "we want to be a certain way, to be a certain sort of person." He claims that if a person plugs into the experience machine, he commits "a kind of suicide." "[T]here is no way he is."

In the third paragraph (pp. 43–44) Nozick says that if you plug into the machine, you "would be limited to a man-made reality, to a world no deeper or more important than that which people can construct." He proceeds to sketch the analogy between plugging into the machine and taking psychoactive drugs. In each case, Nozick acknowledges that readers may reach different assessments: does the subject merely "surrender," or does he take an "avenue to a deeper reality"?

In the fourth paragraph of the section, Nozick engages in speculation about a "transformation machine" and a "result machine." Nozick says that he will "not pursue here the fascinating details of these or other machines." He goes on to offer some speculations:

> Perhaps what we desire is to live (an active verb) ourselves, in contact with reality. (And this, machines cannot do for us.) Without elaborating on the implications of this, which I believe connect surprisingly with issues about free will and causal accounts of knowledge, we need merely note the intricacy of the question of what matters for people other than their experiences. Until one finds a satisfactory answer, and determines that this answer does not also apply to animals, one cannot reasonably claim that only the felt experiences of animals limit what we may do to them. (pp. 44–45)

Different readers come away from this section with different ideas about what Nozick was trying to show. Most philosophers who comment on the passage seem to agree that Nozick presented the example of the experience machine in order to show that some philosophical or psychological theory is false. There is disagreement about the target theory: precisely what was Nozick out to refute? I think there are four main interpretations.[4] According to some, his target was (A) act utilitarianism. According to others it was (B) ethical hedonism as a theory of individual welfare. Others seem to think he was attacking (C) the whole class of mental state theories of welfare. Still others think the target is not in ethics at all. Rather, it is (D) psychological hedonism – a theory about human motivation.[5]

Let us first consider how the argument might be thought to constitute an attack on act utilitarianism.

3.4 UNDERSTOOD AS AN ARGUMENT AGAINST UTILITARIANISM

The discussion of the experience machine comes right after some talk about "utilitarianism for animals"; immediately following it there comes a section in which Nozick mentions that utilitarianism allows us to treat animals as mere means. Perhaps these facts about context have led some commentators to think that Nozick was presenting an argument against utilitarianism in the experience machine passage.[6] There is no evidence in the passage itself that would support this interpretation. In light of things he says elsewhere in the book, it seems clear that Nozick thought that utilitarianism was in deep trouble. He mentions a series of familiar objections.[7] None of these has anything to do with the experience machine. But since so many apparently think that Nozick was attacking utilitarianism, and since he does at least talk about it in the vicinity, it may be worthwhile to consider whether there are hints of an interesting argument against utilitarianism in the experience machine passage.

When we speak of utilitarianism, we are really speaking about a whole family of similar views. Each of these views is a general theory about morally right action. Each purports to state necessary and sufficient conditions for the moral rightness of specific act tokens. Different forms of utilitarianism can be seen as variations on this central theme:

> AU: An act token, a, is morally right if and only if a maximizes actual total utility.[8]

In one place near the beginning of the passage (p. 42) Nozick rhetorically asks: "Should you plug into this machine for life, preprogramming your life's experiences?" The context makes it clear that he thinks the obvious answer is "No. You should not plug in." This gives us a hint of one way to understand the argument.

Let us say that you are in the "Nozick Scenario" if you have been living a fairly pleasant life and can reasonably expect to go on in pretty much the same way; but someone has offered you the opportunity to plug into an experience machine. You have been assured that if you plug in, you will experience a much greater balance of pleasure over pain, just as Nozick has described. Now we can state the argument:

First Anti-Utilitarian Argument

1. If AU is true, then you should plug into the experience machine when in the Nozick Scenario.

2.   But in fact it is not the case that you should plug into the experience machine when in the Nozick Scenario.

3.   Therefore, AU is not true.

This argument is unworthy of extended discussion. There is nothing to be said for premise (1). It seems unlikely that a person floating his life away in a tank would be doing much to enhance the utility levels of his former friends and family.[9] Although the person's own utility level might be fairly high, he would be missing out on many opportunities to provide utility for others. Hence, in anything approaching normal circumstances, the act of plugging in would have relatively low utility. AU then implies that you should not plug in. Premise (1) is just silly.[10]

In the rest of the experience machine passage, Nozick does not say that you should not plug in; rather, he says (or strongly implies) that you would not plug in. This makes it considerably more difficult to see how the premise could be thought to bear on AU. Surely premise (1) of this argument is too preposterous for any discussion.

Second Anti-Utilitarian Argument

1.   If AU is true, then you would plug into the experience machine when in the Nozick Scenario.

2.   But in fact it is not the case that you would plug into the experience machine when in the Nozick Scenario.

3.   Therefore, AU is not true.

AU has no implications concerning what you would do under any circumstances.[11]

Nozick's reflections on the experience machine might be thought to be connected to utilitarianism in a different way. Perhaps the argument goes like this: you would not plug into the experience machine when in the Nozick Scenario. This shows that you value something other than pleasure. And this shows that something other than pleasure has value – in other words, it shows that hedonism is false. But utilitarianism is just the combination of (a) the idea that we should perform the act that maximizes utility, and (b) the idea that the utility of an act is determined hedonistically. Therefore, since hedonism is false, utilitarianism is false. (We may call this the Third Anti-Utilitarianism Argument.)[12]

That would be a tidy little argument, moving smoothly from what seems to be Nozick's central claim ("you would not plug in") to a very interesting conclusion ("utilitarianism is false"). However, there are several serious problems with this interpretation. Foremost among them is that there is no clear evidence in the text that Nozick intended to present this argument. While he does seem to commit himself to the first premise, and he seems to endorse something like the suggested conclusion, there is no hint in the relevant section of *ASU* of the intermediate premises.[13]

The second problem with the interpretation is that the proposed argument would be relevant only to versions of utilitarianism that incorporate a hedonistic axiology. Other versions would be unaffected. Consider, for example, the sort of utilitarianism that ranks outcomes by appeal to the extent to which preferences are satisfied. The current anti-utilitarian argument cannot be revised so as to cast doubt on that sort of utilitarianism. Consider, for another example, the sort of utilitarianism that ranks outcomes by appeal to the extent to which people realize their distinctive human potential. The proposed argument would cut no ice with respect to this theory, either. The same could be said for a wide variety of preferentist, eudaimonist, perfectionist, and pluralist forms of utilitarianism. Thus, in the absence of solid proof that this was the argument Nozick intended, it would be more charitable to seek some other interpretation. Perhaps the argument is meant to refute only those forms of utilitarianism that make use of a hedonistic axiology.

But this leads us to a deeper point about the dialectic. On the latest proposed interpretation, the experience machine argument is intended to refute hedonistic utilitarianism. The argument proceeds by casting doubt on the axiological component of the normative theory. It is silent concerning the basic idea that right acts are ones that maximize some sort of value. It seems to me, in this case, that it would make more sense to view the argument simply as an attack on hedonism. If it refutes hedonism, then by extension it would refute any wider theory that contains hedonism as a part.

3.5 UNDERSTOOD AS AN ARGUMENT AGAINST ETHICAL HEDONISM

Quite a few commentators have thought that Nozick's target in the experience machine passage was ethical hedonism.[14] For purposes of discussion here, I take ethical hedonism to be a theory about personal welfare or wellbeing. To be more precise, I take it to be the view that a person's welfare is directly proportional to the amount of sensory pleasure-minus-pain that he experiences.

One immediate implication of this form of hedonism is that if one possible life has a greater balance of pleasure-minus-pain than another, then the one must have greater welfare value than the other, regardless of other differences between them. This gives us a neat way to understand the point that many readers find in the experience machine passage.

Imagine that you have started out living a certain life, LA (your Actual Life). Things are going reasonably well for you and if you stick with LA you will end up with a fairly pleasant life. Now you are in the Nozick Scenario and someone has offered you a chance to plug into the experience machine. He tells you that if you plug in, you will have many intense and long-lasting episodes of pleasure. You will get to live life LEM (life on the experience machine), which will give you a significantly greater total amount of pleasure-minus-pain. With this as background, we may state a version of the argument that some claim to find lurking in the experience machine passage:

First Anti-Ethical Hedonism Argument

1. If you were in the Nozick Scenario you would not plug in so as to get LEM. You would stick with LA.
2. If (1), then LEM does not have greater welfare value than LA.
3. If LEM does not have greater welfare value than LA, then ethical hedonism is false.
4. Therefore, ethical hedonism is false.

I think (1) is plausible. At least, it is plausible when construed as a claim about what I would do if I were in the Nozick Scenario. If I were given such a choice, I would not choose LEM. For me, the choice would not be difficult. I would prefer to stick with my real life rather than take on a new life on the experience machine. I assume that many others are like me in this respect.[15] But I think there is no reason to accept (2). From the fact that you would be reluctant to choose LEM over LA, nothing follows about the welfare values of the two lives. There are several possible explanations for this. One of the main problems here is epistemic: how can you be sure that the machine would work as advertised? Maybe it is just a scam. Maybe the machine would malfunction. This would give you good reason to avoid plugging in. Refusing to plug in under these circumstances would have no implications concerning welfare values.[16]

Let us revise the example so as to avoid the epistemic difficulties. Let us assume that when you are given the choice of LEM or LA, you know beyond the shadow of any doubt that LEM would contain a substantially greater amount of pleasure-minus-pain. Under these circumstances, would you plug in? We may assume that Nozick would say that you would not.

But even if I were absolutely certain about what would happen to me if I were to plug in, I still might choose to stick with my old life rather than take on a new life in the experience machine. I might do this even though in the imagined circumstances I would know for sure that life on the machine would give me greater pleasure-minus-pain. One simple reason is this: I might think it would be morally wrong to plug into the machine. I have made a bunch of promises to my wife and my daughter and my students and my dog. I might recognize that if I plug in, I will be unable to keep those promises. Under these circumstances, I would probably think it would be morally wrong to choose the pleasant life on the machine and so I would not plug in. But my refusal to plug in would show nothing about the truth of hedonism. Premise (2) remains false.[17]

Let us introduce another adjustment. Let us assume that the subject of the experiment is not only well informed; let us assume in addition that he is completely selfish. Let us assume that he is concerned only about himself. Ordinary selfishness may not be sufficient here; we need to go a bit further: we must assume that the subject is "welfare selfish." He cares only about his own welfare. He does not care about his "moral welfare." Might such a person still refuse to plug in? Would that show that hedonism is false? In other words, what shall we say about this argument?

Second Anti-Ethical Hedonism Argument

1. If you were in the Nozick Scenario, and you knew beyond doubt that LEM would be more pleasant than LA, and you were welfare selfish, still you would not plug in so as to get LEM. You would stick with LA.
2. If (1), then LEM does not have greater welfare value than LA.

3. If LEM does not have greater welfare value than LA, then ethical hedonism is false.

4. Therefore, ethical hedonism is false.

Even with these conditions built into the assumptions, it still seems to me that (2) is open to doubt. One further problem is that you might refuse to plug in because you find the idea of life in the experience machine icky and repugnant. It might just seem too weird and unnatural. In this respect you might be like a patient who refuses some novel medical treatment because it just seems disgusting. He might recognize that undergoing the treatment would be for the best, but he might prefer to remain "naturally" sick.

We can deal with this problem as well. We can stipulate that the subject in the Nozick Scenario has to be fully rational.[18] He cannot allow worries about "ickiness" or "unnaturalness" to deflect him from the course that will maximize his own long-term welfare.

In spite of all this, it still seems to me that premise (2) is open to doubt. You might know for certain that plugging in would be very pleasant, and you might be rational and welfare selfish, but you still might refuse to plug in. This could happen if you do not believe in hedonism. Suppose, for example, that you believe in some form of perfectionism. You think that a person's welfare is determined by the extent to which he conforms to some human ideal. You think this human ideal involves moral, intellectual, aesthetic, athletic, and other achievement. Since you are fully committed to this view about the Good Life, you are not impressed by the offer of a life on the experience machine. "Why would I want that miserable life?" you ask. "I would be much worse off if I were to plug in."

The fact that you would not choose LEM in the imagined circumstances might be thought to show that you do not believe that LEM has higher welfare value than LA, but it does not show that this belief is true.

In order to avoid this sort of difficulty, we need to stipulate that the person in the Nozick Scenario is not already committed to some anti-hedonistic theory of welfare. For so long as we allow that he might be so committed, his choice of LA over LEM might be due to his views about welfare rather than to the fact that LA is actually the better life.

But here we run into profound difficulties. If we say that the subject in the Nozick Scenario simply has no views about what makes for a good life, then it becomes doubtful that he would have any reason to choose to plug in for LEM or to stick with LA. He would presumably have no basis for thinking one life would be better than the other. If we say that the subject accepts hedonism as his theory of welfare, then surely the subject would choose LEM. In this case, premise (1) would be false. If we say that he must accept some non-hedonistic theory of welfare, then he might choose LA, but this would show nothing about the truth of hedonism. The subject's choice would be attributable to his acceptance of a non-hedonistic theory of welfare.

There is another option. We can say that the subject in the Nozick Scenario is "axiologically insightful" – he prefers one life over another only if the one is actually better for him than the other.[19] This rules out the possibility that the chooser might refuse to plug in because he is in the grip of some faulty axiology.

Now we may restate the argument:

Third Anti-Ethical Hedonism Argument

  1. If you were in the Nozick Scenario and you knew beyond doubt that LEM would be more pleasant than LA, and you were completely welfare selfish, and you were rational, and you were axiologically insightful, still you would not plug in so as to get LEM. You would stick with LA.

  2. If (1), then LEM does not have greater welfare value than LA.

  3. If LEM does not have greater welfare value than LA, then ethical hedonism is false.

  4. Therefore, ethical hedonism is false.

Now, it seems to me, we have reached a turning point in the dialectic. With all these extra conditions in place, premise (2) is beginning to seem more plausible. In fact, I find it difficult to imagine how a person with all the traits described here could fail to choose the welfare better life. He cares only about getting the life that will be best for him; he is completely rational; his preferences match the actual values of the possible lives. Every rationale for choosing the less-good life seems to have been ruled out. So if the person were to choose LA, that would support the notion that LA is the better life; and that would refute hedonism.

But once we make these changes in the description of the choice scenario, the plausibility of premise (1) begins to fade. Surely it is now open to the hedonist to say that a chooser like the one we have been describing would choose life in the experience machine. The hedonist would say that since pleasure is the good, any welfare-selfish, knowledgeable, rational person whose preferences match the true values of things would undoubtedly choose the life of pleasure.

It is pointless to insist that you would not plug in. What you would do is irrelevant. We would need to know what a person who is perfectly rational, welfare selfish, knowledgeable, and so forth would do. You are not like that. The idea of a life on the experience machine probably seems totally icky to you.[20,21]

3.6 UNDERSTOOD AS AN ARGUMENT AGAINST PSYCHOLOGICAL HEDONISM

Careful study of the passage will reveal that Nozick does not explicitly claim to be refuting any theory of welfare or of value in general. He never mentions welfare or wellbeing or value or intrinsic value in the passage.[22] Instead, he speaks almost exclusively about certain psychological matters.[23] Thus, for example, he says (pp. 43 and 44) that reflection on the experience machine teaches us something about "what matters to us" or what is "important to us." In other places he suggests that it tells us something about what we desire (p. 43), or what we would choose. All of these remarks more strongly hint that he was interested in a psychological claim about what we value rather than in an axiological claim about what is valuable. We could take him at his word; we could assume that he is just trying to point out that people care about some things in addition to their experiences of pleasure.

It is, of course, perfectly obvious that people care about all sorts of things – what is for lunch, what sort of car they will purchase, who will be elected president, and so on. So there would have been no need for Nozick to bring in an extravagant hypothesis in order to show that experiences of pleasure are not the only things that people care about. We already know that people care about a lot of different things. In order to be worthy of attention, the doctrine in question would have to be a thesis about what people ultimately care about, or about what matters to people ultimately or intrinsically. So understood, the doctrine would imply that if anyone cares about something other than his own experiences of pleasure, he cares about it – in the long run – because he cares about pleasure and thinks the thing would bring some pleasure.

We must not forget about pain. We should note that the only thing that people ultimately care about avoiding is pain.

All this talk about "care" and "importance" and "mattering" is understood to be connected to motivation. When someone cares about something, or when it matters to him, it figures in his motivation. Psychological hedonism may be taken to imply that at least in their serious and considered behavior, people are motivated – ultimately – by their desire for pleasure and their aversion to pain. We might even go so far as to say that psychological hedonism implies that people are always ultimately motivated by a desire to maximize their own pleasure-minus-pain. This ultimate motivation may be hidden – even the agent himself may fail to recognize that he is, ultimately, doing things that he (perhaps at some deeper level) thinks will maximize his hedono-doloric level.

With these thoughts in mind, we may state one form of psychological hedonism in this way:

> PH: Ultimately, each person is motivated solely by a desire to maximize his own hedono-doloric level.

So understood, psychological hedonism is a general thesis in human psychology. It may be what Bentham had in mind in that famous passage where he spoke of the "two sovereign masters, pain and pleasure" who alone "determine what we shall do."

Some commentators have assumed that Nozick appealed to the experience machine in order to refute psychological hedonism rather than ethical hedonism.[24] Nozick never states anything quite like PH; at best his remarks about "what we care about" and "what matters to us" suggest that he might be talking about ultimate human motivation. But we can consider the argument in any case.

In its most straightforward formulation, the argument might simply start from the premise that "you would not plug in to the experience machine" and it might move swiftly from there to the conclusion that psychological hedonism is not true. Thus, the argument might look like this:

First Anti-Psychological Hedonism Argument
1. If you were in the Nozick Scenario you would not plug in so as to get LEM. You would stick with LA.
2. If (1), then you care ultimately about something other than your own pleasures and pains.
3. If you care ultimately about something other than your own pleasures and pains, then PH is false.
4. Therefore, PH is false.

But in this stark form the argument is unpersuasive. Premise (2) is open to question. It could be claimed that your failure to choose LEM is to be explained by the fact that you fear that the machine will not work; you fear that you would not get the promised pleasures or that you would suffer some unexpected pain while plugged in.[25] This would be bad news if you were unable to escape. Imagine how painful it would be to find yourself stuck for life in a tank of water with electrodes attached to your brain. So it is possible that you care only about pleasure and pain, and still would not plug in.

We can avoid this problem by stipulating that the subject in question (namely, "you") is perfectly certain of the outcomes of his choices. Thus, I formulate the argument as follows:

Second Anti-Psychological Hedonism Argument
1. If you were in the Nozick Scenario and were certain that LEM would be more pleasant than LA, still you would not plug in so as to get LEM. You would stick with LA.
2. If (1), then you care ultimately about something other than your own pleasures and pains.
3. If you care ultimately about something other than your own pleasures and pains, then PH is false.
4. Therefore, PH is false.

In this form, the argument is a bit more interesting. Your imagined refusal to plug in must be explainable somehow. Even if we try to explain it by appeal to something completely irrational or to a faulty commitment to a strange axiology or an ultimate interest in being moral, that would not reveal a problem with the argument, for it would show that something other than pleasure is functioning as an ultimate motivator. And that would show that PH is false.

In *Unto Others: the Evolution and Psychology of Unselfish Behavior* Elliott Sober and David Sloan Wilson (1998) interpret Nozick's experience machine argument as an attack on psychological hedonism. They claim that the argument fails. It may be interesting to consider their objection.

Early in the book, Sober and Wilson seem to understand psychological hedonism in a standard way: "avoiding pain and attaining pleasure are the only ultimate motives that people have; everything else we want, we want solely as a means to those twin ends" (Sober and Wilson: 1998, p. 2). Although Sober and Wilson do not formulate the experience machine argument in precisely the way I have formulated it here, their remarks can be taken as a criticism of premise (2).[26] They seem to be saying (in effect) that the psychological hedonist can reject premise (2).

"The hedonist can maintain that deciding to plug into the machine is so aversive [painful?] that people almost always make the other choice. When people deliberate about the alternatives, they feel bad [pained?] when they think of the life they'll lead if they plug into the machine; they feel much better [they have more pleasant feelings?] when they consider the life they'll lead in the real world if they decline to plug in. The idea of life attached to the machine is painful, even though such a life would be quite pleasurable; the idea of real life is pleasurable, even though real life often includes pain. (Sober and Wilson: 1998, p. 285; bracketed interpretive questions added.)

When they explain why someone might find the idea of life on the machine painful, they proceed to cite the very factors that Nozick mentions – separation from the real world, abandonment of projects and commitments, "unreality." But S&W cite these as explanations for the pain the subject would feel as he contemplates making the decision to plug in; they claim that a hedonist can cite these things without abandoning his fundamental hedonistic principles. In other words, S&W are saying that it is consistent with hedonism for the subject to choose the less pleasurable life; it is consistent with hedonism for him to do this since the process of choosing the less pleasurable life is more pleasurable.

It appears to me that S&W have become confused about the theory under consideration. We can clarify this situation by distinguishing between two views. First, there is the familiar form of psychological hedonism that claims that the acquisition of pleasure and the avoidance of pain are our only ultimate motivators; we are always ultimately motivated to perform acts that we believe will maximize our own hedono-doloric balance. This is roughly equivalent to the version of the doctrine that I introduced earlier:

> PH: Ultimately, each person is motivated solely by a desire to maximize his own hedono-doloric level.

A different view would maintain that when people are making decisions, they always choose the decision that is more pleasant to make. According to this view, people are motivated not by the pleasures and pains they anticipate receiving as a result of making a certain decision; rather, they are motivated by the pleasantness or painfulness of the decision-making process itself.

> PH2: Ultimately, each person is motivated to make a choice only if he thinks the process of making that choice would be maximally pleasant for him.

These two views will give divergent results in any case in which the choice that is most pleasant to make is different from the choice that will lead to the outcome containing the most pleasure-minus-pain in the long run. Consider a case in which you know you have a tiny dental cavity. You know that a trip to the dentist will be painful in the near term, but on balance would maximize your hedono-doloric balance. You hate pain – especially when it is coming up soon. Hence, the process of making the decision to go to the dentist is painful. We may assume that it is less painful to make the decision to put it off. So PH2 will say that you will be motivated to choose to put off the visit to the dentist.

But since you know that in the long run you will be better off hedonically if you deal with the cavity soon, PH implies that you will be motivated to go to the dentist soon. Hence, if PH is true (and you know the utilities of your options) you will be motivated to go to the dentist soon.

Since PH represents a more familiar sort of psychological hedonism, I assumed that it would make the most likely target for Nozick's argument. Thus, I formulated the argument so as to have it yield the rejection of PH. S&W also formulate psychological hedonism more or less as PH (on p. 2 of their book), and so one might expect them to interpret Nozick's argument as I have. But then when they get around to discussing that argument (see Sober and Wilson: 1998, p. 285) it appears that they start thinking of psychological hedonism in a new and unfamiliar way – as PH2.

The upshot of all this is that if we understand the allegedly Nozickian argument as I have understood it, the remarks of S&W are irrelevant. They seem to respond to the argument by pointing out that it does not refute a different and unfamiliar form of psychological hedonism.

It seems to me that the form of psychological hedonism I have been discussing (epitomized in PH) is probably the most popular form, but it is not the most plausible. It seems to go obviously wrong in cases involving people who have grown weary of sensory pleasure, or who think that sensory pleasure is disgraceful, or who think that there are more important things than "good feelings." I should like to sketch what I take to be a more plausible form of psychological hedonism. In order to state this, I need to draw a distinction.

There is an important and familiar distinction between sensory pleasure (and pain), on the one hand, and attitudinal pleasure (and pain) on the other hand.[27] Sensory pleasures are feelings; they have "felt intensities"; we feel them in parts of our bodies; they are in these respects like tickles and itches. They are literally sensations. But a person takes attitudinal pleasure in something when he is pleased about it, or enjoys it, or is delighted concerning it. Attitudinal pleasure is not a sensation. We do not feel it in parts of our bodies; it is not like an itch. It is a propositional attitude. To see the difference in a stark case, consider a person who has been suffering from a sensory pain for a long time. Suppose he takes a drug that removes the pain. Suppose that the pain is not replaced by any new and pleasant sensation, but just leaves the formerly painful area feeling numb. The subject might take attitudinal pleasure in the fact that he feels no sensory pain. In this case, the subject takes attitudinal pleasure in a certain fact, but does not feel any sensory pleasure. Attitudinal pleasure and pain always have propositional "objects" like that and that is what makes them propositional attitudes. Sensory pleasures do not have propositional objects.

This provides a new way to understand psychological hedonism. We can assume that whenever a person is confronted with a decision, he will consider his options (although in some cases only briefly or at a low level of consciousness). For each option, there will be some amount of attitudinal pleasure that he takes in the prospect of taking that option. We might elicit this by asking: "How much attitudinal pleasure do you take in the idea that you will take this option?" We can take our new form of psychological hedonism to be the view that when people thus face options, and make decisions, they always decide to take the option in which they take the greatest amount of attitudinal pleasure. We can call this PH3.[28]

It is important to see that a person could take pleasure in an option even though he knows quite well that the option itself does not contain any pleasure. This comes out most strikingly in decisions concerning things that will happen after death. Suppose I am asked whether I prefer to be buried or to be cremated – after I am dead, of course. I realize that I will feel no sensory pleasure or pain either way, but I might take more attitudinal pleasure in the prospect of being buried than I do in the prospect of being cremated.

With this in hand, let us return to the experience machine. Suppose you are given a full and completely persuasive account of what would happen if you were plugged in, and a similar account of what would happen if you were not plugged in. Suppose you were utterly convinced that you would get more sensory pleasure if you were plugged in. Suppose now you are asked whether you want to plug in. Suppose you consider the options. You see that you would get more sensory pleasure if you were to choose to plug in, but at the same time you take less attitudinal pleasure in the prospect of living out the rest of your life in a tank, connected by electrodes. So you say that you would not plug in.

In this case, Nozick's reflections on the experience machine would not show that the most plausible form of psychological hedonism (namely, PH3) is false. For in the example, as described, if you choose to remain in your actual life, you in fact do choose the option in which you take greater attitudinal pleasure. Oddly, in this case, you take greater attitudinal pleasure in the option that you know will itself contain less sensory pleasure.

3.7 SUMMING UP

Some readers note that Nozick's discussion of the experience machine occurs in a context in which he is talking about utilitarianism for animals. These readers think that Nozick used the thought experiment concerning the experience machine as part of an argument against utilitarianism. I presented several different possible forms the argument might be thought to take. The first two arguments are completely unpersuasive; the third focuses only on the hedonistic component of hedonistic act utilitarianism. In spite of the facts about context, it seems to me that there is no convincing evidence that Nozick intended to present any such argument. Final verdict: bad arguments; not in the text.

Very many readers seem to think that Nozick was trying to refute ethical hedonism. They think that when Nozick concluded that certain things "matter to us" beyond the things we could get in the experience machine, he meant to say that certain things in addition to pleasures have direct impact on our welfare. I presented several arguments, each starting with a premise to the effect that we would not choose life in the experience machine and ending with the conclusion that ethical hedonism is false. The arguments differed in the conditions they imposed on the characteristics we are to imagine the subjects having while making the choice. In some cases, it seemed to me, premise (2) was false. In other cases, it was premise (1). None of the arguments seems persuasive. Again, I am not convinced that Nozick intended to present any of these arguments. Final verdict: bad arguments; probably not in the text.[29]

A few readers think that Nozick was trying to refute psychological hedonism. Perhaps when he talks about "what matters to us" he means "what ultimately motivates us." Again, the argument could be interpreted in a variety of different ways. Some forms of psychological hedonism might be refuted by the argument so construed – but these forms of psychological hedonism are pretty implausible to start with. A more interesting form of psychological hedonism would remain unrefuted. The textual evidence in support of this interpretation is debatable. Final verdict: unimpressive arguments; not clearly in the text.

My own view concerning the experience machine is this: it is a wonderfully provocative thought experiment; it can provide the basis for lots of interesting and useful discussions in introductory ethics classes. It makes people think about what they really care about. I have no settled view about what Nozick was trying to establish. Perhaps it was nothing more than this: typical human beings care about being in contact with reality, and displaying actual character traits in their actions, and having actual achievements; thus, they care about more than merely having the inner experiences associated with these things. Animals might be like us in these respects.[30] Maybe, therefore, we should not assume that animals care about nothing beyond the quality of their inner experiences. This might have some implications for the notion that some form of utilitarianism accounts for our obligations to animals. I leave it to others to assess the plausibility and significance of the argument so construed.

APPENDIX

In spite of the fact that Nozick never mentions either intuition or intrinsic value in the experience machine passage, some commentators persist in saying that the passage contains an argument that turns essentially on a claim about our intuitions about the intrinsic values of two lives. (Nozick's own remarks in later writings tend to suggest this sort of view.) Let us consider a typical interpretation of this sort.

First we must describe the essential features of two possible lives. Following what was said in the text of the chapter, let us say that LEM is a marvelously pleasant life in an experience machine. The subject is completely fooled. He thinks he is writing great novels, making lots of friends, and reading interesting books. In fact, however, he is floating in a tank with electrodes connected to his brain. For comparison, we say that LA is a moderately pleasant life in the real world. The subject never writes any great novels, makes only a moderate number of friends, and enjoys reading only a few fairly good books. However, he is in contact with reality, he has actual (modest) achievements, and he does not live in a purely man-made reality.

We stipulate that the lifetime hedono-doloric balance of the person who lives LEM is significantly greater than the lifetime hedono-doloric balance of the person who lives LA. As before, ethical hedonism is understood to be the view that the welfare value of a life is entirely determined by the amounts of sensory pleasure and pain in the life, in such a way that the welfare value of a life is directly proportional to the hedono-doloric balance of that life. The welfare value of a life is understood to be a form of intrinsic value.

We may now state the argument as follows:

1.   If ethical hedonism were true, the welfare value of LEM would be greater than the welfare value of LA.
2.   But it is not the case that the welfare value of LEM is greater than the welfare value of LA.
3.   Therefore, ethical hedonism is not true.

Let us agree that the defender of this argument attempts to defend premise (2) by saying that it is all a matter of "moral intuition." When he reflects with due care on LEM and LA, he can just "see" that the intrinsic welfare value of LEM is lower than the intrinsic welfare value of LA.

I have to admit that I find this latest argument to be fairly interesting. But anyone who is skeptical about moral intuition or intrinsic value would surely find it much less interesting. Among those who have no problem with moral intuition and intrinsic value, the hedonists will claim that they just "see" that (2) is false. So it is a controversial argument. But there is one point that all readers should agree upon: Nozick did not present this argument in the experience machine passage. He never mentioned moral intuition. He never mentioned intrinsic value. These are essential features of the argument presented here, but are not features of Nozick's argument.

On the other hand, he did say various things about whether his reader would (or should) choose to plug in. Something about choosing to plug in seems to be an essential feature of Nozick's argument. Yet there is no mention of any such choice anywhere in the argument presented here. Choice simply plays no role in this argument. Thus, the text of *ASU* provides no justification for attributing this argument to Nozick. Final verdict on this argument: possibly an interesting argument; definitely not in the text.

NOTES

I am very grateful to Kristian Olsen for generous assistance on earlier drafts. I am also grateful to Ralf Bader and Owen McLeod for extensive critical comments and suggestions.

1. He returns to the topic later in *The Examined Life, Philosophical Explanations,* and "The Pursuit of Happiness," as well as in other writings. I will focus here on the passage in *ASU*.

2. Although, as Ralf Bader reminded me, Nozick elsewhere claims that this appearance might be misleading.

3. It is interesting to compare Nozick's description of the subject in the experience machine with J. J. C. Smart's discussion of the "bald-headed man with electrodes protruding from his skull." In both cases, the electrodes are imagined to be connected to a machine in such a way as to induce pleasant experiences. And in both cases, the question is whether the life of the subject would be a good one, or one we would desire. Smart's discussion of the "electrode man" first appeared in his 1961 book *An Outline of a System of Utilitarian Ethics.* The passage reappears on p. 19 of his contribution to *Utilitarianism: For and Against,* which was published in 1973. *ASU* was published in 1974. Nozick does not mention Smart in section 3 of *ASU,* and he does not cite Smart in his bibliography or index.

4. In addition to the four views mentioned here, there are some "outliers." Sober and Wilson seem to claim that Nozick appealed to the experience machine in an effort to refute *psychological egoism* (see Sober and Wilson: 2000, p. 199). Another commentator says that Nozick was trying to show that a person's welfare level is not determined by how happy he is. He takes the target to be eudaimonism (see Jollimore: 2004, p. 333). Griffin says that the target is a sort of hybrid of hedonism and preferentism as a theory of welfare (see Griffin: 1988, p. 9).

5. I should mention as well that some commentators claim that the example of the experience machine is designed to establish a positive thesis about welfare. "This thought experiment [the experience machine] shows that a valuable life involves certain character traits, the exercise of certain capacities, and having certain relations with others and to the world and, hence, that value cannot consist in psychological states alone" (Brink: 1989, p. 224).

6. This sort of interpretation seems to be endorsed by MacNiven: 1993, p. 4; Railton: 1984, pp. 148–149; Teichman and Evans: 1999, pp. 91–92; among others. Smart's example of the electrode man was explicitly intended to figure in an objection to utilitarianism; perhaps some readers assume that Nozick must have been following suit.

7. In a brief passage (pp. 41–42) Nozick alludes to the repugnant conclusion, the Ten Little Indians, person-affecting problems, problems about the evil of killing. Elsewhere he makes clear his objections to utilitarianism as a theory of distributive justice. None of these objections turns essentially on intuitions brought out in the experience machine passage.

8. One variant would make use of the concept of satisficing instead of maximizing; another variant would employ the notion of expected utility instead of actual utility. There are dozens of variations.

9. Nozick comments on this point, first in *ASU* and then later in *The Examined Life*. I discuss the relevance of his remarks in note 17.

10. I leave it to the interested reader to determine whether any other form of act utilitarianism would be refuted by an argument of this form. So far as I can tell, no recognized form of utilitarianism implies that you should plug in. Premise (1) remains false under all reinterpretations.

11. Again, I leave it to the reader to consider whether some other form of act utilitarianism might give rise to a more plausible version of premise (1).

12. Railton seems to interpret the argument in this way (see Railton: 1984, pp. 148–149).

13. Nor, I should note, is there any mention of the conclusion *in the experience machine passage itself*.

14. See, for example, Attfield: 1987, p. 33; Brink: 1989, pp. 223–224; Crisp: 2006, p. 620; Driver: 2007, p. 33; Goldsworthy: 1992, p. 14; N. Lemos: 1994, p. 202; Sobel: 2002, p. 243; Sumner: 1996, p. 94; Tannsjo: 2007, pp. 79–80.

15. But this premise has been challenged. Torbjorn Tannsjo points out that many people take mind-altering drugs (see Tannsjo: 1998, p. 112). These drugs can be seen as pharmacological experience machines. They cause the subject to have feelings of pleasure associated with dreamy, delusional, hallucinatory, unrealistic, drug-induced experiences. Felipe De Brigard (De Brigard: 2010) claims to have given some questionnaires to his students. In one series of tests, he asked them if they would choose life on the experience machine over their actual lives. Though the testing was all make-believe, and one may assume that the students all knew that the whole business was little more than a joke, apparently quite a few of them said they would opt for the machine.

16. A number of commentators have focused on this problem with the argument. See, for example, Sumner: 1996, p. 95. Sumner asks, "What happens if there is a power failure?" Crisp: 2006, p. 635 alludes to the same point. He dismisses the question about whether people would

choose to plug in, since their choices might be influenced by "differing attitudes to risk." Goldsworthy: 1992, p. 18, emphasizes this point, saying that a reasonable person might choose not to plug in because of fear of "catastrophic, unimaginably horrible consequences of malfunction or abuse." Sober: 2000 makes a similar point.

17. For a persuasive presentation of this objection, see Kawall: 1999, pp. 381–387. Sumner makes a similar point, noting that "welfare tracks only one dimension of the value of a life" (Sumner: 1996, p. 96). See also Shaw: 1999, p. 51. A similar point is made in Haslett: 1990, as well as in Silverstein: 2000, p. 290. Silverstein points out that when he returned to this topic in *The Examined Life* Nozick emphasized some details of his description of the Nozick Scenario and thereby overcame this difficulty (see Silverstein: 2000, p. 291). Specifically, Nozick asked us to imagine that we are given assurances that others will also have the option of plugging into experience machines, and so we need not worry about failing to fulfill our moral obligations if we choose LEM. (As Ralf Bader reminded me, Nozick had already made this point in *ASU*, p. 43.) However, it seems to me that the imagined clarification of the Nozick Scenario does not overcome the difficulty. A person might still worry about fulfilling his moral obligations even if he were convinced that others would be plugging in. For example, consider someone who solemnly promised his mother that he would rescue her if her experience machine should happen to malfunction. Believing that others would be in experience machines (or would have the option of plugging in) would not relieve him of his feeling of obligation to keep out of the machine so as to be available for rescue operations, should they be necessary. And even more obviously, suppose he knows that others have been given the opportunity to plug in but have chosen to remain unplugged. His feeling of obligation to them would be unaffected. See Nozick: 1989, p. 105.

18. It would be difficult to give a fully satisfactory account of what is meant here by "rational." I beg the reader's indulgence.

19. Thanks to Owen McLeod for encouraging me to pursue this line of argument.

20. In his paper on this topic, Felipe De Brigard (De Brigard: 2010) describes an experiment in which his students were asked whether they would choose to plug in to an experience machine. Before announcing the choices they would make, the students were given make-believe accounts of what they would get if they chose to plug in. De Brigard claims that the results of his experiment are relevant to Nozick's argument. But it should be clear that no amount of this sort of empirical data would bear on premise (1) of the latest argument. The students

(unless De Brigard's classes are very unusual indeed) were not "completely rational," or "completely welfare selfish," and they surely were not "completely convinced" that they would get the life they chose. They knew perfectly well that it was all just a bit of fantasy. So far as I can tell, there is no empirical experiment that would either confirm or disconfirm (1). It is a philosophical claim about the connections between rationality, knowledge, welfare selfishness, and axiology, on the one hand, and choice on the other.

21. Some have taken the target of Nozick's attack to be the whole class of mental state theories of welfare (e.g., Kagan seems to say this, and he explicitly mentions Nozick in a note associated with this passage [see Kagan: 1998, pp. 35–36]). Mental state theories of welfare include sensory hedonism, certain versions of the "happiness theory" (aka eudaimonism), and all other theories that identify the ultimate atoms of personal value as "inner states." Such theories imply that if two lives are alike internally – if everything "feels the same" to the people living the lives – then those lives must be alike in welfare value. Since I have already spoken at length about the implications of the argument interpreted as an argument against ethical hedonism, and what I said about hedonism would carry over for other mental state theories of welfare, I will say no more than this here: there is nothing in the experience machine passage that casts any serious doubt on mental state theories of welfare.

22. He uses the word "best" in one instance. And in the following section he mentions utilitarianism, although it is not clear how this is supposed to relate to what he says in the discussion of the experience machine. It is also interesting to note that in his commentary on the experience machine in his later *The Examined Life* he explicitly says that the example of the experience machine is intended to shed light on a question about *value* (see Nozick: 1989, p. 105). In this context he mentions the idea that "plugging in constitutes the very best life." Ralf Bader (in personal correspondence) has pointed out several other instances in which, in later writings, Nozick suggested that he took himself to be presenting an argument about the value of a life in the experience machine passage.

23. These *seem* to be matters of psychology, but, as Matthew Silverstein emphasizes, it is possible that when Nozick says that something "matters to us" he means not just that we care about it, but that it is in fact good for us. See Silverstein: 2000, p. 286.

24. Elliott Sober discusses the experience machine at some length in his article "Psychological Egoism" (Sober: 2000). He seems to think the argument can be used against psychological hedonism. In two papers

on this topic, John Lemos consistently indicates that he interprets the argument in this way. See J. Lemos: 2002 and J. Lemos: 2004. Felipe De Brigard seems to assume this interpretation. He explicitly mentions psychological hedonism as the target of Nozick's argument on p. 3 of his paper "If You Like It, Does It Matter If It's Real?" (De Brigard, 2010). Others including Torbjorn Tannsjo seem to read the passage in a similar way. It's not clear to me that these people would understand psychological hedonism precisely as I have here.

25. Sober mentions this problem in Sober: 2000, p. 137.

26. Which says that if you would choose your actual life over the experience machine life, then psychological hedonism is false.

27. For an extended discussion of this distinction, see Feldman: 2004, ch. 4.

28. It is conceivable that S&W had something like this in mind when they talked about pleasure taken in the making of a decision.

29. Many readers think that Nozick was not trying to refute just ethical hedonism. Rather, he was trying to refute all mental state theories of welfare. Since he talks broadly about "how experiences feel from the inside" and not narrowly about pleasure, and since he never explicitly mentions hedonism, this interpretation is more plausible than the preceding one. But the arguments would be just as inconclusive. Final verdict: bad arguments; not clearly in the text.

30. Although it must be acknowledged that it is pretty wild to assume that a cow or a chicken is deeply concerned about the extent to which she is having actual achievements or displaying excellent character traits.

Part II **Anarchy**

4   Nozickian arguments for the more-than-minimal state

4.1   INTRODUCTION

The first and longest part of Robert Nozick's *Anarchy, State, and Utopia* (*ASU*) is substantially devoted to a defense of the minimal (nightwatchman) state against the challenge of the individualist anarchist. In this chapter I explore the contest between Nozick and the individualist anarchist by examining responses that Nozick offered, could have offered, or should have offered to the anarchist challenge. I conclude that the best Nozickian response to the anarchist challenge vindicates a state which is more than minimal because, although it provides only the service of rights protection, it funds the production of its services by *requiring* at least some of the recipients of those services to purchase those services. In this introductory section I will provide a sketch of the structure of this exploration.

Nozick begins *ASU* with the well-known proclamation that "[i]ndividuals have rights, and there are things no person or group may do to them (without violating their rights)" (p. ix). He immediately adds: "So strong and far-reaching are these rights that they raise the question of what, if anything, the state and its officials may do. How much room do individual rights leave for the state?" (p. ix). Pursuing these questions, the individualist anarchist maintains with considerable plausibility that, if one takes these individual rights as seriously as Nozick thinks one should, one must reject even the minimal state in favor of a system of competing private protective agencies. For even the minimal state – which is solely concerned with the protection of individual rights – must attain and maintain something like a monopoly over the protection of rights within its claimed territory simply in order to be a state. And, the

89

anarchist contends, the attainment or maintenance of this monopoly will violate certain of the rights that advocates of the minimal state believe should be respected and protected. The crucial right that the anarchist invokes is the right of individuals to act as executors of the law of nature – the right of individuals to act to protect and enforce their own rights and (even) to sell their services as rights protectors and enforcers to individuals who choose to purchase those services. The anarchist's complaint is that "when the state monopolizes the use of force in a territory and punishes others who violate its monopoly ... it violates moral side constraints on how individuals may be treated" (p. 51). The individualist anarchist challenge to Nozick's endorsement of the minimal state is particularly acute precisely because Nozick himself affirms the state of nature right of individuals to protect and enforce the first-order rights to life, liberty, and property.

Before proceeding further we must deal with a complication that Nozick introduces with his distinction between what he calls the "minimal state" and what he calls the "ultra-minimal state." As Nozick defines these terms, the ultra-minimal state exercises a type of monopoly over the provision of rights protection in its territory; the minimal state *in addition* charges some people more than it otherwise would charge them for its protective services and with the difference extends those services to at least some further inhabitants of its territory. Nozick maintains that, along with objecting to the (ultra-minimal) state's suppression of competing protection agencies, the anarchist objects to the (minimal) state's "forcing some to purchase protection for others" (p. 51). On Nozick's depiction, the anarchist holds that, whereas the ultra-minimal state is only guilty of illicitly establishing a monopoly on rights protection, the minimal state is also guilty of pressing some individuals to pay for protection for others. This sets the stage for Nozick to assert that his principle of compensation (which I shall discuss in sections 4.2 and 4.3) elegantly provides an answer to both (purported) anarchist objections. For that principle is said both to justify the (ultra-minimal) state's suppression of independent rights protectors *and* to require that the (minimal) state charge its paying customers more than it otherwise would to finance protection for some of those suppressed independents. However, the idea that a major concern of the anarchist is that states charge their paying clients more than they otherwise would so as to fund protection for others is a fiction created by Nozick so that the principle of compensation can be celebrated for killing two anarchist objections with a single blow.

The anarchist does, of course, object to the state forcing *any* purchases. Indeed, we shall see that as the archist–anarchist debate develops the permissibility of forced exchanges becomes the pivotal issue. However, no individualist anarchist specifically focuses on and complains about the "redistributive" feature that in Nozick's terminology distinguishes the minimal from the ultra-minimal state. This is largely because what Nozick calls the minimal state is not on the radar screen of any individualist anarchist; it is not on that radar screen largely because it is not advocated by any known partisan of the minimal state. The theorists who the individualist anarchists think of as partisans of the minimal state and who think of themselves as partisans of it – for example, Auberon Herbert in the late nineteenth century and Ayn Rand in the mid and later twentieth century – endorse what Nozick calls the ultra-minimal state. So the justifiability of the feature that Nozick takes to distinguish what he calls the "minimal state" – namely, its charging its paying customers more in order to fund protective services to some non-payers – is at best a distracting side issue. For this reason, I follow all the other parties to the archism–anarchism debate by understanding the "minimal state" to be quite simply the state that maintains its monopoly on the provision of rights protection – albeit without forcing anyone to purchase the services it offers.[1]

I begin this exploration with the main response that Nozick actually offers to the anarchist – the response that turns on the principle of compensation. I contend that this actual response is unsuccessful. I then move on to a response that can be readily extrapolated from the attenuation of rights that is supposed to underwrite the principle of compensation. I argue that this extrapolated response achieves a pyrrhic victory over the anarchist. The victory is pyrrhic because of the heavy philosophical costs that the minimal statist must sustain to achieve it. The *least* of these costs is that the deployment of the extrapolated response seems to vindicate a state that is more extensive than the minimal state because it *taxes* recipients of its protective services to fund the production of those services. In actuality, this extrapolated response and attenuation of rights on which this response is based may well support a state that is even more extensive than the minimal taxing state. It may well support a state that engages in more than the protection of individuals' rights and that taxes the beneficiaries of these additional activities in order to finance them. Finally, the attenuation of rights that lies behind the extrapolated response seems to betray the core understanding of rights that characterizes Nozickian libertarianism. Because of the philosophical costs that are attached to the extrapolated response, I go on to explore whether a more constrained response is available to the archist that might meet the anarchist's challenge without incurring *all* of the philosophical costs that are incurred by the extrapolated response. I describe two versions of a constrained response and maintain that the second "anti-paralysis" version yields a victory for the archist that is markedly less pyrrhic than that won through wielding the extrapolated response. This victory is less pyrrhic because, although it lends support to the more-than-minimal minimal taxing state, it does not lead beyond the minimal taxing state to the even more extensive mutual advantage state; moreover, it does not seem to betray the core understanding of rights that characterizes Nozickian libertarianism.

Let us pause here to summarize the projected structure of the essay and to review our terminology. In section 4.2, we shall look at Nozick's actual response (AR) to the anarchist challenge. We shall see that the AR depends upon Nozick's appeal to a principle of compensation but that, even if this principle is accepted, its deployment fails to vindicate the minimal state (MS). In section 4.3, we shall pause to examine the shift in Nozick's understanding of the character of rights that is supposed to underwrite the principle of compensation. This shift in the conception of rights is the basis for the extrapolated response (ER) to the anarchist. In section 4.4, I describe ER and argue that it succeeds too well because it seems to vindicate not merely the minimal taxing state (MTS) but the even more extensive mutual advantage state (MAS). And, in section 4.5, we shall look at two versions of a constrained response (CR), each of which arguably succeeds to just the right extent by vindicating the MTS.

Of course in *ASU* Nozick sets out to vindicate the MS, not the MTS. So, how can it be said that from a Nozickian perspective the CR – which vindicates the MTS – is the response which *succeeds to just the right extent*? Part of the answer is that the Nozickian has to go where the best Nozickian argument takes him. If the CR is the response that it would have been reasonable for the Nozick of

ASU to make to the anarchist challenge and that response vindicates the MTS, then the endorsement of the MTS can be described as "Nozickian." Another part of the answer is supplied by noting that there is a shift in focus as the archist–anarchist debate develops. This shift is from the permissibility of a protective agency suppressing the provision of protective services by other agencies to the permissibility of a protective agency requiring individuals to purchase protective services from it. If the really important dispute between the archist and the anarchist is about the latter permissibility, then victory for the archist will be victory for the MTS rather than for the MS and the Nozickian responder to the anarchist challenge must reconcile himself to the MTS.

4.2 THE FIRST ROUND: NOZICK'S RESPONSE AND THE MINIMAL STATE

Nozick and his individualist anarchist interlocutor share a host of Lockean state of nature premises. Individuals have natural rights to do as they see fit with their own persons and to acquire and exercise the rights of private property.[2] Furthermore, through certain types of interaction with other agents – typically, contractual interaction – individuals can acquire particular rights against other agents to the delivery of specific goods or services. Indeed, all rights to the delivery of particular goods or services must be acquired through some form of rights–generating interaction. Since there are no natural, that is, original and unacquired, rights to the delivery of specific goods or services, there is no natural right to the delivery of protective services. Whether Josh's right against Bekah is a natural right against being beaten or an acquired right to some material object or a contractual right that Bekah perform some service for him, Josh's possession of that right provides no basis for affirming that he has a right against any third party that this party protect him against Bekah's violating the right he has against her. Mary's failing to come to Josh's defense when Bekah is about to beat him or deprive him of his rightful possession or fail to deliver a contracted service does not itself violate any right that Josh possesses against Mary unless Josh has acquired that right to protective services through some rights generating interaction with Mary. In the absence of such a rights generating interaction, Josh is, of course, at liberty to act as an executor of the law of nature. But he will have no claim on the assistance of strangers – much less on the assistance of specialists in the business of rights protection.

So how is a state of nature individual like Josh to acquire rights to others providing him with the service of rights protection? The standard Lockean move is, of course, to postulate a *social contract* in which at least a significant percentage of individuals agree to authorize some common agent – for example, "political society" – to act on their behalf as the common executor of the law of nature. In return for this authorization *and* for the individual's agreement to help fund this protective agency each social contractor acquires a right to protective services.³ However, anyone who, like Nozick and the individualist anarchist, is impressed with the virtues of competitive market provision of desired services will question the core presumption of this standard appeal to a social contract, namely, that all individuals who seek to purchase protective services will converge on the same supplier of those services or that people's desires for such services are likely to be best satisfied if there is only one supplier for them to converge upon.⁴ The contrary presumption of those impressed with the market provision of goods and services and with the diversity among persons in the strength and focus of their preferences for rights protection is that consumers of protective services will be better served by competing suppliers.

However, a system of competing market providers of rights protection seems to be subject to the same inconveniences that Locke ascribes to individuals acting as self-protectors in the state of nature. Protective services (or what purport to be protective services) provided by particular independent suppliers may not accord with settled and known law, may not accord with the judgments of indifferent judges, and may not be backed by sufficient force (relative to the force which might stand in opposition to the offered services).⁵ Nevertheless, before abandoning market provision and jumping to a social contract,

[w]e also must consider what arrangements might be made within a state of nature to deal with these inconveniences ... Only after the full resources of the state of nature are brought into play, namely all those voluntary arrangements and agreements persons might reach acting within their rights, and only after the effects of these are estimated, will we be in a position to see how serious are the inconveniences that yet remain to be remedied by the state, and to estimate whether the remedy is worse than the disease. (pp. 10–11)

Since these are inconveniences for prospective customers of protective services, suppliers of these services will seek to make arrangements that allow them to offer more convenient protective services. So, for example, each supplier of protective services will seek to assure prospective clients that the client's rights that it proposes to protect against clients of other suppliers will be recognized by those other suppliers. Each supplier will want to be able to assure its protective clients that procedures for the peaceful settlement of disputes between it and its competitors and its clients and the clients of its competitors are in place. And each supplier will include within its agreements with competing firms' arrangements for the cooperative enforcement of the substantive and procedural claims on which they have converged and of the judgments that arise out of the procedures they have mutually endorsed. As the individualist anarchist will be especially eager to insist, if there is a market demand for known law, indifferent judges, and reliable enforcement of acknowledged rights, arrangements necessary to the satisfaction of that demand will be made by those who seek to profit from meeting that demand. Nozick, it seems, should join the anarchist in projecting the emergence of a complex network of articulated norms, jointly accepted procedures, arbitration institutions, and cooperative enforcement arrangements that would add up to a convenient legal order.[6] Indeed, it seems to be precisely respect for the right of each supplier of protective services to bring its product to the competitive market that conduces to this convenient legal order. Similarly, effective arrangements for the suppression of "outlaw" agencies will be generated to the extent that the economic demand for protection of the peaceful enjoyment of life, liberty, and property exceeds the economic demand for aggression, enslavement, and predation. So Nozick's proper reminder that one must explore the resources of the state of nature before placing one's bet on some sort of social contract seems to vindicate the anarchist's projection of a non-state regime of rights protective agencies and cooperative associations.

Nozick often seems to want to counter this perception of a more or less normal competitive market in protective services with the idea that monopoly in the provision of protective services is natural. Nozick asks: "Why is this market different from all other markets? Why would a virtual monopoly arise in this market without the government intervention that elsewhere creates and maintains it?" (p. 17). His answer seems to be that it is highly disadvantageous for an individual to depend for his protection on a small isolated protective agency or small isolated network of such agencies. It is much better for an individual to be hooked into a comprehensive network for the enforcement of commonly recognized norms and procedures than to face the prospect of violent conflict with those he transacts with; hence customers for protective services will only select protection agencies which are integrated into such a network. However, Nozick is mistaken in his belief that this means that "competing companies are caught in a declining spiral" (p. 17). This only means that competing companies that do not network with their competitors are caught in such a spiral – as would a cell phone manufacturer that made cell phones that could only connect with other cell phones from that manufacturer.

Sometimes Nozick seems to want to leap from the modest conclusion that one can expect that each or almost each (surviving) protective agency will be connected to a more or less comprehensive network of protective agencies to the bolder conclusion that one can expect a minimal state (with a natural monopoly on the provision of protective services) to arise in the state of nature. For instance, Nozick declares that, "the self-interested and rational actions of persons in a Lockean state of nature will lead to single protective agencies dominant over geographical territories; each territory will have either one dominant agency *or* a number of agencies federally affiliated so as to constitute, *in essence,* one" (p. 118, emphasis added).[7] Yet surely a network of agencies that are affiliated in the ways we have just discussed but that compete with one another for customers on the basis of the particular packages of services they offer and the prices for those packages is *not* in essence a state. It would no more be a state than those competing (but coordinating) cell phone manufacturers would be a single firm.

Moreover, an appeal to the idea that rights protection lends itself to natural monopolization would not meet the anarchist challenge *in the way* that Nozick wants. The anarchist insists that for any agency to attain a monopoly in the provision of rights protection in a given territory it must impermissibly suppress competing suppliers of protection. The natural monopoly response is that there is no impermissible suppression by the aspiring monopolist *because there is no suppression*; since this market is different, monopoly arises naturally *without suppression*. Nozick, however, wants to agree with the anarchist that suppression of competing suppliers is necessary for an agency to attain its monopoly position; hence, what he really has to challenge is the *impermissibility* of that necessary suppression. Against the claim of the anarchist that this suppression is impermissible, Nozick needs to argue that on closer inspection it is not. The prohibitions that an aspiring minimal state must engage in to arrive at and maintain its position as the monopoly supplier of protective services are not *really* violations of the rights of independent self-protectors or independent suppliers of protective services.[8]

We have already noted the permissibility of prohibiting the activities of outlaw agencies that engage in or shield rights violating activities. Even in the absence of a satisfying philosophical account of this, it seems reasonable to understand this permissibility to extend to the prohibition of activities that pose a high risk of violating or shielding the violation of rights. In contrast, it seems that it is not permissible to prohibit activities that pose only a low risk of rights violation. This leaves unsettled the permissibility of the prohibition of activities that are less risky than high risk conduct but more risky than low risk conduct. Nozick's AR proceeds by construing the anarchist as holding that only independent agencies engaged in rights violating activities or activities with a high risk of being rights violating may permissibly be suppressed and by countering this anarchist stance with an argument for the permissibility of suppressing mid-range risky activities as well. The permissibility of suppressing these mid-range risky activities turns on Nozick's principle of compensation that asserts that "those who are *disadvantaged* by being forbidden to do actions that only *might* harm others must be compensated for these disadvantages foisted upon them in order to provide security for the others" (pp. 82–83). This principle – the basis of which will be explored in the next section – does not merely say that, *if* possibly harmful actions are forbidden to an agent's disadvantage, *then* compensation must be paid for that disadvantage. Rather, such prohibitions are permissible as long as compensation for disadvantages accompanies them.

Wielding this principle a protective agency (or set of "federally" affiliated agencies) that is already relatively strong will permissibly prohibit competing agencies or self-protectors from engaging in activities that pose even mid-level risk of violating rights. The already strong ("dominant") agency will announce and enforce its policy of proceeding forcefully against any other protective agent that does not restrict its activities to those which the strong agency judges to be of no or low risk.[9] Its proceeding in this way will be permissible as long as it compensates any party who is disadvantaged by these prohibitions. In this way, a dominant protective agency will permissibly monitor and control the provision of protective services in the area in which it operates. These ways of exercising power over and constraining its competitors makes that agency the monopoly provider of protective services. In Nozick's terminology, this mode of rising to monopoly status makes the agency an "ultra-minimal" state. The compensation this ascendent agency must then extend to the parties who are disadvantaged by its prohibitions will take the form of free or discounted rights protection packages (see p. 110) – financed out of somewhat higher charges to its regular paying customers. In Nozick's terminology, in extending this morally required compensation, the ultra-minimal state becomes a minimal state. In the more standard terminology of this essay, through the exercising of this power and constraint over its competitors the dominant agency permissibly becomes a minimal state.

Many questions may be raised about Nozick's AR. For example, if the dominant agency is itself a complex network of competing agencies affiliated through many numerically and qualitatively distinct bilateral agreements and cooperative structures does it become a state even if under the principle of compensation it puts all *non-affiliated* agencies out of business? Let us suppose, however, that the dominant protective agency that embarks on the prohibition of too risky competitors under the banner of the principle of compensation is a single firm in the business of selling rights protection. Would the degree of monitoring and constraining *other* agencies (or self-protectors) that is justified by the principle of compensation bestow a state-like monopoly upon that unified dominant protective firm? Contrary to Nozick, the answer seems to be, no.[10] For there is plenty of room for competition with the dominant agency *within the bounds of that agency's reasonably imposed constraints* on the riskiness of its competitors's services. Competing agencies can operate within those constraints while still offering distinct protective services or packages of services or distinctive pricing to draw costumers to them.

Recall how varied different customers' preferences for protective services are. Some want comprehensive coverage; others want only catastrophic coverage. Some want the services of firms which specialize in protecting contractual rights; others are drawn to firms that specialize in protecting trade secrets. All sorts of contingencies of time and place will make patronage of one particular protective agency preferable to some individuals and patronage of another preferable to others (see Mack: 1978). Imagine one cell phone manufacturer enforcing certain performance standards on its competitors so that its customers will not face even mid-level risks of not being able to connect telephonically with the customers of these other manufacturers. Such enforcement (however justified or unjustified) would leave plenty of room for competition between the standard enforcing manufacturer and the monitored manufacturers – unless, of course, the monitoring firm would continually adjust its enforced standards so as to forbid effective competition (rather than forbidding riskiness) whenever competition threatens to occur. However, were the dominant protective agency so to adjust its constraint of its potential competitors, it would show itself to be an outlaw agency. Hence, the AR on behalf of the minimal state fails.

We should take note of another response by Nozick that seems to be independent of the principle of compensation. This response turns on the contention that state–of–nature individuals possess procedural rights against being subject to others' mid-level risky rights protective activities; the dominant agency merely enforces these rights. The key premise for this contention is that an agent who employs procedures for determining the liability of another (to defensive, restitutive, or retributive measures) without knowing the reliability of those procedures acts wrongly. On the basis of this premise Nozick asserts that such actions are "wrong and impermissible" (p. 106); and from the impermissibility of those actions Nozick infers the recipient's procedural right against their performance. "On this view, many procedural rights stem not from rights of the person acted upon, but rather from moral considerations about the person or persons doing the acting" (p. 107). Unfortunately, from the procedure being impermissible *in some sense that is implied by its being wrongful*, it hardly follows that the coercive suppression of the procedure is permissible. If it did follow, Nozick would be well on his way to the anti-libertarian position that there is no right to do wrong.

4.3 BETWEEN ROUNDS: NOZICK'S ATTENUATION OF RIGHTS

We need to pause here to examine the basis that Nozick offers for the principle of compensation. For this basis can also serve as a ground for the ER – which we will take up in section 4.4. Recall the basic structure of the debate between the libertarian archist and the individualist anarchist. The anarchist identifies some sort of conduct that seems necessary for an agency to become or maintain itself as a state and asserts that this conduct violates rights. The libertarian archist responds by claiming that, contrary to first appearances, this sort of conduct does not truly violate rights because the relevant rights are not as robust, not as demanding of constraint, as one might at first think. In the case of the AR, the principle of compensation embodies the idea that the independent's right to engage in mid-level risky protective activities is not as robust, not as demanding of constraint, as one might at first think. However, the basis offered by Nozick for the principle of compensation involves a much more general attenuation of rights.

This more general attenuation of rights is developed in Chapter 4 of *ASU* on "Prohibition, Compensation, and Risk" (see Mack: 1981 and Arneson: 2005a). Near the beginning of this chapter Nozick poses the surprising question:

Are others forbidden to perform actions that transgress the boundary [that are defined by a person's rights] *or encroach upon the circumscribed area, or are they permitted to perform such actions provided that they compensate the person whose boundary has been crossed?* (p. 57, italics in original)

This is surprising because the reader may well have thought that it *follows* from there being such a moral boundary that actions transgressing it are forbidden. Certainly that is the suggestion of both Nozick's opening declaration of rights that may not be violated and his talk about rights as moral side constraints that mark the *inviolability* of persons (see pp. 30–33). In contrast, Nozick's approach in "Prohibition, Compensation, and Risk" takes the essential content of an agent (say, Josh) having a right to X against another agent (say, Bekah) to be that it is impermissible for Bekah to deprive Josh of X *if and only if* Bekah fails to compensate Josh duly for the loss of X. Josh's right to X does not pure and simple forbid Bekah's depriving Josh of

X; it merely requires that Bekah's depriving Josh of X be accompanied by her duly compensating him for his loss of X. Josh's right to X vindicates forbidding Bekah from taking X only if that right is conjoined with some special condition that makes problematic the determination of what the due accompanying compensation would be.

Nozick discusses two sorts of condition that render problematic the identification of what the due compensation for such a taking would be. First, the best measure of due compensation to Josh for the transfer of X to Bekah would be the exchange price for X that Josh and Bekah would settle upon were there antecedent negotiation and agreement between them concerning the transfer of X. This is by far the best way to determine what the division of the benefits of the exchange should be. (After all, Nozick's basic critique of "distributive justice" is that there is no independent standard for what the division of the benefits of cooperative interaction ought to be.) If instead Bekah seizes X, the best that can be done to identify due compensation for Josh is to attempt to identify what Josh and Bekah would have settled upon had prior negotiation and agreement been required. Since this is a far inferior way of identifying due compensation, it makes much more sense to require prior negotiation and agreement. However, to require prior negotiation and agreement is to *prohibit* the taking. Thus, concern for due compensation recommends prohibiting the taking of X *as long as prior negotiation and agreement are feasible*. Where market transactions are feasible, concern for due compensation *in effect* elevates rights to markers of things that may not be done to people.

Second, if the taking or the boundary crossing is feared (or generates fear of further takings or boundary crossings), the prospect for subsequent due compensation for that taking or crossing is substantially diminished. If Josh fears having his arm broken, he may well refuse a payment for permission to break his arm that is large enough to leave him feeling duly compensated if he receives that payment after his arm is broken. Here too there seems to be no good substitute for prior negotiations for determining due compensation. Moreover, according to Nozick, the failure to prohibit feared takings or boundary crossings exacerbates problems of uncompensated fear – because non-prohibition will result in crossings being feared that will not in fact ever eventuate. Since these feared of crossings will not in fact eventuate, there will be no one from whom compensation for that fear can reasonably be demanded. Where takings or crossings are feared, concern for due compensation *in effect* elevates rights to claims about what may not be done to individuals. In contrast, if neither of these two conditions are present, an agent's right remains in its default position, that is, it remains merely a claim to receive accompanying due compensation for the taking or crossing.

How does this apply to the permissibility of a dominant agency's suppression of mid-level risky actions on the part of independents? (Recall that, by hypothesis, these actions are not risky enough to count as straightforward rights violations.) The right of an independent protector to engage in such a risky activity remains the default position claim to be duly compensated for the loss imposed in precluding that activity. This is because in cases of this sort neither of the two types of difficulty in identifying accompanying due compensation obtain. Hence, there is no reason to insist that the dominant agency enter into prior negotiations with the independent protector in order to secure that protector's abstention from the risky activity. First, according to Nozick, there is no difficulty of determining what should be the division of the benefits of the exchange in which the clients of the dominant agency receive the independent's abstention from mid-level risky activity. Nozick supports this with the surprising contention that the independent protector's abstention from mid-level risky action does not benefit those clients. Since those clients do not benefit from this abstention by the independent protector, there is no need to identify the proper division of benefits from the transaction between the dominant and the independent agency. Second, the dominant agency's prohibition of these risky actions is not itself feared.[11] Hence, the right of the independent remains in its default position and it may permissibly be infringed as long as due compensation accompanies this infringement. Since recipients of abstentions from others' mid-level risky actions do not benefit from those abstentions, the recipients do not *in virtue of such benefit* owe compensation to those who are forced not to engage in those risky actions. However, if those who are forced to forego risky actions which might well not have violated anyone's rights are *disadvantaged* by being subject to that force, then those on whose behalf that force was used owe the subjects of that force compensation for those disadvantages. Hence, the principle of compensation.

Here we are primarily concerned with Nozick's overall suggestion that to have a right to X is in essence to have a right to due
compensation if X is taken from one rather than with the principle
of compensation itself. For, as we have seen, even given this principle Nozick's AR does not succeed against the anarchist and it is
the general suggestion of "Prohibition, Compensation, and Risk"
that provides the basis for the ER to the anarchist. Nevertheless, we
should note one particular problem with Nozick's claim that the clients of the dominant agency do not benefit from the prohibition of
the independent's mid-level risky activities (and, hence, that agency
does not have to engage in prior negotiation with the independent so as to determine the proper division of benefits of exchange).
According to Nozick, the clients of the dominant agency do not
benefit from the independent's abstention if that abstention merely
provides those clients with "relief from something that would not
threaten if not for the possibility of an exchange to get relief from
it" (p. 85). However, a standard, run-of-the-mill protective agency
will not set itself to perform protective activities merely in order to
sell its abstention from those activities; it will set itself to perform
those activities in order to offer those activities to its current and
prospective clients. Hence, if the dominant agency secures abstention from *these* activities, its clients are provided with relief from
something, namely, those risky activities, that does not threaten
merely because of the possibility of exchange to get relief from it.
Thus, it is not true that the clients do not benefit. So, it seems, one
should hold that the division of benefits argument for prior negotiation *does* apply to the dominant agency securing these abstentions
and, therefore, the dominant agency must engage in prior negotiation with these independent agencies to secure their abstention
from mid-level risky activities.[12]

4.4 ROUND TWO: THE EXTRAPOLATED RESPONSE AND THE MUTUAL ADVANTAGE STATE

The failure of Nozick's AR should lead the archist to revisit the
premises of the archist–anarchist debate as it is depicted by Nozick.
For that depiction may grant some crucial premise to the anarchist
that the archist can profitably challenge. And there is indeed such
a common premise. The premise is that there is no special problem

with the provision of the service of rights protection through voluntary market interaction; rights protection is just another service susceptible to market provision. To the extent to which individuals value their rights being protected, they will be willing to pay for this service and, hence, it will be produced and supplied to a suitable extent by some agent – or, better yet, by a confederation of competing agents – seeking payment in exchange for the delivery of rights protection. Rights protection is a marketable economic good comparable to laptop computers, fine meals at fancy restaurants, and haircuts. Clearly the individualist anarchist subscribes to this view. So too does the Nozickian minimal statist. For a striking feature of the minimal state is that it does not engage in forced exchanges of the services provided by it and payments from the recipients of those services. The MS derives all of its revenue from voluntary contracts for the sale of its protective services.[13] It eschews taxation. In this way the minimal state is fundamentally a market and not a political institution. (Nozick, however, tends to underplay the non-political character of the minimal state. He skirts past the fact that the minimal state as it appears within *ASU* is essentially a firm with managers, employees, proprietors or stockholders, marketing strategies, and customers; it does not have a constitutional structure, legislative bodies, political parties, electoral campaigns, or citizens.[14])

That rights protection is an ordinary marketable service is a premise that the archist may profitably challenge – on the familiar grounds that protective services have the crucial feature of public goods, namely, that if they are produced it is impossible or very costly to exclude individuals who have not themselves paid for the goods from benefitting from their production. More precisely, the relevant concern is *not* that the service will get produced and that some people will free ride upon those who voluntarily pay for the service's production. Indeed, Nozickian libertarianism rejects a principle of fairness that requires that all riders pay (see pp. 90–95). Rather, the problem is that so many potential purchasers of protective services may seek to free ride on others' voluntary funding of those services (or may judge that there is no point in joining the too small number of those agreeing to pay for those services) that those services will not get funded (or will be radically under-funded).

Of course many goods or services that non-payers cannot (feasibly) be prevented from enjoying do nevertheless get voluntarily funded. People dining in restaurants to which they will not soon be returning tip their waiters and thereby help fund the public good of there being enough well-disposed waiters even though those people would get no less service were they not to tip. Given appropriate conventions or contractual arrangements, a service from which persons cannot (feasibly) be excluded were they not to pay for it may nevertheless be voluntarily funded (to an acceptable extent) (see Mack: 1986). Individualist anarchists will want to argue that, despite initial appearances, *protective* services – including even national-scale defense – will be supported without its beneficiaries being required to purchase them (cf. Schmidtz: 1990a and Stringham: 2007). If the anarchists succeed in making that difficult argument – and I for one wish them well – the common marketability premise of the archist versus anarchist debate as Nozick depicts it will be vindicated and there will be no room for the archist to shift the focus of that debate by challenging that common premise.

Nevertheless, because of their public goods features, it is sufficiently plausible that protective services would not be voluntarily funded (at more than very sub-optimal levels) for the Nozickian archist to press the anarchist about the stance he must take if those services would not be voluntarily funded (at more than very suboptimal levels). The anarchist must then say that individuals have rights and in virtue of those rights they are not to be required to purchase protective services even if the alternative is that each individual will be subjected to more extensive infringements of his rights than would be involved in his being required to pay for those protective services. Although the greater yet infringement of rights that (by hypothesis) will occur if individuals are not required to purchase protective services is a very discomforting prospect for the anarchist, he will still insist that forcing individuals to purchase these services is an impermissible violation of their rights. He will insist that the Nozickian archist must also reject mandatory purchase of protection services. However, this challenge provides the Nozickian archist with the opportunity to argue – in accordance with his general strategy against the anarchist – that what appears to be a violation of rights is on closer inspection not really a violation. To exploit this opportunity the Nozickian archist can turn to the overall attenuation of rights developed in Chapter 4 of *ASU*. What emerges is the ER.

Consider the right of an individual to those of her holdings that would be taken from her in exchange for protective services within a scheme of required payments for such services. According to the overall attenuation of rights, in its default position that right is a claim against her being deprived of those holdings without receiving due compensation for that deprivation. By itself the right does not prohibit this taking; the right is not violated if the taking is accompanied by due compensation. The right will *in effect* rise to a right that the holdings not be taken and will mandate prior negotiation and agreement only if some condition is present that makes the determination of due accompanying compensation problematic. But no such condition is present. First, the fear condition does not obtain. Such takings are no more feared by those subject to them than the suppression of mid-level risky protective services are feared by those who otherwise would provide these services. Second, the division of the benefits of exchange consideration in favor of prior negotiation and agreement does not come into play.

Recall that we are assuming that protective services cannot be successfully marketed. Given that assumption, requiring prior negotiation and agreement in order to determine the proper division of the benefits of exchange (of protective services and payment) will be futile – precisely because there will be no settled upon agreement. So, in these cases, attempting to identify what the recipient of protective services would have agreed to pay for those services *if she had to pay to get those services in order to receive them* is not a less apt way of determining the proper division of the benefits of exchange than requiring prior negotiation and agreement. If the public good feature of protective services does render the marketing of those services infeasible, then the case for requiring prior negotiation and agreement does not get off the ground and the individual's right to the relevant holdings remains in its default position. Hence, no right to the holding is violated if its seizure is accompanied by the provision of protective services as extensive as the holder would have bargained for in exchange for that holding. For that provision will be due compensation for the taking.

This vindication of requiring individuals to purchase protective services does not seem quite to get us to a vindication of the state. For it seems that no agency would have a monopoly over this liberty to require payment for its provision of protective services. However, only a dominant agency (or a dominant set of closely affiliated agencies) could plausibly claim to be exercising this liberty. For only such an agency (or network) will be collecting payments from a high enough percentage of individuals to raise the funds necessary for the production of the protective services the provision of which will duly compensate those individuals.[15]

The ER seems to vindicate the MTS; and for the Nozickian libertarian this may not be too much of a philosophical cost to pay for defeating the anarchist challenge. However, there are further and more difficult to bear costs that come with the ER and the attenuation of rights that underwrites the ER. To begin with, the argumentation takes us beyond the MTS to the MAS that also imposes taxes on individuals to fund *non-protective* goods and services insofar as such goods or services would not be funded through voluntary market agreements because of their public goods character. For such takings of holdings from individuals are presumably not feared and the goods or services provided to each individual will duly compensate her for the taking (as long as each individual would have voluntarily agreed to the payment that is in fact assigned to her if she would have faced exclusion from enjoying that good or service had she not agreed to pay for it). The Nozickian archist will typically join the anarchist in arguing that many goods and services that are proclaimed to be public goods and not susceptible to voluntary market funding can in fact be financed through voluntary agreement. Nevertheless, if the archist can demand that the anarchist take seriously the possibility that protective services will not be susceptible to voluntary market funding, the archist must take seriously the possibility that some *non-protective* goods or services will not be susceptible to such voluntary funding. The Nozickian archist who appeals to the ER and its underlying attenuation of rights may find himself committed to taxation to finance mosquito abatement (with dispensations for individuals who like mosquitos).

Worse yet from the perspective of Nozickian libertarianism, the ER and the associated attenuation of rights requires the rejection of principled anti-paternalism, namely, the view that individuals must be allowed to live their own lives in their own chosen way even when boundary-crossing interference with their choices would genuinely benefit them.[16] At least the prohibition on *non-feared* and genuinely beneficial interference must be dropped – because the gain to the subject of interference will duly compensate her for the cost to her of the non-feared interference. Against this contention it might be argued that there is no barrier to prior negotiation and agreement between the aspiring intervener and the prospective subject of his intervention. The aspiring intervener can offer the benefits of that intervention in exchange for that subject's permission to intervene. The benefit that is great enough to induce the prospective subject to agree to the intervention is her due compensation for being subject to the intervention. Hence, in the determination of due compensation for the intervention, prior negotiation and agreement are to be preferred over boundary crossing accompanied by non-negotiated compensation; and this requires the prohibition of non-consensual intervention.

However, this argument fails because, by hypothesis, the prospective subject of the intervention either does not understand what benefits her or is unmoved by that understanding. It is the aspiring intervener who, by hypothesis, is more moved by a correct understanding of what is beneficial to the prospective subject and to what degree. Hence, that person's judgment rather than prior negotiation and agreement is the more apt determinant of what counts as due compensation to the subject of the beneficent intervention. Thus, the boundary-crossing involved in non-consensual intervention is *permissible* if it is accompanied by duly compensating benefits for the subject of the intervention. Since a state will, presumably, exercise this liberty to engage in paternalist interventions only when doing so accords with the preferences of its (other) clients, the exercise of this liberty will fit under the umbrella of the MAS.

The fact that the ER and attenuation of rights that underwrites it render paternalist interference permissible highlights the nature of the attenuation of rights that Nozick proposes in "Prohibition, Compensation, and Risk." One feature of this attenuation is that Nozick moves from a conception of rights as being at their core claims that are protected by property rules (that forbid boundary-crossings) to a conception of rights as being at their core claims that are protected by liability rules (that allow crossings as long as liability for due compensation is paid). This does not accord well with the deeply propertarian tone of Lockean-Nozickian libertarianism. For instance, in condemning imposed slavery on the basis of self-proprietorship or self-ownership the Lockean-Nozickian does not mean merely to say that slaves do not receive due compensation for their enslavement. They do not mean to say that, if only we could be sure that a slave is receiving at least as much compensation as would have induced him to agree to enslavement, we could be confident that this enslavement is permissible.

What ultimately matters on the less robust, less constraining, liability rule conception of rights is whether a boundary-crossing on net moves its subject below a certain level of wellbeing or utility. Boundary-crossing is morally problematic solely because it tends to depress the level of wellbeing or utility of the subject of the crossing. On this less robust conception, it seems that it must be the value of the prospective subject being at the specified level of wellbeing or utility that grounds that individual's right.[17] In contrast, on the more robust conception of rights that Nozick proclaims at the outset of *ASU, non-consensual* boundary-crossing is morally problematic because it is up to the right-holder to decide whether that boundary will be permissibly crossed – whatever the effects of that boundary-crossing will be on her level of wellbeing or utility. To possess a right is to have this choice, this jurisdiction, over the domain defined by the right. This focus on the subject's choice or jurisdiction and the wrongfulness of overriding this choice or trespassing on this jurisdiction – whatever the value of the upshot of the overriding or trespass – is essential to the deontic character of rights that Nozick seeks to articulate in the language of inviolability and side constraints. On this deontic understanding of rights, due compensation for the *harm* that results from a boundary-crossing does not negate the *wrong* done in overriding the right-holder's choice or jurisdictional authority. It is to block this wrong that boundary-crossings are prohibited.[18] The abandonment of this understanding of rights is the philosophically deepest cost of responding to the anarchist challenge by invoking the ER and the associated overall attenuation of rights.

4.5 ROUND THREE: CONSTRAINED RESPONSES AND THE MINIMAL TAXING STATE

Can the Nozickian offer a more constrained response to the anarchist's challenge with respect to the forced purchase of protective services – a response that has significantly lower philosophical costs from the Nozickian perspective? Two possibilities are worth considering. The first basically accepts the basic apparatus of "Prohibition, Compensation, and Risk" and merely seeks to constrain what counts as due compensation for boundary-crossing. The second version does not seek to build upon that apparatus. Rather, it proposes a constrained specification of persons' property rights such that, if it is true that persons' rights (including their property rights) will be more extensively infringed unless they are subject to some non-consensual takings of their holdings, their property rights do not include rights against those takings.

For the Nozickian rights constitute a special dimension of morality that protects individuals from non-consensual interference by other agents. To engage in such interference is to inflict a special sort of wrong upon right-holders – a wrong that is quite distinct from merely setting back their interests. So, for example, Bekah may set back the interests of her business competitor Josh by attracting his customers without at all inflicting the special sort of wrong involved in rights violation. The special character of the injury involved in rights violation suggests a constraint on what sort of compensation is due for rights infringing action. If the injury is in the currency of a boundary crossing, the compensation must consist in the prevention of boundary crossing. Only then will the purported compensation be commensurate with the injury. Due compensation for an infringement upon Josh's rights must then take the form of an offsetting prevention of a more extensive violation of Josh's rights.

This "commensurate compensation" version of the CR seems to work out very nicely for the libertarian archist. It does get the archist to the MTS rather than the MS. Still, if it is true that in the absence of forced purchases of protective services, those services would not be funded (or would be substantially under-funded) – that is to say, if it is true that a (non-taxing) MS would fail to provide the services that the advocate of the MS anticipates – the archist may quite reasonably take arrival at the (taxing) MTS to be a philosophical *bonus*. Moreover, the commensurate compensation response does keep the door shut against takings to finance non-protective public goods. For the enjoyment of non-protective goods will not constitute *commensurate* compensation. Furthermore, the commensurate compensation constraint for boundary crossings allows the archist to retain principled anti-paternalism (with a class of exceptions to be mentioned). For, in the standard case of paternalist interference, the injury from which the subject is protected is not an infringement of the subject's rights. Hence, what the subject gains from standard paternalist interference is not commensurate with the sort of injury she undergoes. Thus, on the basis of this constraint on due compensation for boundary crossings, standard paternalist interventions are not justified. The exceptions to this anti-paternalism are those cases in which interference with the subject prevents her from exposing herself to more extensive (non-consensual) boundary crossings. Notice, however, that *these* permissible paternalistic boundary crossings are simply variants upon what the MTS already does in requiring persons to purchase protective services. For what the MTS already does can be described as paternalistically preventing people from exposing themselves to more extensive violations of their rights through their too clever attempts to be free riders on others' payment for protective services.

Still, the commensurate compensation version of the CR does incur the deeper philosophical costs involved in taking rights at their core to be claims that are merely protected by liability rules rather than property rules and to be protective of the right-holder's wellbeing or utility rather than the right-holder's choice or jurisdiction. Indeed, the overall attenuation of rights from which the ER proceeds may itself *exclude* the plausible-sounding constraint that we have been considering. For that constraint depends on the idea that boundary crossing involves a special sort of injury that is distinct from merely setting back the wellbeing or utility of the subject of the crossing. However, if boundary crossing is wrong simply in virtue of its setting back the wellbeing or utility of its subject, then it seems that boundary crossing will be permissible whenever the injury it inflicts will be accompanied by a sufficiently extensive countervailing enhancement of the subject's wellbeing or utility.

Perhaps, however, the Nozickian can offer a version of the CR against the individualist anarchist without building upon the general attenuation of rights developed in "Prohibition, Compensation, and Risk." Perhaps the Nozickian can make room for the permissibility of takings if they are necessary for the funding of protective services for those subject to the takings without abandoning the conception of rights embodied in *ASU*'s opening proclamation of rights, that is, a conception according to which *in their default position* rights are claims protected by property rules. The basic strategy, in contrast to that employed in "Prohibition, Compensation, and Risk," would be to explain why in certain special circumstances specific rights take a more attenuated – perhaps a much more attenuated – form than rights take in their default position. One approach within this strategy would proceed in terms of what we may call the "anti-paralysis postulate." According to this postulate, when working out the detailed specification of person's rights, one is to avoid specifications that systematically morally preclude individuals from exercising their rights or from conducting their lives in ways that a specification of their rights is supposed to protect. The intuitive idea that the detailed specification of rights – insofar as that is the job of philosophical reasoning – must be guided by the purpose for which rights are to be recognized as a crucial dimension of morality.

Here are three instances of the anti-paralysis postulate at work. First, suppose we are considering whether an agent's rights over her own person and (legitimately acquired) possessions remain fully intact if she is in the process of violating the rights of others. If we hold that they do remain fully intact, then we must deny that others have rights of self-defense and we must hold that in many circumstances individuals under attack must submit to the violation of their rights. To avoid a specification of rights that yields this conclusion, we must hold that the aggressor's rights do not remain fully intact. But note that it does not follow that the aggressor's rights totally disappear. The aggressor may, for example, still have rights against defensive force which is not necessary to defeat his aggression.

Second, suppose we are considering what (if anything) persons' original equal right to natural material comes to – or, more particularly, whether individuals possess original joint-ownership in the earth. If we hold that they do, we will have to conclude that no individual will permissibly do anything with any natural material without everyone else's permission. Since such universal permission will never be obtained, no individual will ever permissibly do anything with any natural material. Original joint-ownership would render nugatory any right to use or acquire natural material. The anti-paralysis postulate tells us that these consequences are reasons for rejecting original joint ownership of nature. Actually, we should note a helpful complication here. Strictly speaking, the anti-paralysis argument I have just given is only an argument against persons possessing original joint rights to the earth which are protected by property rules. For only such rights *forbid* all individuals from doing anything with any portion of the earth without everyone else's consent – even if such an individual duly compensates others for her use of their natural material. So a further argument would be needed to rule out an original joint right to the earth that was merely protected by a liability rule.[19]

Third, suppose we are considering whether persons are to be understood as having rights against others performing actions that pose any risk – however low – of violating those persons' rights. Such a specification of persons' rights would also be paralyzing. Rather than enhancing persons' peaceful enjoyment of their rights, this specification would systematically diminish each person's sphere of permissible and morally protected action; it would systematically morally preclude individuals from activities that rights are supposed to protect. The anti-paralysis postulate tells us, then, that individuals are not to be understood as having rights against all low-risk activities by others.

To apply this pattern of reasoning to the archist–anarchist dispute, suppose (again) that, in virtue of the public goods feature of rights protection, rights-bearers would be substantially less able to coordinate so as to protect their rights if their rights are understood to preclude their being required to contribute to the funding of protective schemes. If that is the case, a plausible specification of their rights would *not* include a right *protected by a property rule* against being required to contribute to such a scheme. For, given our supposition, a specification that includes a right *protected by a property rule* against being required to contribute would systematically diminish the prospects for the non-violation of each of those rights-bearers' rights. So, "anti-paralysis" considerations support a *limited attenuation* of these rights-bearers' property rights. If a forced exchange is really needed for the funding of needed protective services (which will more extensively protect each individual from rights violations than the forced exchange itself will infringe), then the right of each of those individuals against being subject to the projected taking shifts downward from a right protected by a property rule to a right protected by a liability rule. Hence, a provider of protective services may require recipients of its services to pay for those services – as long as such a system of forced exchanges is really necessary for the financing of (more than sub-optimal) protection of individuals' rights *and* the extent of protection provided to each such individual fulfills the provider's liability to provide compensating protection. (If any of these conditions are not met, the coercive taker violates the rights of those individuals.)

In this way, the MTS archist can defeat the anarchist's contention that the minimal state violates individuals' rights when it requires individuals to purchase its protective services. Note further that this anti-paralysis CR does not undercut libertarian anti-paternalism. For *rights* (taken as claims protected by property rules) are not better served by allowing beneficial (but unchosen) interferences with persons' lives. More fundamentally, the anti-paralysis CR avoids the overall attenuation of rights – from claims protected by property rules to claims protected by liability rules – that Nozick seems to commit himself to in "Prohibition, Compensation, and Risk." The anti-paralysis approach seeks to spot islands of rights attenuation within a sea of robust rights rather than islands of robust rights within a sea of attenuated rights. For this reason, the anti-paralysis CR is the best Nozickian response to the anarchist challenge even though it takes the Nozickian one step beyond the minimal state.

NOTES

I have benefited from presenting this essay at a conference on Reappraising *Anarchy, State, and Utopia* at King's College London and at the University of Virginia. I especially thank Alexander Cohen, Loren Lomasky, and John Simmons for pressing me on my apostate acceptance of certain forced takings.

1. Nozick seeks to bolster his proposal that what everyone else calls the "minimal state" should be seen as merely the "ultra-minimal state" by claiming that a necessary condition of an institution being a state is that "it protect[s] the rights of everyone in the territory" (p. 113). But surely this is a strange claim. If it were true, it would follow that no state has ever slaughtered its own subjects – because if that agency did slaughter its own subjects it would not be a state!
2. On the natural right to acquire property, see Mack: 2010.
3. See Locke: 1960, sections 88 and 130.
4. Nozick is also eager to challenge the social contract account because it involves a visible hand explanation of the state whereas invisible-hand explanations have more charm.
5. See Locke: 1960, sections 123–127.
6. What is projected is not the most reliable system of rights enforcement that money can buy; for people will be interested – to different degrees – in spending money on competing goods and services.
7. Note also the problematic use of "federally" to describe the nature of the affiliation. See also the use of "federal" on p. 16.

8. More precisely, these prohibitions will not be violations of rights if they do not disadvantage those subject to them or if those subject to them are compensated for any disadvantages that are engendered.

9. It is not that only this agency *may* permissibly suppress mid-level risky activity; it is that only the already strong ("dominant") agency *will* permissibly do so (see pp. 108–110).

10. This is not merely for the reason – acknowledged by Nozick – that the dominant agency would not seek to monitor and constrain the packages of services offered to its non-clients for their protection against other non-clients (cf. pp. 109–110).

11. Surely Nozick needs this claim – albeit I cannot find an explicit statement of it.

12. Nozick recognizes that in the standard case the independent "does have some motive other than selling abstention." Still, this independent's abstention leaves the dominant agency's clients no better off than they would be if the independent "didn't exist at all." Nozick holds that the satisfaction of this latter condition combines with the mid-level riskiness of the independent's activity to vindicate the suppression of that activity (with compensation for disadvantages imposed, if any) (cf. p. 86). There is no explanation of how these two conditions combine to yield this vindication.

13. The minimal statist will argue that the *permissible* suppression of independent rights protective activity does not render individuals' purchases of its protective services non-voluntary.

14. There is a sense, therefore, in which a state that does no more than Nozick's minimal state but which has a political–constitutional structure is more of a state than Nozick's minimal state; it is more state-like.

15. In the early 1980s I laid out this argument to Nozick and asked him if he had anything like it in mind when he developed the attenuated understanding of rights in chapter 4 of *ASU*. He said that he had not.

16. In his preface, Nozick tells us that one of the two noteworthy implications of his doctrine is that the state may not use force "in order to prohibit activities to people for their *own* good or protection" (p. ix).

17. Nozick seems to be drawn to this essentially interest conception of rights by his (surprising) tendency to think that in the final analysis wrongness in action has to be accounted for by the disvalue – indeed, the disutility – associated with that action. See Gaus: 2002.

18. And, perhaps, boundary-crossings are punished in order to negate this wrong.

19. Perhaps no argument is really needed to rule *out* any original right to the earth if no argument can be found to rule *in* any such right.

5 Explanation, justification, and emergent properties: an essay on Nozickian metatheory

5.1 INTRODUCTION

In some ways, *Anarchy, State, and Utopia* (*ASU*) has been a victim of its own success. For over thirty-five years it has been one of the most provocative works in political philosophy, and the preeminent defense of Lockean libertarianism. Almost all readers have read it with an eye to its conclusions. Statists and redistributionists see it as something to be combated and defeated; libertarians start out to defend it or, at least, modify it in constructive ways. Given this it is hardly surprising that the second part of *ASU*, arguing against the redistributive state, has been the focus of by far the most extensive, and famous, discussions. One shudders to think of how many essays have been written on Nozick's witty, four–page, Wilt Chamberlain example.[1] The first part of *ASU*, in which Nozick argues against the anarchist, showing that minimal state is (in some sense) justifiable, has received much less attention. Eric Mack's contribution to this volume is an insightful analysis of Nozick's substantive case against anarchism, and how it might be modified to achieve success.

If within *ASU* the first part generally goes unnoticed, within that part Nozick's path-breaking analysis of invisible-hand explanations is almost entirely ignored in political philosophy.[2] Readers focus on Nozick's substantive claims, and not what he calls his "abstract" and "metatheoretical" comments about explanation and justification (p. 3). This is partly Nozick's own doing; he directs readers away from his metatheoretical comments about the benefits of state of nature theories and invisible hands to his substantive account of the state of nature and the rise of the minimal state (p. 4). The proof of his method, he suggests, is in the pudding. I wish to take just the opposite course: I plan to examine the proof without the pudding. Or, rather, I wish to ask what Nozick would have proved if the pudding came out just as he hoped. If Nozick's argument against anarchism had fully succeeded, what would it have shown? Contrary to the view of most commentators, I shall argue that it would have shown *a lot*. If the argument had succeeded, Nozick would have provided a powerful account of the realm of the political and demonstrated its moral permissibility and justifiability independent of collective choice or actual history. That is, Nozick would have fulfilled some of the core ambitions of political philosophy.

5.2 A SHORT SUMMARY

In what follows, then, I assume that Nozick's argument in the first part of *ASU* ("State of Nature Theory, or How to Back into a State without Really Trying") is entirely successful. To recall, the starting point of the analysis is a non-political, Lockean, "state of nature." There are only individuals with their Lockean rights to life, liberty, and property. Following Locke, Nozick holds that each has executive power: she can enforce her own rights, punish transgressors, seek just compensation, and assist others in doing so (p. 10). Again closely following Locke, because individuals are judges in their own cases, their self-bias will lead them to err in their own favor: they will overestimate the harm done to them, and interpret rights claims in their own favor (p. 11). Conjoined with the executive power of each, we can expect disagreement and conflict about what is just. As I have argued elsewhere, Hobbes, Locke, and Kant all share the conviction that individuals, employing their private judgment about the dictates of justice, will inevitably disagree, and will be led to conflict (see Gaus: in press-a). At this point the social contract tradition appeals to a collective agreement according to which

all private judgment of every particular Member being excluded, the Community comes to be Umpire, by settled standing Rules, indifferent, and the same to all Parties; and by Men having Authority from the Community, for the execution of those Rules, decides all the differences that may happen between any Members of that Society, concerning *any matter of right*; and punishes those Offenses, which any Member hath committed against Society, with such Penalties as the Law has established. (Locke: 1960, section 87, emphasis added)

Famously, Nozick does not appeal to such an agreement. Instead, he proposes an "invisible hand" mechanism according to which each individual, acting only to best secure her own rights and interests, acts in such a way that the unintended outcome of a complex social interaction is, essentially, the Lockean state. Private judgment about the demands of morality is excluded, and some possess sole authority to adjudicate the differences that may happen between any members of that society concerning any matter of right, and punish those offenses, which any member has committed against society with such penalties as the political authority establishes. This result, Nozick argues, emerges in the state of nature because individuals will realize that relying solely on self-enforcement of their rights claims will be ineffective and dangerous for all the reasons that Locke pointed out. But the first obvious response is not to rush headlong into the state, but to form self-protective groups, in which individuals would agree to defend and enforce each other's rights. These groups, though, would have serious disadvantages:

(1) everyone is always on call to serve a protective function ... and (2) any member may call out his associates by saying that his rights are being, or have been, violated. Protective associations will not want to be at the beck and call of their most cantankerous or paranoid members, not to mention members who might attempt, under the guise of self-defense, to use the association to violate the rights of others. Difficulties will also arise if two different members of the same association are in dispute, each calling upon his fellow members to come to his aid. (pp. 12–13)

More entrepreneurial and judicial protective agencies would arise to cope with these problems. So that a person is not constantly on call to engage in time-consuming and potentially dangerous enforcement activities, the protective agency would sell its enforcement services; people could buy a policy and so free themselves of actually engaging in enforcement and punishment. In order to cope with the problem of cantankerous, paranoid, and criminal members, the agency would only act when, on the basis of its own settled standing rules, it decides that its clients have been wronged. At first there is no reason to think that these rules will be, in Locke's terms "indifferent, and the same to all Parties" – some agencies may have rules that manifestly favor their own clients. But while such agencies may be favored by cantankerous, paranoid, and criminal members, others will see their premiums going up as the agency constantly seeks to enforce biased claims on others. Most will abandon such agencies for those with more "indifferent" rules and procedures, which will tend to minimize enforcement costs and, so, premiums.

The next crucial step in Nozick's story is the rise of a dominant agency. Although he does not explicitly invoke the idea, rights enforcement has important increasing returns features: the more others join a specific agency, the greater the benefits of others doing so.[3] If everyone is a client of the same agency, all disputes will be internalized and so all disputes will be settled by its own standing rules and it will never actually have to battle other agencies. For these and other reasons (cf. pp. 15–18), we can expect a territory to come to be dominated by a single protective agency or a few acting as a combine.

At this point an "ultramininal state" has arisen. Nozick thinks it falls short of our normal notion of a state because some individuals may have refused to join it for idiosyncratic reasons (some people after all still use Word Perfect despite the increasing returns of using Word). These individuals would either enforce their own rights or be members of boutique agencies; the dominant association would not defend them. The final step in the evolution of the state is for it to claim the right to judge whether non-members are employing rules and adjudication procedures that it deems fair; if it decides that such procedures are unacceptable it may ban their use against its members provided compensation is paid to the independents. This leads to two of Nozick's most complex and controversial arguments in Part I. First, that provided compensation is paid the dominant agency may prohibit procedures that, on its view, run too great a risk that its members will be treated unjustly and, second, that adequate compensation can consist of providing protection services. If the dominant protection agency does this, he argues that it has evolved into a minimal state, claiming the sole authority to judge when coercion may be employed, and "taxing" some (its members) to pay for the protection of others (compensated independents).[4] We seem to have come very close to the Lockean state in which the dominant agency has authority for the execution of rules, decides all the differences that may happen between any members of that society concerning any matter of right; and punishes those offenses, which any member hath committed against society, with such penalties it has established.

5.3 THE INVISIBLE-HAND EXPLANATION OF THE STATE

5.3.1 *Nozick's analysis of invisible-hand explanations applied to his account*

Nozick not only emphasizes that this account of the rise of the state constitutes an invisible-hand explanation, but spends a good deal of time analyzing the general idea of invisible-hand explanations. The core of an invisible-hand explanation is that (1) a certain pattern of human activity P arises which was produced by the intentional actions of the participants but (2) at least in the pure case no one acted with the intention of bringing about P.[5] (As Nozick remarks: "No one, as they buy protection services from their local protective agency, has in mind anything so grand" as the creation of a Lockean state [p. 132].) Nozick identifies two mechanisms that can produce P from a set of actions and intentions not aiming at P: "filtering processes wherein some filter eliminates all entities not fitting a certain pattern, and equilibrium processes wherein each component part adjusts to local conditions, changing the local environments of others close by, so the sum of the local adjustments realizes a pattern" (Nozick: 1991, p. 314).[6]

The account of the rise of the state employs both mechanisms. Nozick supposes that people seek to act justly. To be sure, from an objective point of view some people act wrongly: after all, there is a dispute about rights claims and we must suppose that on a Lockean account one of the parties is, objectively, wrong. Nozick – and here he is faithfully following the social contract tradition – supposes that while there is an objective moral truth in such disputes, when we employ our reason we disagree. As Hobbes put it, no man's reason constitutes right reason; that the use of private reason about objective morality leads us to disagree is perhaps the fundamental claim of the social contract tradition.[7] So rather than saying that each person acts rightly or morally, we can say that, overwhelmingly, people employ their private reason to act "within good faith" in interpreting the law of nature (p. 17). If state of nature/social contract theories take disagreement of private reason as the fundamental fact that makes individual rights enforcement unstable, an account of the rise of the state as a solution to this problem (whether via an invisible hand or a collective agreement) must retain this assumption.[8] An account that iterates interactions in a way that filters out bad-faith motivation will ensure that pattern P has been arrived at without anyone acting badly (on the importance of this, see section 5.4). If we are seeking to understand how individual rights-bearers might solve their problem under the assumption of disagreement in private reason, but have doubts about the central design approach characteristic of the social contract (section 5.3.4), then we may model them as interacting as morally as they reasonably can be expected to (but otherwise realistically, being mostly concerned with their own costs and benefits), and then subject to this filter, see what pattern emerges.

The rise of the dominant protective agency is an equilibrium filter – not in the sense of equilibrium in neoclassical economics in which the system will arrive at, and return to, the same equilibrium under a wide variety of conditions, but in the sense of a path-dependent system that can arrive at multiple equilibria.[9] Any agency might rise to dominance; and whatever agency does so constitutes an equilibrium. Given that some agency is dominant, there will be no incentive to defect given the increasing returns features of adjudication (section 5.4.4).[10] Thus as a system travels along some path, some protective agencies are filtered out, leading to an equilibrium with one dominant agency.

5.3.2 How invisible-hand explanations demystify emergent properties

In Edna Ullmann-Margalit's analysis a successful invisible-hand account tells a "story," typically characterized by several stages, in which the actions of individuals are the ordinary and expected (see Ullmann-Margalit: 1978, pp. 270–271). Prosaic action in the story is a strong point: we do not assume people do extraordinary things to get the right result, they only do what people normally would be expected to. Thus in Nozick's account of the rise of the ultra-minimal state, people act to protect themselves, they do not wish to spend a lot of time being called out to protect others, they are worried about being at the beck and call of the quarrelsome and contentious, and they seek to get good value for their money. Overall, they are what we might call reasonably self-interested folk who are willing to act within their understanding of morality. Ullmann-Margalit holds that the power of an invisible-hand account is that, on the basis of the prosaic, an unexpected, surprising, pattern emerges:

What is surprising – even startling, sometimes – about invisible-hand explanations is, I suggest, their very existence: the fact, that is, that what one would have thought had to be the product of someone's intentional design can be shown to be the unsought and unintended product of dispersed individual activity ... among the marks of the good invisible-hand explanations are ... the fluency and naturalness – the very lack of surprising elements in – the description involved. (Ullmann-Margalit: 1978, pp. 271–272)

An effective invisible-hand explanation shows the emergence of a new and unexpected property (P) out of the prosaic properties of the account, which appear themselves not to have P implicit in them. The argument for the ultra-minimal state certainly qualifies, and Nozick himself is clear that this is an invisible-hand explanation (see p. 22; Nozick: 1991, p. 314; see also Ullmann-Margalit: 1978, pp. 264–265). It is far less clear that the argument from the ultra-minimal to minimal state is a compelling invisible-hand account, although many have supposed that the entire analysis leading up to the minimal state is an invisible-hand explanation (see Miller: 2002; Lind: 1989). On the one hand, Nozick suggests that the minimal state is already implicit in the ultra-minimal (see p. 25), so we might conclude that the invisible-hand explanation of the minimal state just *is* the explanation for the ultra-minimal state. Yet the actions and reasoning of the dominant protective agency in prohibiting unauthorized enforcement by independents is too close to aiming at P to constitute a satisfying invisible-hand explanation of P: the agency is seeking to gain a monopoly on the authorization of coercion, and its complex compensation reasoning (see Chapter 4 of *ASU*) is anything but prosaic. It is not very surprising that the outcome of the dominant agency's reasoning is a claim to minimal, Lockean, statehood.

Invisible-hand explanations are so powerful because they fully explain an emergent property. The resulting P property is surprising because – at least before the account is given – we cannot see how P is latent in the filtered, rather prosaic, actions of a number of people. In complexity theory, P is an emergent property of system S when

S is composed of elements $\{e_1...e_n\}$ and our best micro knowledge of the elements does not attribute to them the property of producing P. In his *System of Logic* Mill proposes three features of an emergent property P:[11]

(1) P is not the sum of $\{e_1...e_n\}$;
(2) P is of an entirely different character than $\{e_1...e_n\}$;
(3) P cannot not be predicted or deduced from the behavior of the members of $\{e_1...e_n\}$ considered independently (i.e., apart from their interactions in S).

Thus it is said that waves are an emergent property of H_2O. The properties studied by hydrology are not the sum of the properties of hydrogen and oxygen (as opposed to a mechanical force, which may be seen as the sum of its causes); waves are of a very different character than a chemical compound, and the properties of an individual water molecule do not allow us to deduce the relevant laws concerning waves. Of interest for us is that emergent properties are distinguished from mere "resultant" properties on the grounds that, while a resultant property is the expected outcome of S, an emergent property is novel and, given our understanding of $\{e_1...e_n\}$, unexpected or surprising (see Auyang: 1998, p. 177).

Invisible-hand accounts are thus explanations of emergent properties.[12] Indeed they are especially informative explanations of such properties. Claims about emergent properties can sometimes seem rather mysterious: we might know that P emerges from $\{e_1...e_n\}$ in S, but the way in which it does so may be unexplained.[13] Thus it is plausible to see consciousness as an emergent property of the brain, but it is not clear how much this actually explains. It tells us the sort of explanation we are looking for, but we have not yet seen how consciousness emerges. In contrast, an invisible-hand account provides the motivations, filters and equilibrium concepts such that we can model the emergence of P from an S composed of $\{e_1...e_n\}$.

5.3.3 Actual, hypothetical, and counterfactual invisible hands

An important feature of emergent properties is that the macro property P emerges from a wide variety of values for $\{e_1...e_n\}$. That is, if P is an emergent property of S, there are many states of the micro elements $\{e_1...e_n\}$ that produce P. To return to the standard example of waves, the same wave action can be produced by different water molecules; switching e_i for e_j (and so replacing system state S_2 for S_1) will have no effect: the same P will be produced by either S_1 or S_2.[14] The core idea here is the micro-unpredictability (we cannot say what any specific element will be doing at any particular time, or with whom it will be interacting), is combined with macro-predictability: we nevertheless can predict that P will arise anyway (see Smith: 1998, p. 13). Thus in Nozick's invisible-hand account, it does not matter, in any particular system S, what protection agency gains dominance, what people are independents, who is paranoid, and so on. If we think of each of the actors as being specified by different values (degree of contentiousness, risk aversion, liability to misinterpret rights, entrepreneurial skill, skill in winning conflicts, amount of property held, etc.), then for a wide range of these values, the values can be varied (some S's may have a high standard of entrepreneurial skill, others a lower average) and permutated (it does not matter whether person e_i has entrepreneurial skill value x and e_j y, or vice versa), and yet P will still be the emergent property.

This is of the first importance, for we are now ready for (our first) somewhat surprising result: the fact that the account is hypothetical, rather than being a weakness, is a strength in our analysis of P. Suppose that we possessed a complete historical account of the rise of some specific ultra-minimal state. We could specify the specific actors involved and the roles they played. Suppose further that the record revealed that everyone acted in good faith, according to their plausible understanding of natural law. What would this show? Not very much: we would know that pattern P actually did arise from system S_1, but we would not know much about P. Does it only emerge upon this particular specification? What changes in the values of the system members and their interactions are consistent with P emerging? We would, as it were, have one data point, but our understanding of the way that P emerges on S would be very limited indeed. On the other hand, a hypothetical account can be seen as a *model*; by not specifying many of the values, we can run the model and see to what extent the micro specifications of $\{e_1...e_n\}$ in S do and do not affect the emergence of P. That the invisible-hand "story" gives rise to P when only specifying broad prosaic motivations under plausible filters and equilibrium concepts gives us greater confidence that we know the processes by which P emerges on S.

But, it may be objected, if in the real world P did not emerge by the invisible-hand process from S, but from an alternative process, then we have not really understood *our* pattern P. Suppose in our world P emerged because it was the object of an explicit social contract; in such a case it was the result of design, not an invisible hand. So in the end, it might be insisted, history does matter. We need to be clear here; the problem is not that our invisible-hand account is hypothetical – the worry now is that it is counterfactual. To what extent is our model still a good explanation if we know that some specific P did not emerge from the invisible hand? According to Ullmann-Margalit, showing that the genesis of P was not via the invisible hand is not definitive in whether the invisible hand explains P.

[E]ven if the invisible-hand explanation turns out not to be the correct account of how the thing emerged, it may still not be devoid of validity with regard to the question of how (and why) it is *maintained*. Not every product of design, especially if we are dealing with a complex social pattern or institution, is successful and lasting. The ascertainment that there is (was) a designing agent, therefore, even when conjoined with the ability to identify him and to spell out his rationale, does not take us very far towards illuminating the nature of its success and stability. The availability, on the other hand, of a cogent invisible-hand story of how the pattern in question could have arisen – given the specific circumstances, some common-sense assumptions concerning the drives of the individuals concerned, and the normal course of events – may, I believe, contribute to our understanding of the inherently self-reinforcing nature of this pattern and hence of its being successful and lasting. (Ullmann-Margalit: 1978, p. 275)

Given the rather prosaic actions that underlie P on the invisible-hand account, the fact that the efficient cause of P was some intentional process that, perhaps, short-circuited the invisible hand, does not show that P is not maintained or sustained by the invisible hand. Insofar as the invisible hand is based on a compelling equilibrium analysis, attributing to it a sustaining function will be especially plausible.

Nozick makes a far stronger claim for counterfactual invisible hands:

A theory of a state of nature that begins with fundamental general descriptions of morally permissible and impermissible actions, and of deeply based reasons why some persons in any society would violate these constraints, and goes on to describe how a state would arise from the state of nature will serve our explanatory purposes, *even if no state ever actually arose in that way.* (p. 7, emphasis in original)

Ullmann-Margalit is willing to endorse the invisible-hand account even though states were not produced by the process as long as they are sustained by it; but she insists that if our explanation is to be true whatever claims we make about the facts must be true (Ullmann-Margalit: 1978, p. 274). Nozick is much more willing to embrace counterfactual explanations. He allows that a perfectly good (he does not say "true") explanation of P may be process-defective (p. 8).[15] Suppose the facts are as postulated by the invisible-hand account, and the laws involved in the invisible-hand explanation are perfectly true, but some non-invisible-hand process always intervenes and produces and sustains P via its own processes. Nozick holds that, given that we have shown that P would emerge and be sustained as a result of the invisible-hand process were it not for the intervention, we have gone a long way toward explaining P.

Although we certainly would learn a lot about P from seeing how it would emerge out of an invisible-hand process even if in fact it never does, we would have to inquire why our invisible hand always gets preempted by another process. And although we learned that P *could* be an emergent property of the invisible hand, in our world it would not be. (That is why we have learned a good deal about P, but not much about P-in-our-world.) Such a case might arise for a neoclassical economist in a world economy run by a central planning God; she could give an account of how the invisible hand *could* produce an equilibrium, but God always beats the invisible hand to it. Although our economist does know something important about the property of equilibrium states, she does not explain economic equilibrium in her world. Consider, though, a less radical case of the invisible hand as a process-defective explanation. Assume that in our society P is not produced or even sustained by the invisible-hand process. God runs our economy, and so we have a centrally planned command economy with perfectly efficient prices, but the rest of the world runs things the old-fashioned way.[16] Nevertheless the invisible-hand explanation may still be the best account of what property P is about in our world. God would not be the best explanation of the property of economic equilibrium, for this process produces P only under exceptional and fragile circumstances[17] (when we are God's chosen people, and until we disobey), whereas (let us suppose) an alternative, invisible-hand process, produces P under a wide variety of parameters (think again about the importance of hypothetical models). Although it would be wrong to say that P can *only* be an emergent property of the invisible hand in S, it would still be true that the best understanding of P is as such a property, for it is the most robust explanation of the rise and/or maintenance of P in our world – it produces/sustains P under a wide variety of S specifications. Thus even under some counterfactual conditions the invisible hand would be our best explanation.

5.3.4 Explanatory political theory: the political order as an emergent property

Nozick tells us that invisible-hand accounts provide "fundamental explanations" of a realm because they "make no use of any other notions of the realm" (p. 19). A property P is fundamentally explained when there is a convincing account of how P is an emergent property of $\{e_1...e_n\}$ in S. Nozick's invisible-hand account starts with a prosaic individual-level activity subject to a high level of social interaction given some filters and equilibrium concepts, and then (assuming all goes well in the story) shows that statehood (or, at least, ultra-minimal statehood) is an emergent property. Thus the idea of statehood would be fully explained and explicated without employing basic concepts such as sovereignty, social order, political power, or political authority. Although today political philosophers are often obsessed with normative claims, we should not forget that a longstanding aim of political theorizing is to understand the realm of the political. We should not succumb to the temptation of dismissing invisible-hand theories as *merely explanatory*,[18] and so largely besides the point in political theory. A traditional view – which has much to recommend it – is that before political theory can ask whether the state is justified, it must have some grasp of what the core properties of statehood and the political are.[19]

Now a dominant strain in modern political philosophy is to view the state as an artifice, created to solve human problems. "The state, conceived of as artificial, is to be understood as created for our ends, our protection, our defense" (Morris: 1998, p. 5). While to view the state as an artifice does not necessarily require that it is the product of intentional design, this view of the state easily lends itself to the design perspective: if the state is an artifice with a point, then we may suppose that it came about in order to secure the relevant aims. Hobbes's and Locke's social contract theories sought not simply to justify the state, but to explain how it arose out of the state of nature. Seeing how our ends were frustrated, we designed an institution for our protection and defense. Thus, on this view, the realm of the political was intentionally designed to solve a set of human problems. Recall Hobbes:

The only way to erect such a common power, as may be able to defend them from the invasion of foreigners, and the injuries of one another, and thereby to secure them in such sort as that by their own industry and by the fruits of the earth they may nourish themselves and live contentedly, is to confer all their power and strength upon one man, or upon one assembly of men, that may reduce all their wills, by plurality of voices, unto one will ... This is more than consent, or concord; it is a real unity of them all in one and the same person, made by covenant of every man with every man, in such manner as if every man should say to every man: I authorise and give up my right of governing myself to this man, or to this assembly of men, on this condition; that thou give up, thy right to him, and authorise all his actions in like manner. This done, the multitude so united in one person is called a COMMONWEALTH; in Latin, CIVITAS. *This is the generation* of that great LEVIATHAN, or rather, to speak more reverently, of that mortal god to which we owe, under the immortal God, our peace and defence. (Hobbes: 1994, p. 109 [ch. xvii, para. 13], emphasis added)

The traditional social contract explication of the political is just the sort of intentional design account that, we might say, is an explanation of the first look: seeing that the state solves problems, we explain it as the result of people seeking to solve the problems. The concepts constitutive of the political are, as it were, inventions of the political. A whole new set of concepts – authorization, political authority, united wills and judgments, political power – all arise out of the insight that they are required to solve this problem. Not only is such an explanation of the political rather thin, it opens the way to a deep anarchist objection that the idea of the political is simply an error, or a piece of ideology perpetuated by those who wish to rule over others. Contrast this to a successful invisible-hand account. Here the realm of the political is the emergent property of prosaic human actions under a large range of system states. It comes very close to establishing the claim that the political is the natural result of free and normal human interaction.

5.4 DOES NOZICK'S INVISIBLE HAND JUSTIFY?

5.4.1 The minimal justificatory claim

That the political realm is something like the inevitable result of prosaic human action would not show that the state or the realm of the political is justified. Nozick is explicit that "the notion of invisible-hand explanation is descriptive, not normative. Not every pattern that arises by an invisible-hand process is desirable, and something that can arise by an invisible-hand process might better arise or be maintained through conscious intervention" (Nozick: 1991, p. 314). Yet it is natural to refer to "Nozick's invisible-hand justification of the political state" (Lind: 1989). In what way is the invisible-hand explanation part of the justification of the political state? That is our key question.

The most obvious answer is that because one of the filters (section 5.3.1) is a moral filter – people are assumed to act out of good-faith concern for the rights of others – we can be assured that the rise of the political is not *necessarily* the result of intentional rights violations. Nozick is very clear that he seeks to answer the anarchist who claims "that any state necessarily violates people's moral rights and hence is intrinsically immoral" (p. 6). To anarchists such as Bakunin, the state necessarily depends on exploitation: slavery is its essence (Bakunin: 1971, pp. 137ff.). Nozick demonstrates that, at a minimum, the political can emerge on a system characterized by prosaic action under the constraint that people make a good-faith effort to do the right thing. Thus, in opposition to the classical anarchists such as Bakunin, Nozick has shown that political properties – the realm of the political – can be accounted for even when filtering out manifestly exploitative and unjust action. So unjust and exploitative action cannot be essential to the political. Thus the claim that the political is inherently unjust is defeated. We have at a minimum, then, a possibility proof that the political can arise without manifest rights violations, and that the realm of the political is not essentially unjust.[20]

5.4.2 Legitimacy as an emergent property

The possibility proof is a significant result, but it only serves to defeat the sort of unqualified criticism of the state advanced by Bakunin – that it is *necessarily* unjust. I believe our analysis of the Nozickian invisible hand and its emergent properties allows us to make a much stronger claim, directed at a much wider array of anarchists: namely, that moral legitimacy is a property of ultra-minimal states generally. Recall that we have seen that a hypothetical invisible-hand account is best understood as a model, in which a wide variety of values of $\{e_1...e_n\}$, resulting in a wide variety of specifications of system S, all produce the same emergent property P – the set of properties of the ultra-minimal state. We have also seen that the invisible-hand account leading to P filters out manifestly impermissible action, so all these specifications of S will lead to the emergence of a pattern P that is permissible. One understanding of the idea of state "legitimacy" is that the coercive actions of the state to enforce the law are morally permissible.[21] What the Nozickian invisible hand shows, then, is that political legitimacy is an emergent property of prosaic human action under the constraint that people make a good-faith effort to act within the moral law.

This is a truly striking result. Political theory has typically supposed that the question "Is the state legitimate?" is one that must be answered at the political level: it is a question to be posed by political theory within the political realm. Nozick's argument is designed to demonstrate that the legitimacy of the ultra-minimal state arises from non-political interactions, and emerges upon a wide variety of social states. There is an instructive contrast here to Hayek, whose invisible-hand-evolutionary account of social order Nozick cites (pp. 336–337). For Hayek, an "order of actions" is an emergent property of a system of rules under conditions of generally free action.[22] As a selectionist, Hayek proposes mechanisms by which competition between societies selects rules that provide for effective orders. As an emergent property, an effective social order can arise from a variety of rules and social settings. Nozick's account is different; it specifies the rules (Lockean moral constraints), and then shows that these rules under prosaic motivations and concerns (1) lead to the emergent property of the ultra-minimal state and (2) select only such states that are legitimate. Thus Nozick demonstrates that a legitimate political order is an emergent property for all populations of Lockeans.

5.4.3 Objection 1: hypotheticals, counterfactuals, and legitimacy

David Schmidtz plausibly argues that a hypothetical story cannot justify through emergence. Schmidtz contrasts a "teleological" justification, which "seeks to justify institutions in terms of what they accomplish" from an "emergent approach [which] takes justification to be an emergent property of the process by which institutions arise" (Schmidtz: 1990a, p. 89). On Schmidtz's analysis the emergent approach – which he identifies with both social contract and invisible-hand accounts (Schmidtz: 1990a, p. 91) – looks to what has actually taken place to justify the state. Schmidtz is adamant that hypothetical models cannot justify via emergence; if society S has not actually gone through the process, we cannot say that there has been an emergent justification of P via the process. If a hypothetical emergence account does appear justificatory it is only because we take the emergence story as indicating that there is an implicit teleological justification of the state. In a hypothetical story hypothetical emergence occurs because we can see the hypothetical agents would do what satisfies their goals, including constructing a state (see Schmidtz: 1990a, p. 101).[23] But then it is the goals, not the emergence, which is doing the justificatory work.

Our analysis paints a considerably more complex picture. Again, we must be careful to distinguish hypotheticals and counterfactuals. That the explanatory account is a hypothetical model rather than an actual account is a great strength, for we see that ultraminimal statehood is an emergent property of a wide variety of societies, not just one. This increases our confidence that the best explication of these properties is as emergent. The question is whether we still can conclude that ultra-minimal statehood is an emergent property under counterfactual conditions – when we know that a specific P did not arise via the invisible hand. Now here we must take care to also distinguish purely explanatory from normative contexts. Recall that in purely explanatory contexts I considered three different views of the place of counterfactuals. (1) Ullmann-Margalit holds that if the invisible hand sustains this P, even if it did not bring about this P, we could still see this P as an emergent property. (2) I pressed further: even if we live in an outlier society in which some other process has preempted the invisible hand, the best explanation of P in our world (including our P) is that it is an emergent property, although we have to admit that it can arise, and has arisen, in other ways, as it did in our case. If in one case the conditions explaining P are unstable and/or unusual, and in another account P is the normal result of prosaic actions, the latter is the preferred general explanation of the nature of P. (3) Lastly, we saw that Nozick wishes to push further still: even if the invisible hand is always preempted by some other process, we still have explained the nature of P by knowing that in lieu of this other process (or these other process; p. 8 fn.), P is an emergent property of the invisible hand.

Although I was skeptical of Nozick's full embrace of counterfactuals in purely explanatory contexts, it is unobjectionable in what we might call normative-explanatory theory.[24] In political theory we are often interested in explaining a realm or idea in a normative context. We are interested in the idea of rights, or democracy, or the state, and so we wish to see how an explanation of a realm or concept accounts for the current understanding of our practices, where one of the aspects of the current understanding is that the realm or concept has normative significance. Now one of our concerns is the nature of a legitimate and just state – one that is not the result of immorality, exploitation, or oppression. In Rawls's theory, we inquire about such a state by considering the political principles reasonable and rational people would select in a fair original choice situation (Rawls: 1999a, pp. 15–19). Nozick's concern is the properties of the state in a society populated by people who are acting on the basis of their own costs and benefits but who are also basically moral – let us call them "reasonable and rational Lockeans." Perhaps there never has been a society of such Lockeans (or a society of reasonable and rational Rawlsians); if so non-counterfactual analysis will only explicate the realm of the political under Lockean injustice and/or irrationality. By applying the filter on manifestly non-Lockean action, Nozick can propose an answer to the question at the core of political philosophy since Plato's *Republic*: what are the properties of a just state? That there has never been such a state does not show that there cannot be an explanation of what its properties would be. What Nozick shows is that the properties of a just and legitimate state are those that would emerge from the prosaic actions of rational and reasonable Lockeans, and that it would be a minimal state.

This may appear *too* striking. The invisible hand legitimates *P* even though there never has been a *P* produced by the invisible hand! Readers may recoil at this, but I believe that is because they read Nozick's account too simply, as simply a story about legitimation via consent. Schmidtz, I think, does so, and this is why he can see invisible hand and traditional social contract accounts as both emergent, when it is quite clear that the social contract does not offer a fundamental emergence explanation.[25] Nozick's aim is to provide a fundamental explanation of the properties of the legitimate state. Because it is partly an explanatory project, Nozick's concern is to model the conditions under which such a state would arise; because it is also a normative project, the conditions are appropriately counterfactual in filtering out manifestly anti-Lockean motivations, while otherwise postulating prosaic actions and concerns.

5.4.4 Objection II: the failure of true justification

Thus far I have been focusing on the question of moral legitimacy, that is, the moral permissibility of the state's use of force. Nozick, though, actually suggests three possible ways in which one might "justify the state": "If [a] one could show that the state would be superior to the most favored situation of anarchy, the best that could be hoped for, or [b] would arise by a process involving no morally impermissible steps, or [c] would be an improvement if it arose, this would provide a rationale for the state's existence; it would justify the state" (p. 5).

Nozick's analysis seems to focus almost exclusively on (b).[26] But what of (a) and (c)? David Miller has strenuously argued that Nozick fails to "show that the emergence of the state is not only something that might happen, permissibly, but that would be desirable if it did" (Miller: 2002, p. 15).[27] Miller recognizes that invisible-hand explanations are path-dependent (section 5.3.1), so a society could arrive at a suboptimal, ultra-minimal state.

If agency A gets off to a flying start, either because it runs the best advertising campaign, or because it appeals to those clients who are the quickest to see the advantages of a professional protective service, or for whatever reason, other clients may switch to A *not* because they like its organization or the procedures it uses but because of the advantages in being a client of the largest agency in town. If A eventually turns into a minimal state, its claim to legitimacy resides solely in the fact that it discharges the functions appropriate to a minimal state; it cannot claim to have been *chosen* by the people it serves, by virtue (for instance) of the superiority of its methods to those of its erstwhile rivals. (Miller: 2002, p. 17)

In contrast, Miller argues, in a traditional social contract account, although Lockean contractors "may not end up with the form of government that each of them prefers ... at least the majority's preference will prevail" (Miller: 2002, p. 17). Because the invisible hand is path-dependent in this way, it would seem that we can get worse results than would be delivered by the traditional, collective, social contract. It seems that if our aim is to justify the state by showing that it is an improvement over the state of nature – that it is a truly desirable condition – then the invisible-hand process cannot ensure this.

We need to distinguish four possible outcomes of the invisible-hand process that might cause worries. In order of increasing seriousness:

(1)   There is a legitimate minimal[28] state that the majority holds is inferior to a state that could have been arrived at by a contract;

(2)   There is a legitimate minimal state that is Pareto-inferior to a state that could have been arrived at by a contract;

(3)   There is a legitimate minimal state that is not Pareto-superior to the state of nature;

(4)   There is a legitimate minimal state that is Pareto-inferior to the state of nature.

Re (1): Miller invokes the first option in the above quote. He is certainly right that a path-dependent process driven by increasing returns is by no means guaranteed to satisfy majority preferences (reflect on how many people use the Windows operating system just because so many others use it). However, it begs the question against Nozick to hold that in a Lockean contract the majority would at least have its preferences satisfied. Nozick assumes no such majoritarian values. If some have majoritarian values and others do not, there is no reason why majoritarianism should rule. Indeed even in

Locke the majoritarian phase supposes a prior unanimous consent to enter a civil society (Locke: 1960, ch. VIII).

It is also worth stressing that, unlike Nozick's invisible-hand account, there is no reason to suppose that the outcome of a simple majoritarian choice will be a Nash equilibrium. In Nozick's tale, at the end of the day no one has a unilateral incentive to defect on the minimal state – either one has joined because the benefits of membership exceed the costs, or one has been compensated for membership. With a simple majoritarian choice, although the majority may get what it wants, there is no reason to suppose that the minority will not have an incentive to defect and go their own way.

Re (2): Of course if everyone has majoritarian preferences that would be different, for now we would have our second case in which the path-dependent process leads to a Pareto-inferior outcome. In such a case the invisible hand leads to a non-majoritarian state P, whereas everyone prefers the majoritarian P'. There is no reason to think this might not happen. In a path-dependent process protective agency A may be eliminated by B at time 1, and B eliminated by C at time 2, yet if people were confronted with a choice between A and C it is possible that all would prefer A to C. Miller would, presumably, hold that an explicit contract would not select a Pareto-dominated state, and leaving aside information and transaction costs, this seems generally true. If, however, everyone actually prefers another state to that which has emerged from the invisible hand, there is no reason why the members of a Nozickian society could not contract into this different state. Indeed, the entire point of Part III of *ASU* is to allow groups to contract into more-than-minimal states that appeal to them. At a limit, if everyone in a society wished to contract into such a state, they certainly could. Similarly, if they all preferred the creation of a new minimal state to the present one, they could (consistent with their current contracts) contract into a new state.[29]

Although explicit unanimity requirements are good at avoiding Pareto-dominated options in a set of eligible choices, they have difficulty in showing that there is any state that is acceptable to parties stuck in the state of nature. It is unlikely that any specific state will be most preferred by everyone in the state of nature. Consider Table 1.

Here there is no unanimous view of the best state. Betty would rather stay in the state of nature than have D, and Charlie would

Table 1

Alf	Betty	Charlie
A	B	C
B	C	B
C	A	D
D	S of N	S of N
S of N	D	A

rather stay put than live under A. They can all agree that either B or C would be better than staying in the state of nature, but neither Pareto dominates the other (again, it begs the question to say that the majority prefers B to C; suppose Charlie is a libertarian). In the end, even an explicit contractual view is unlikely to employ the unanimity rule in deciding which of the eligible options to choose.

Re (3) and (4): It would be more worrisome if there was a legitimate state that was not Pareto-superior to the state of nature – that is, at least one person would prefer life in the state of nature to membership in the state. If this occurred some might claim that the state may be permissible but it cannot be justified to them. It is important to see that, even if successful, Nozick's compensation argument would not show that such a complaint could not be made. To see this, suppose that the individualistic state of nature is S_1; S_2 is a condition with a dominant protective association that allows independents to use their own procedures, but always wins in any dispute with them; while S_3 is characterized by a dominant protective association that has turned itself into a minimal state by prohibiting independent procedures of which it does not approve. Let us grant that the move from S_2 to S_3 is justified via the compensation argument, so that the independents are not worse off in S_3 than in S_2. But we see that this does not ensure that the independents are not worse off in S_2 than in S_1; perhaps they enjoy being independents and it is easier to be one in a world composed entirely of small independent groups. So the move to S_2 – to a dominant protective agency – made some of our independents worse off by making the life of an independent less pleasant.

This possibility alerts us to the problem with understanding "better off" in terms of desires or a wide-open notion of preference – which is perhaps why Nozick does not really explore options (a) and (c). If Alf has preferences over other people's action, then Betty's exercise of her rights will often make him worse off simply because he has a preference that Betty not do what she has a right to do.[30] But surely Nozick cannot say that a condition in which all are acting within their rights, but some prefer others not do so, fails to be justified because the latter group is "worse off." In Lockean theory the only clear and uncontroversial sense of Betty being worse off in situation S_2 than in S_1 is if her rights and claims to the fruits of the earth are less honored and protected in S_2 than in S_1.[31] It might appear that this leads us to the conclusion that so long as everyone acted permissibly (i.e., honored rights) in moving from S_1 to S_2, no one can be worse off in S_2 in the sense relevant to Lockean political justification. This would seem to mean that the permissibility of the move from S_1 to S_2 (Nozick's option [b]) implies Miller's stronger notion of justification (Nozick's [a] and [c]): the move from S_1 to S_2 was justified because it was permissible. This would be wrong: we must allow that, at least in principle, an unintended consequence of each person's permissible actions may be a pattern (S_2 or S_3) in which the protection of rights is more uncertain than in the state of nature (S_1).[32] All would be good reasonable and rational Lockeans (and so each would be acting permissibly) but, from the perspective of honoring rights, each may yet be worse off (say because they have equilibrated on a really inefficient ultra-minimal, or minimal, state).

If we evaluate the state of nature and the minimal state simply in terms of whether one's rights are honored, Nozick must argue that, with regard to rights protection, most will be better off and none worse off than in the state of nature. The Lockean thesis is that this indeed will be the case because in a world of independents justice will be systematically distorted by self-bias; as we move to more impartial systems, Locke argued, we achieve superior justice (Locke: 1960, section 89) even though one may disagree with many judgments of the state (or dominant protection agency). If Locke – and indeed the entire social contract tradition – was right about this, then Nozick is well-positioned to claim that the minimal state (which is simply an organization for the effective enforcement of rights) is not simply permissible, but Pareto-superior to the state of nature. Moreover, although enforcement of individual claims can be understood as a purely private good (the individual gets her own rights enforced), insofar as effective enforcement acts as a deterrence of future violations, this has general public good features: those who do not buy policies as well as those who do receive the general benefits of deterrence. Consequently, in S_1 – a world of independents – there will be underinvestment in deterrence; as one agency comes to dominate, the benefits of providing deterrence will be internalized among its members, and so it will more efficiently invest in deterrence as opposed to merely enforcement activities. Thus we have additional reason to suppose that justice will be better enforced under a dominant agency. To be sure an incompetent minimal state – one that was worse at enforcing justice than individuals in the state of nature – would not be Pareto-superior, but the point of the invisible-hand account is that there is a market mechanism that would filter out really bad providers of impartial justice (here it seems far superior to the contract story, which requires a one-time central plan to set up a state). And, of course, if the minimal state is Pareto-superior to the state of nature it cannot be Pareto-inferior to it, so possibility (4) can also be dismissed.

I conclude that if Nozick's derivation of the minimal state is successful the minimal state is not simply justified in the sense of being morally legitimate, but justified in the sense that most are better off and none worse off in terms of their rights to life, liberty, and property than they would be in the state of nature.

5.5 CONCLUSION

Nozick's argument against the anarchist constitutes a major advance in political theory. *If* we accept his Lockean premises and *if* his argument goes through as intended (admittedly, two pretty big "ifs") he would have explicated the realm of the politically legitimate as an emergent property of prosaic actions of individuals given certain filters and equilibrium concepts. One of these filters is on clearly immoral action. We are, after all, interested in the nature of the legitimate state, not an oppressive one. *The legitimate state is an emergent pattern produced by the prosaic actions by reasonable and rational Lockeans.* Although the hypothetical invisible-hand account is based on the free choice of individuals, the case for legitimacy is not based on consent, but on the emergent properties of the ultra-minimal state as it arises under the moral filter. Nozick's argument against the anarchist is not a tweak on the traditional social contract story; it is a fresh beginning in political theory, exploring the nature of emergent explanations, and how they can figure into justifications. In answering the anarchist he provides an entirely new approach to the ancient inquiry into the properties of the just and legitimate state.

Readers may resist this. Of course, they may insist, at the end of the day Nozick must be proposing some version of consent theory, and it must really matter whether people have actually consented! The problem, in my view, is that readers simply have not taken seriously enough that Nozick's starting point is explanatory political theory. A reading of the book that does not give a crucial role to explanatory political theory is, I propose, ultimately incoherent. Everyone knows that *ASU* gives pride of place to the "invisible hand," but the invisible hand is explicitly part of explanatory political theory. One simply cannot stress the invisible hand in *ASU* and ignore explanatory political theory. The deep interpretive question is the relation between explanatory political theory and justification. On the interpretation I have proposed, Nozick's normative political philosophy shows that one of the emergent properties of a system of free interaction among reasonable and rational Lockeans is a justified ultra-minimal state with moral legitimacy.

NOTES

1. Most famously, perhaps, G. A. Cohen's "Robert Nozick and Wilt Chamberlain: How Patterns Preserve Liberty" (in Cohen: 1995, ch. 1).
2. I add within "political philosophy" as those concerned with social explanation and evolutionary theory have recognized its importance. See, for example, Ullmann-Margalit: 1978; Vogel Carey: 1998.
3. See Arthur: 1994. See also *ASU*, p. 17.
4. See, however, Eric Mack's contribution to this volume.
5. Nozick allows that there may be impure cases in which some participants intend *P* (p. 352 n. 7). Cf. Ullmann-Margalit: 1978, p. 287 n. 9.
6. On filters see also *ASU*, pp. 21–22 and 312–318.
7. I argue this further in Gaus: in press-b.
8. Douglas Lind argues that Nozick does not consistently follow it; in Lind's view Nozick sometimes appeals to a Hobbesian state of nature

riven by conflict and lack of trust (see Lind: 1989, p. 64). I believe that Lind fails to appreciate the intractable conflict in Locke's state of nature arising from disagreement in private reason: "though the Law of Nature be plain and intelligible to all rational Creatures; yet men being biassed by their Interest, as well as ignorant for want of studying it, are not apt to allow of it as a Law binding to them in the application of it to their particular Cases" (Locke: 1960, section 124).

9. In this sense Nozick's invisible-hand account is very different from Adam Smith's. David Miller recognizes this; because the equilibrium is path-dependent there is no convincing reason to think the equilibrium arrived at will be optimal (Miller: 2002, p. 17). I consider this issue in section 5.4.4. Multiple equilibria often are associated with complex systems; the extent to which standard microeconomics can model them is a matter of controversy. For an excellent defense of the ability of standard microeconomic reasoning to model these cases, see Durlauf: in press.

10. David Miller doubts this (Miller: 2002, pp. 20ff.). Again, I am assuming in this chapter that Nozick's pudding is perfectly done.

11. Cf. Mill: 2006, pp. 370–373 and 438–440. I am following here Auyang: 1998, pp. 173–174.

12. Durlauf rightly stresses this in Durlauf: in press.

13. This is Durlauf's complaint against many complexity models in economics.

14. Durlauf deems this the property of "universality" (see Durlauf: in press).

15. Nozick also considers how fact-defective and law-defective explanations may satisfy our explanatory interests (p. 8). See section 5.4.3.

16. This relates to the famous socialist calculation debate between, on the socialist side, Oscar Lange and on the other the Austrians – von Mises and Hayek. For a nice summary from the Austrian perspective, see Vaughn: 1994, ch. 3.

17. This is the worry about Nozick's supposition of an invisible-hand process that always gets pushed aside by another process, and so is always process-defective.

18. I believe that David Miller does so; see Miller: 2002, pp. 14ff.

19. Morris notably follows this method in Morris: 1998, ch. 2.

20. David Schmidtz notes this in Schmidtz: 1990a, p. 102.

21. We can contrast such legitimacy to justified state authority in the sense that citizens have an obligation to obey the state. See Christiano: 2008, pp. 240–241.

22. I analyze Hayek's evolutionary account and its relation to emergent properties in Gaus: 2006. For a careful analysis of Hayek's idea of an "order of actions" see Mack: 2006.

23. Note here the similarity to the traditional account of the social contract as artifice (section 5.3.4).

24. I am here considering what Nozick calls "fact-defective" accounts (see p. 7).

25. In fairness to my good friend David Schmidtz (and one should *at least* be fair to one's friends!) his analysis is presented as general, and does not explicitly address Nozick. Although I disagree with his analysis of emergence, his essay remains one of the most thoughtful analyses of emergent justifications in political philosophy.

26. This is noted by Lind: 1989, p. 62.

27. Miller's criticism is more wide-ranging than I can consider here; especially interesting is his proposal that we can construct a preference ordering over modes of justification. It would take us too far afield to consider this idea.

28. I have been stressing that the invisible-hand process certainly leads to an ultra-minimal state; I have been more skeptical about its relation to the minimal state. However, Nozick clearly thinks that the minimal state is superior to the ultra-minimal, and permissible steps would lead to it. Since Nozick's stopping point is the minimal state, I deal with Miller's objections in relation to it.

29. Of course the transactions costs would be very high, but we have bracketed those.

30. I further explore this problem in Gaus: 2009.

31. Two problems arise here. (1) It may seems that the "proviso" on appropriation of property necessarily refers to a person being made "worse off" in a sense that does not refer to her rights and claims. Much depends here on the details. Nozick, to be sure, talks about "worsening" of another person's situation through appropriation (see p. 178); however we may follow Locke in specifying the worsening in terms of claims to available resources and fruits of the earth (see Locke: 1960, ch. IV). (2) Nozick's compensation argument requires some measure of being as well off in one condition as another. If the dominant agency is compensating people for not being able to exercise their judgment rights, surely there must be some measure of wellbeing besides being able to exercise one's rights. This is the most perplexing issue in the first part of *ASU*. On the view I have proposed here, a person would have to be compensated in terms of how well his rights are honored

and protected, but it may seem that it is just this matter about which the independents disagree. I tend to think that a consistent account could be worked out along these lines, but of course I cannot do so here.

32. Following Philip Pettit, we might call this an "invisible backhand" as in a Prisoner's Dilemma (see Pettit: 1996, p. 270).

Part III **Justice**

6 Nozick's libertarian theory of justice

In *Anarchy, State, and Utopia* (*ASU*), Robert Nozick sketches and motivates a libertarian theory of justice and then uses it to argue that a minimal state, but nothing stronger, can be just. In this chapter, I focus on explaining and assessing his libertarian theory. My focus will be on laying out the basics and identifying how they can be challenged. I shall not address his argument for the minimal state.[1]

6.1 JUSTICE

Although Nozick frequently (and confusedly) writes of (moral) justifiability, permissibility, and legitimacy, it is clear that his main focus in the book is on justice.[2] He never, however, explains the concept of justice. We shall therefore start by clarifying the concept of justice relevant to Nozick's theory. What is his theory about?

The term "justice" is used in many different ways by philosophers: as fairness (comparative desert), as moral permissibility (or justifiability) either of distributions of benefits and burdens or of social structures (e.g., legal systems), as enforceable duties (duties that others are permitted to enforce), as the duties that are owed to individuals (as opposed to impersonal duties, owed to no one), and as the *enforceable* duties owed to individuals. It is clear that Nozick restricts justice to the fulfillment of the duties owed to individuals, but it is unclear whether he restricts it only to enforceable duties.

For you to *owe someone a duty* is for that person to have a *claim-right* against you that you perform, or not perform, some action. This means that you wrong that individual if you fail to fulfill that duty. As long as rights are understood inclusively, justice in the sense of duties owed to individuals is a broad topic. It covers all moral duties except those that apply independently of both the wills and interests of individuals (e.g., a duty not to eat bananas that holds even if everyone consents to eating one and it is in everyone's interest to do so). On this broad view of claim-rights, children and animals with interests can have rights, and thus can be owed duties – even if they do not have autonomous wills.

Nozick understands justice to hold just in case rights are respected.[3] Rights, however, are sometimes understood merely as duties owed to the right-holder (mere claim-rights), and sometimes more narrowly as *enforceable* duties owed to the right-holder. Suppose that I owe my mother a duty to attend her birthday party, but neither she, nor anyone else, is permitted to use force against me to get me to attend. In the narrow sense, she has no right that I attend and I do her no injustice if I do not, whereas, in the broad sense, she has such a right and I do her an injustice if I do not attend. It is, as we shall see, unclear which way Nozick understands rights and hence justice.

Nozick explicitly rejects the view that all obligations, even all obligations owed to others, are enforceable (p. 91). Our question here, however, is whether all *rights*, as he understands the concept, are enforceable. In one passage, where he is arguing against the enforceability of all obligations owed to others, he seems to endorse the view that rights need not be enforceable: "Yet rights of enforcement are themselves merely *rights*; that is, permissions to do something and obligations on others not to interfere" (p. 92). This supports the view that he thinks that one could have a right that others do something without it being permissible to enforce that right.[4] This is, however, the only passage in *ASU* in which he discusses this issue. In *Philosophical Explanations* (seven years later), he writes: "a right is something for which one can demand or enforce compliance" (Nozick: 1981, p. 499). Given that demanding (e.g., verbally demanding) need not involve enforcement, this too suggests that he understands the concept of a right not to entail enforceability. Instead, it seems to consist of duties owed to one (as opposed to impersonal duties or duties owed to someone else), since those are the duties for which one can demand fulfillment. It seems, then, that rights, as Nozick understands them, are not necessarily enforceable. They are simply duties owed to the holder. Thus, if justice is respect for rights, then justice is simply a matter of fulfilling the duties owed to individuals.

Things are not, however, quite this simple. In *Philosophical Explanations*, Nozick writes: "Political philosophy, as I see it, is mainly the theory of what behavior legitimately may be enforced, and of the nature of the institutional structure that stays within and supports these enforceable rights" (Nozick: 1981, p. 503).[5] His reference to enforceability suggests, again, that rights need not be enforceable (although, of course, it could simply be for emphasis). Nonetheless, given that he clearly takes justice to be a core topic in political philosophy, this passage suggests that justice is only concerned with enforceable duties owed to individuals.

In short, Nozick is not very clear on how he understands the concept of justice. Although he typically writes as if justice is a matter of respecting rights, he seems also to hold that justice is a matter of respecting enforceable rights. This is problematic, given that he seems to deny that rights are necessarily enforceable.

Overall, it seems best to interpret Nozick as understanding justice narrowly as a matter of the enforceable duties owed to individuals and to interpret his typical references to rights as references to enforceable duties owed to right-holders. This understanding makes his libertarian project more defensible, because it makes it less ambitious. His topic is not what it is morally desirable to do, not what morality requires us to do (which may include impersonal duties), and (probably) not even what duties we owe individuals. It only concerns what enforceable duties we owe individuals. Justice in this sense addresses but a small part of morality.

One further clarification of Nozick's concept of justice is needed. Is it a matter of not infringing rights or of not violating rights? A right is *infringed* just in case the boundaries that it protects are crossed without suitable authorization (e.g., permission or non-setback to the right-holder's interest). A right is *violated* just in case it is infringed and there is no conclusive justification for the infringement. Thus, for example, lightly striking an individual may infringe his rights of bodily autonomy, but it may not violate these rights, if it is necessary and sufficient to save millions of lives. Infringing someone's rights can be permissible (when there is a suitable justification), but it typically leaves in place some kind of rectification duties (e.g., to apologize or compensate) that also apply in the case of violations.

Justice can be understood as non-infringement of (enforceable) rights or as non-violation thereof. Both are important topics and people use the term "justice" in both ways. Because, as we shall see below, Nozick holds that rights are absolute (with one possible exception), he denies, on substantive grounds, that rights are ever permissibly infringed. Thus, we may take him to be addressing the broader concept of justice as the non-infringement of enforceable rights.

Justice in the sense of not infringing the enforceable duties that we owe individuals, then, is Nozick's core topic. Particular theories of justice identify a specific set of rights and claim that, as a substantive matter, they exhaust the enforceable duties that we owe individuals. Below, we shall examine both the general and the specific character of the rights that Nozick invokes.

6.2 NEAR ABSOLUTE CHOICE-PROTECTING RIGHTS

Nozick invokes a libertarian theory of rights. Before examining the specific content of these rights, we shall examine some general features of the rights he believes that we have.

Nozick holds that certain kinds of individuals have certain *natural* rights. These are rights possessed in virtue of possessing some natural features (e.g., being human, or being capable of autonomous choice) that is independent of conventional (e.g., legal) or instrumental considerations (e.g., rule utilitarianism or rule contractarianism).

Rights in the broad sense can protect the choice (consent) of the right-holder, her interests (e.g., wellbeing), or both. Consider, for example, the right, against me, that I not strike your body. A standard kind of choice-protecting conception would hold that this right consists of it being wrong for me to strike your body without your valid (e.g., free and uncoerced) consent. The right protects your choices (or will) in the sense that the protection can be waived by your valid consent (as you might do to participate in a friendly boxing match). By contrast, a simple kind of interest-protecting conception of the right, against me, that I not strike your body holds that this right consists of it being wrong for me to strike your body when it is against your interests. The right protects your interests in the sense that the constraint against striking you does not apply when it is in your interests (e.g., when the only way to prevent you from being hit by a car is to push you out of the way).

Conceptually, rights in the broad sense can be choice-protecting, interest-protecting, or both. Nozick, however, assumes, as a substantive matter, that we have choice-protecting rights. Indeed, he never even considers the possibility of rights being interest-protecting. This is not surprising, since the choice-protecting conception is the most familiar one, and the contrast between the two conceptions has been significantly developed since Nozick wrote the book. (For a superb analysis, see Kramer, Simmonds, and Steiner: 1998.)

Nozick addresses the question of what kinds of rights we have by asking (p. 48): "What are constraints based on?" This is a somewhat confusing way of asking about rights, since moral constraints need not be grounded in rights. Conceptually, there can be impersonal constraints, which are constraints that apply even when everyone consents and benefits (e.g., a constraint against killing humans no matter what). Nozick's answer, however, makes reasonably clear that he is focusing on rights-based constraints. He suggests that moral (rights-based) constraints are based on some combination of the right-holder being rational, having a free will, being capable of guiding its behavior by moral principles, and having "the ability to regulate and guide its life in accordance with some overall conception [of its life] it chooses to accept" (pp. 48–49). Simplified, this boils down to the requirement for some kind of autonomous agency. Some such requirement underlies the choice-protecting conception of rights, but it is not an essential part of the interest-protecting conception. For the latter, the requirement is some kind of capacity for interests (e.g., wellbeing). On the interest-protecting conception, mammals and infants are possible right-holders even though they have no capacity for autonomous choice.

If Nozick is to defend a theory of justice in the broad sense, he cannot simply assume that rights protect autonomous choices. He needs to argue, on substantive grounds, that there are no interest-protecting rights. This, however, he does not do.[6] This, then, is one limitation of his argument. Nozick could, of course, retreat simply to defending a theory of justice in the narrow sense of choice-protecting rights, but this would rob his argument of considerable generality.

Nozick takes a stance on a second issue about rights: whether basic rights (such as the right against aggression) are absolute (conclusive and unconditional), conditionally conclusive (conclusive, but only under certain conditions), or *pro tanto* (having some weight but can be overridden by countervailing considerations). He claims that the rights that we have are almost absolute (conclusive either unconditionally or almost so). He leaves open the possibility that rights can be permissibly infringed in order to avoid cases of "catastrophic moral horror" (p. 30 fn.).

Nozick supports this view by rightly claiming that "[s]ide constraints upon action reflect the underlying Kantian principle that individuals are ends and not merely means" (pp. 30–31). This is compatible with an interest-protecting conception of rights. Far more controversial, however, is his associated claim that "they may not be sacrificed or used for the achieving of other ends without their consent. Individuals are inviolable" (p. 31). This not only presupposes a choice-protecting conception of rights, it also assumes that rights are absolute. It is possible, however, for rights to provide strong *pro tanto* protection to individuals (e.g., never overridden by non-rights considerations) without that protection being absolute. Protection of other people's rights may sometimes take precedence. For example, it may be permissible for me to take your gun without your permission in order to protect ten innocent people from being killed by a murderer.[7]

In a related vein, Nozick claims: "The root idea, namely that there are different individuals with separate lives and so no one may be sacrificed for others, underlies the existence of moral side constraints" (p. 33). Again, we can agree that the fact that individuals have separate lives, with the capacity for wellbeing, provides good reason for thinking that they have some kind of rights protecting their lives. Hedonistic utilitarianism, for example, is mistaken in holding that all that matters is some social aggregate (e.g., total happiness). The distribution of wellbeing *to individuals* and other features matter. This, however, does not require that individuals have rights that are absolute or nearly so. They might simply have rights that are conclusive but highly conditional. Or the rights might be relatively strong *pro tanto* considerations. The separateness of persons can be recognized in a variety of ways, and appeal to absolute rights is only one very strong such way. Nozick is correct that:

"there is no social entity with a good that undergoes some sacrifices for its own good. There are only individual people, different individual people, with their own individual lives" (pp. 32–33). This, however, does not establish that rights are absolute.

6.3 ENTITLEMENT THEORIES

So far, we have addressed the concept of the justice of actions. Justice is also, however, applied to states of affairs (e.g., distributions of goods) and to institutions (e.g., the state). Because we are not here addressing Nozick's arguments about the justice of the state (or other institutions), we shall focus on his views about the justice of states of affairs.

As a substantive matter, Nozick implicitly assumes *proprietarianism*, the view that all enforceable moral rights are moral property rights (rights over things). The justice of a state of affairs is, on this view, a matter of whether individuals have a right to their holdings (the objects in their possession broadly understood): "The complete principle of distributive justice would say simply that a distribution is just if [presumably: and only if] everyone is entitled to the holdings they possess under the distribution" (p. 151).[8] Although proprietarianism is a controversial view, Nozick does not defend it.

More specifically, Nozick invokes an *entitlement theory* of justice, a particular kind of proprietarian theory, specified by the following kinds of principle:

1. *Justice in acquisition*: Principles specifying the conditions under which an individual can come to have rights over a previously unowned thing.
2. *Justice in transfer*: Principles specifying the conditions under which an individual having rights over a thing can transfer those rights to another.
3. *Justice in rectification*: Principles specifying how the rights of people change in virtue of a past injustice (rights-infringement).

One puzzling aspect of this schema is that it does not explicitly mention anything about *preventive justice*. What rights do individuals have to prevent others from violating their rights? For example, does an innocent person have a liberty-right to kill a person attempting to kill her? To cover these issues, which Nozick clearly intends to cover, let us lump preventive justice with rectificatory justice. The third principle thus becomes:

3. *Justice in prevention and rectification*: Principles specifying how the rights of people change in virtue of a past, present, or future injustice (rights-infringement).

A second puzzling feature of this schema is that it makes no mention of the *initial rights* that individuals may have prior to acquisition and transfer. A very natural thought is that individuals typically have certain rights over their bodies (e.g., a right not to be killed or struck). How does this fit in Nozick's schema? One possibility is that these rights are acquired through the relevant acquisition or transfer procedures, but this seems implausible. Rights over one's body do not seem to depend contingently upon engaging in whatever actions are required for acquisition or transfer. Instead, it seems that individuals start their lives (at some suitable point) with these rights. They seem to be initial rights.

Nozick was probably focusing on rights over external objects (non-persons), and for this purpose it is quite plausible that there are no initial rights over such things. It is reasonably clear that he was implicitly assuming that individuals have certain initial rights (e.g., over their bodies). Let us therefore add a fourth kind of principle to the entitlement theory schema:

4. *Initial justice*: Principles specifying the initial rights that individuals (of certain sorts) start with.

On entitlement theories, then, individuals start with certain rights, acquire rights in previously unowned things, transfer some rights to others and receive some rights from others, and lose or acquire some rights to rectify any past injustices. This is very schematic and can be filled in many ways. Nozick, we shall see, fills it in with a libertarian theory. First, however, let us consider the procedural nature of entitlement theories.

6.4 PROCEDURAL THEORIES OF JUSTICE

Justice, on an entitlement theory, is past-regarding in that the rights an individual has depends on what the past was like (who acquired what, who transferred what, who violated whose rights, etc.). Nozick is surely correct that what moral rights one has depends on what the past was like. For example, whether I have a moral right to a certain car in my possession depends on what the past was like. If you were the rightful owner, and I validly purchased it from you, then I have a right to the car. If, on the other hand, I simply stole it from you, then I do not.

Entitlement theories are, however, past-regarding in a very specific way. They are *purely procedural theories of justice* in the sense that they hold that "[a] distribution is just if it arises from another just distribution by legitimate means. The legitimate means of moving from one distribution to another are specified by the principle of justice in transfer [and the principles of acquisition, and prevention/ rectification] ... Whatever arises from a just situation by just steps is itself just" (p. 151; see also pp. 207–208). A purely procedural theory of justice derives the justness of distributions from the justness of the prior situation and the justness of the steps taken from it (with special procedures required to restore justice when an unjust step takes place).[9]

Nozick defends entitlement theories by appealing to his famous Wilt Chamberlain example (cf. pp. 160–164), which is intended to show that theories that are not purely procedural involve unacceptable continual interference with people's lives.[10] Suppose that everyone starts with a just initial set of holdings (on one's preferred theory of justice, say equality of some sort). Now suppose that Wilt Chamberlain, a famous basketball player, agrees to play basketball in return for 25 cents from each spectator and the spectators voluntarily agree. Suppose that, over the course of the season, a million fans voluntarily purchase tickets and there are no other financial transactions. Chamberlain now has (at least) $250,000 more than each of the fans. Whatever non-purely procedural principle of justice was invoked for the initial holdings (egalitarianism, utilitarianism, desert theory, etc.), it would only be by accident if it were still satisfied. Thus, if justice is to be maintained, there must be continual redistribution among individuals. This, Nozick claims, is implausible. Given that the distribution arose from the voluntary choices that individuals had with respect to resources that they were, by assumption, entitled to control, how could the result be unjust? Moreover, such redistribution involves continual interference with people's lives, and it seems implausible that justice would require this. Nozick concludes that principles of justice that are not purely procedural must be rejected.

Do theories of justice that are not purely procedural necessarily require continual interferences with people's lives in some empirical (non-moral) sense? They do require at least some occasional interference, but the real question is whether non-procedural theories require *significant* continual interference with people's lives. Some certainly do. For example, a theory that requires equal wealth *at all times* would be continually adjusting people's wealth levels, sometimes in significant ways. Non-procedural theories, however, need not (as Nozick recognized, cf. p. 164) be concerned with *difficult to achieve* states (such as maximal equality) *at each time*. Consider a principle that holds that justice requires that each person have *enough annual income for basic subsistence*. Under moderate abundance, if people start with a just share, this will not require frequent significant adjustments to the distribution.[11]

Moreover, even entitlement theories involve continual interference with people's lives. Those who are not entitled to given resources are threatened with punishment if they use them without permission, are prevented from doing so if they attempt to do so, and are punished if they do so. The real issue for Nozick, I think, is, not interference with people's lives but rather, the idea that, if one has certain (e.g., initial) rights over certain resources and one exercises them in a way that respects the rights of others, then the result must be just (and interference unjust). Let us explore that issue.

To start, note that almost any principle of justice (e.g., utilitarian or egalitarian) can be used as the basis for a purely procedural (or starting-gate) theory of justice. One simply applies the principle to determine initial shares and then allows unrestricted transfers after that. For example, the initial holdings (assuming unrestricted transfer rights) may be divided up to efficiently promote expected equality of wellbeing (e.g., giving Wilt a much smaller share of the non-human assets to offset his superior human assets). The Wilt Chamberlain example has no purchase against such theories.

Of course, unrestricted transfers *by gift* are problematic in the context of *multiple generations*. Unrestricted gifts (including bequests) will prevent individuals from starting at the desired starting position (e.g., equal opportunity for wealth or wellbeing). Because Nozick's Wilt Chamberlain example involves only market transfers, and not gifts, it is compatible with significant taxation of gifts to equalize (for example) the starting positions of non-initial generations. That, however, would miss Nozick's real point, which is that there should be no restrictions on voluntary transfers generally. That may be plausible in the single generation case, and it may even be plausible generally for market (rather than gift) transfers. It is much less clear, however, that there should be no restriction on gift transfers in the multiple generation case.[12]

Suppose, however, that we accept that there are no restrictions on voluntary transfers and therefore restrict our attention to entitlement theories that impose no such restrictions. If I have some rights over a given resource, and I have and exercise the unrestricted moral power to transfer it to you, does it follow that you *fully own* the resource? It does not. I may not fully own the resource to start with, and the rights that I transfer to you may not be sufficient to give you full ownership. For example, if there is a public right of way on my land (and hence I have less than full ownership of the land), you do not acquire full ownership of the land when I transfer my ownership to you. The key question here concerns the content of the initial rights that individuals have and of the moral powers they have to appropriate (acquire rights over previously unowned resources). If the initial rights are limited in various ways, or the rights that can be acquired through appropriation are also limited, then rights that can be acquired through unrestricted transfer may also be limited.[13]

To make this concrete, suppose that the initial rights people have and the rights that they can acquire through appropriation are always conditional on the holder not possessing more than 150 percent of the per capita market value of resources. The excess share, let us suppose, belongs to the king. A million people below this benchmark may consensually transfer the conditional right to 25 cents to Wilt Chamberlain. The transfer is consensual and thus fully valid. What is transferred, however, is a conditional right (since that is all that was initially possessed), and, if Wilt Chamberlain ends with more than 150 percent of a per capita share of wealth, his excess share belongs to the king, and not to him. Justice thus requires a redistribution of holdings (although not of rights).

In sum, even if consensual transfers of rights are unconditionally justice-preserving (and they are not on some possible entitlement theories), the rights so transferred need not be unconditional. They may be subject to on-going limitations. As a result, even though consensual transfers are perfectly valid, that does not entail that the resulting distribution of holdings is just. The on-going limitations may require a redistribution. Indeed, something like this, we shall see, is true on Nozick's own libertarian theory. Let us, finally, turn to that.

6.5 LIBERTARIAN RIGHTS

Nozick invokes the following libertarian version of the entitlement theory:

(1)   *Justice in initial rights:* Each agent initially has full control-ownership of her person.

(2)   *Justice in acquisition:* Each agent who claims control-rights in unowned resources and mixes her labor with them (or something like that) has those rights over the resources to the extent compatible with a Lockean proviso that enough and as good be left for others.

(3)   *Justice in transfer:* If an agent has certain rights over a resource, and she validly (e.g., without force or fraud) consents to transfer those rights to someone else, then the other person acquires those rights, if (a) the other person validly consents to the acquisition, and (b) the transfer satisfies the Lockean proviso.

(4)   *Justice in prevention and rectification:*
  (a)   An agent who violates the rights of another owes her compensation for the loss of wellbeing from the violation.
  (b)   An agent is permitted to use suitable force, and to authorize others to use such force, to prevent another from violating her rights.
  (c)   All agents have some kind of right (either individually or jointly) to punish those who violate rights.

We shall examine each of these principles carefully below.

6.5.1 Justice in initial rights: control self-ownership

Nozick endorses:

Justice in initial rights: Each agent initially has full control-ownership of her person.

Although libertarianism is generally taken to be committed to the thesis that agents fully own themselves, Nozick uses the term "self-ownership" only once in the entire book (p. 172, in his discussion of taxation and forced labor). As we shall see, however, it is clear that he means to endorse at least full *control* self-ownership. (Here and below, I assume a choice-protecting conception of rights for illustration.)

Self-ownership is simply a special case of ownership. It is the case where the owner and the thing owned are one and the same. We can thus start with the general notion of *control* ownership of a thing, which is at the core of *full* ownership of that thing (cf. p. 171). The other incidents of full ownership are the rights of transfer, rights to prevent and rectify violations, and immunities to loss. Control ownership, like ownership generally, can take stronger or weaker forms, but I shall focus on full control ownership (the strongest form). Control-ownership of a thing consists of the following: (1) the claim-right, against all others, that they not use the object without one's valid consent; (2) an unrestricted liberty-right, against all others, to use the object (no one else's permission is needed); and (3) the moral power (a kind of right), against all others, to authorize the use of the object (no one else's permission is needed). Full control-ownership of a thing does not mean that one is permitted to use it in any way one wants. Using the baseball bat one fully owns to smash someone's head is not permitted, but this is because it violates the other person's rights (e.g., to her body) – not because using the bat as such was wrong (as it would be if it belonged to someone else).[14] (See pp. 171–173, 281–282.)

Nozick does not use the term "control self-ownership," but he claims that the fact that individuals have separate existences leads to the libertarian constraint against aggression (see p. 33). He never explicitly clarifies what counts as aggression, but it clearly includes use of another's person (e.g., body) without her valid consent (e.g., rape, assault, homicide). He also holds that individuals are entitled to their natural talents (their natural personal endowments; cf. p. 225). Although this is not conclusive, it seems reasonable to hold that Nozick is committed to at least full control self-ownership.

Control self-ownership reflects the separate existences of individuals. It gives individuals special rights of control over the use of their person. Most people accept it as at least a *pro tanto* principle. Nozick, as we have seen, accepts it as an almost-absolute principle.

Indeed, except for the one footnote on p. 30 (where he leaves open the possibility that the infringement of rights may be permissible where necessary to avoid catastrophic moral horror), Nozick writes as if all rights are absolute. For brevity, I shall write as if he is committed to the absoluteness of the rights he invokes and leave the possible qualification implicit.

While *pro tanto* control self-ownership is relatively uncontroversial, absolute control self-ownership is highly controversial and rejected by most. It has two problematic implications. Suppose that the only way to save a thousand lives is to remove one of one's hairs to produce an antidote to a fatal disease afflicting them. Control self-ownership says that (1) one is at liberty not to remove any hairs (i.e., one owes no one a duty to do so) and (2) one has a claim-right that others not remove any of the hairs (without one's permission). This is very plausible as a *pro tanto* consideration that may be overridden by stronger countervailing considerations, but it is intuitively implausible that this liberty and claim-right are absolute.

The force of the above objection can be softened if one grants that agents have some initial duties to aid others and only insists that these duties are not enforceable. This involves rejecting the moral liberty that is part of control self-ownership, but it maintains the right against interference even when one fails to provide the required aid. This response softens the first objection, but does not eliminate it, since many hold that we have enforceable duties to aid others. Moreover, this response does not address the second objection (the duty of others not to remove one of your hairs without your permission).

A more general response to the above objection involves the following: (1) pointing out the radical implications of recognizing an obligation to aid others, or a liberty of others to use one's person for such purposes, even in the special cases where the benefit to them is great and the cost to one is small (since life is full of such situations); (2) appealing to a very strong normative separateness of persons; (3) insisting on *initial* full control self-ownership, but allowing that individuals can lose some of their full control self-ownership in virtue of their use or appropriation of natural resources (discussed below); and (4) insisting that, although it has some counterintuitive implications (like all robust principles), its theoretical plausibility more than offsets them. Although I believe that something like this is plausible, I shall not pursue it here.

6.5.2 Justice in acquisition: appropriation subject to the Lockean proviso

Nozick endorses:

Justice in acquisition: Each agent who claims control-rights in unowned resources and mixes her labor with them, or something like that, has those rights over the resources to the extent compatible with satisfying a Lockean proviso that enough and as good be left for others.

Almost all libertarian theories hold that one can acquire property rights over an unowned thing as long as one performs an appropriate action with respect to that thing and certain provisos are satisfied. Different versions differ in their specifications.

Three general points should be kept in mind about the conditions on acquisition. First, one acquires rights over a resource, when one performs a suitable action (e.g., labor mixing), only when that object is *unowned*. Mixing my labor with your Cadillac by washing its windows without your permission does not give me any rights to your car. Second, even if, say, labor-mixing is required, one presumably must also *claim* (e.g., by some public act) rights over the object to acquire them. Merely clearing a space in the forest to sleep for a night during a trip does not automatically make you the owner. Third, the ownership of things acquired by acquisition need not be, and is probably rarely, *full* ownership. This is both because some rights over a resource may have already been claimed by others (e.g., there may be an established right-of-way on some land that someone appropriates) and because the appropriator may not claim all the available rights (either because she does not want them or she did not think to claim them). The strength of property rights in external things (other than persons) is thus historically contingent.

Nozick does not take a firm stance on what kind of action is needed with respect to the resource. He focuses on labor-mixing (Locke's view), finds it problematic, but never endorses an alternative. The main problem that Nozick identifies is that of determining the boundaries of the "object" with which one mixes one's labor: "If an astronaut clears a place on Mars, has he mixed his labor with (so that he comes to own) the entire planet, the whole uninhabited universe, or just a particular plot?" (p. 174). (Note that first occupancy/possession theories have similar problems.) Nozick offers no answer to this question. A more plausible approach, I think, is to drop the labor-mixing requirement and simply require that the individual publicly *claim* rights over a specified (delimited) set of resources. In any case, we shall, following Nozick, assume that some solution has been found for determining the boundaries of the object to which one acquires rights.

Let us turn now to what kind of proviso limits the acquisition of rights over unowned resources. *Radical right-libertarianism* (e.g., Narveson: 1988, ch. 7; Narveson: 1999, p. 118; Rothbard: 1978, pp. 31–36) imposes no proviso. The first person to mix her labor (or: occupy, possess, discover, or claim) with a resource comes to own it. This, however, is implausible. Prior to someone's acquisition of ownership of a given unowned resource, others are at liberty to use it (e.g., walk on a path). Although it may be plausible that they can be deprived of this liberty when it does not disadvantage them, it is not plausible that they can always be so deprived when it disadvantages them.[15] Nozick agrees (cf. p. 175), and following Locke (1960, ch. 5), he imposes a proviso that "enough and as good be left for others." Nozick (pp. 174–182) interprets this proviso as requiring that no one be worse off (in wellbeing) than she would be if the resource remained unowned.[16]

Nozick is surely right that his version of the Lockean proviso is a necessary condition for acquisition of rights over unowned things. It is, however, arguably too weak to be the only necessary condition. As he himself asks: "Why should one's entitlement extend to the whole object rather than just to the *added value* one's labor has produced?" (p. 175). Nozick dismisses this question in a single sentence by claiming: "No workable or coherent value-added property scheme has yet been devised, and any such scheme presumably would fall to objections (similar to those) that fell the theory of Henry George [a nineteenth–century left-libertarian]" (p. 175). There is, however, no problem in principle here. One can allow that the appropriator obtains rights over the entire object, but insist that this is conditional on her paying back to the members of society the competitive value (based on supply and demand; for example, based on an auction or a competitive market) of the rights she has claimed over the resource in its *unimproved* state. This leaves the appropriator any profits or benefits that she can reap from the improvements (valued added). Obviously, the details need to be worked, but there is no problem in principle. Moreover, although the ideas of Henry George (like all moral theories) are controversial, they have not been decisively refuted.[17]

Within libertarianism, there are many possible views about how strong a proviso there is on acquisition. As we saw above, radical right-libertarianism rejects any proviso. The first one to perform the relevant action (e.g., labor-mixing) acquires rights over the resource, with no constraints on how others are affected. Nozick imposes the weak constraint that no one be made worse off than if the resource remained unowned. There are at least two more egalitarian provisos. *Equal share left-libertarianism* imposes the proviso that one leaves enough for others to have an equally valuable (e.g., in terms of financial value) share. *Equal opportunity for wellbeing left-libertarianism* imposes the proviso that one leaves enough for others to have an equally valuable opportunity for wellbeing (and thus requires that larger shares be left for those whose opportunities for wellbeing are otherwise limited).[18] In short, the proviso that Nozick adopts on appropriation is but one of several live possibilities. Much more argument is needed to establish his version of libertarianism.[19]

It is worth noting that, whatever the content of the proviso is (as long as it is not empty), a plausible version would allow the appropriator to keep any excess share as long as she pays back to others the competitive (e.g., financial) value of the excess share. This debt, which could take the form of a periodic rental payment rather than a one-time lump sum payment, could provide the basis for wealth taxation of rights over natural resources.

Before turning to Nozick's views on justice in transfer, we need to address one final aspect of the proviso: does it apply only at the time of appropriation or is it an on-going limitation on the property rights involved? Nozick is clear that it is the latter:

Each owner's title to his holding includes the historical shadow of the Lockean proviso on appropriation. This excludes ... his using it in a way, in coordination with others or independently of them, so as to violate the proviso by making the situation of others worse than their baseline situation ... Thus a person may not appropriate the only water hole in a desert and charge what he will. Nor may he charge what he will if he possesses one, and unfortunately it happens that all the water holes in the desert dry up, except for his. This unfortunate circumstance, admittedly no fault of his, brings into operation the Lockean proviso and limits his property rights. Once it is known that someone's ownership runs afoul of the Lockean proviso, there are stringent limits on what he may do with (what it is difficult any longer unreservedly to call) "his property." (p. 180)

I believe that Nozick is exactly right about this. Whatever the proviso is, it is not a one-time test (at the time of appropriation); it is an on-going limitation. Thus, the ownership in external objects is never full. It is always subject to the restrictions imposed by the proviso. It may be satisfied at one time but not at a later time. This point, I believe, has not been adequately appreciated in the literature. It is often supposed that the proviso is merely a one-time condition.[20]

6.5.3 Justice in transfer: full transfer rights

Nozick endorses:

Justice in transfer: If an agent has certain rights over a resource, and she validly (e.g., without force or fraud) consents to transfer those rights to someone else, then the other person acquires those rights, if (a) the other person validly consents to the acquisition, and (b) the transfer satisfies the Lockean proviso.

Nozick does not explicitly state that the valid consent of the transferee is required for the validity of a transfer, but he surely intends it be present. One does not acquire property rights merely because someone else decides to transfer them to one. One must accept the transfer. Nor does Nozick explicitly discuss what is required for valid consent, but it is clear that he requires something like the absence of force and fraud.

Nozick believes that the same proviso that applies to acquisition also applies to transfers: "A theory which includes this proviso in its principle of justice in acquisition must also contain a more complex principle of justice in transfer ... If the proviso excludes someone's appropriating all the drinkable water in the world, it also excludes his purchasing it all" (p. 179). Nozick is, I believe, confused here. Once he recognizes (as indicated above) that the proviso is an on-going limitation on acquired rights, there is no need for that proviso also to apply to transfers. If others have appropriated certain resources, those rights are limited, on an on-going basis, by the proviso. When they transfer them to you (e.g., by gift or sale), the rights you acquire are also so limited. There is no need for the acquisition proviso to apply to transfers. (Note that the proviso applies only to rights initially acquired through appropriation. There is no proviso, within libertarian theory, on initial self-ownership and thus there is no proviso restricting the transfer of such rights.)

Justice in transfer claims that all rights are fully transferable. This is not a conceptual truth. One can have control rights over an object (e.g., a rented apartment, or a primogeniture estate) without having any rights to transfer those to others. Still, if one fully owns an object, this includes full transfer rights. This is roughly Nozick's idea.

If the rights of *self-ownership* are fully transferable, then one can transfer ownership of oneself to someone else (by gift or sale) and thereby become her slave. Nozick clearly believes that individuals have such rights. He explicitly says that they do (see p. 331), and his discussion of people selling shares in themselves (see pp. 281–287) implicitly presupposes that they do. *Involuntary* enslavement, of course, is a gross violation of full self-ownership, but *voluntary* enslavement is something that full self-ownership allows. Intuitively, of course, this seems problematic.

If one thinks that a main concern of justice is to protect the *having* of effective autonomy, or to *promote* the having, or exercising, of effective autonomy, then voluntary enslavement will indeed seem problematic. On the other hand, if one thinks that a main concern of justice is to protect the *exercise* of autonomy, it is not. A well-informed decision to sell oneself into slavery (e.g., for a large sum of money to help one's needy family) is an exercise of autonomy. Indeed, under desperate conditions it may even represent an extremely important way of exercising one's autonomy. The parallel with suicide is relevant here. In both cases an agent makes a decision that has the result that she ceases to have any moral autonomy and thus ceases to exercise any. In both cases it will typically be one of the most important choices in the agent's life. I would argue that, assuming no conflicting commitments, protecting the agent's *exercise* of her autonomy in such a case overrides any concern for protecting or promoting her *continued possession* of moral autonomy.

One has the right to choose to cease to be autonomous (by dying or by losing rights of control). Thus, genuine voluntary enslavement is arguably not problematic. It is simply the limiting case of the sorts of partial voluntary enslavement that occurs when we make binding commitments and agreements (e.g., to join the military).[21]

Before concluding, let us briefly consider Nozick's claims about rights to prevent and rectify rights violations.

6.5.4 Justice in prevention and rectification

Nozick endorses:
Justice in prevention and rectification:

(a)   An agent is permitted to use suitable force, and to authorize others to use such force, to prevent another from violating her rights (see pp. 127–130).

(b)   An agent who violates the rights of another owes her compensation for the loss of wellbeing from the violation (see pp. 135–137).

(c)   All agents have some kind of right (either individually or jointly) to punish those who violate rights (see pp. 135–142).

Nozick's discussion of these issues is very schematic and leaves a wide range of important issues unresolved. Still, almost everyone will agree that individuals have some rights to prevent the violation of their own rights (although there will be disagreement about the exact content of those rights). His claim that individuals have rights to compensation is more controversial, but I believe that he is correct on this (although again the devil is in the details). I shall not, however, pursue these issues here.

The claim that individuals, either individually or collectively, have a right to *punish* wrongdoers is controversial, even among libertarians. Many libertarians (e.g., Rothbard: 1982 and Barnett: 1977, 1980 and 1998) would argue that rectification rights are limited to the extraction of compensation for wrongful harm. Sometimes, punishment may be a necessary part of compensation (e.g., where it is the only way of minimizing the harm to the victim), but where it is not, some libertarians would argue that there is no right to punish. The crude idea is that even wrongdoers maintain some of their rights of self-ownership. Although harming them is permissible where necessary to reduce their wrongful harm to others, it is not permissible if it benefits no one (as with purely retributive punishment). I believe that this view is correct, but I shall not pursue it here. I merely flag it as one more issue left unresolved by Nozick.[22]

Because of the indeterminacy of full ownership with respect to the prevention and rectification rights (and the corresponding immunity to loss of rights), there is room within libertarian theory for radically different views. Nozick sketches a framework, but the hard work is in articulating and defending a specific set of rights.

6.6 CONCLUSION

Nozick argues (1) that a non-consensual minimal state can, if it arises in the right way, be just (violate no one's rights) and (2) that no stronger form of a state can be just. His argument is based on the assumption that individuals have the libertarian rights that we have discussed. Whether his argument is successful if individuals do have such rights is a topic that will be discussed in other chapters.

Nozick does not fully articulate his libertarian theory nor adequately defend it. Still, the book is full of stimulating examples and important ideas for moral theory. It was clearly a major impetus for others to explore more systematically the core ideas. There are many ways of contributing to philosophy and this is surely one of them.[23]

NOTES

1. For superb introductions to Nozick's book, see Wolff (1991) and Bader (2010).
2. Some of the many references to permissibility, justification, or wrongness occur on pp. ix, xi, 36, 38, 114, and especially 52. References to legitimacy occur, for example, on pp. 52, 134, 232, and 333.
3. Some of the many references which at least implicitly restrict justice to respect for rights occur on pp. ix, xi, 6, 12, 13, 23, 28, 114, and 149.
4. In discussing this passage, Steiner: 1981, 1982; Miller: 1981; and Wilson: 1981 each agree that Nozick is denying that rights are necessarily enforceable, although they disagree about whether he is right about that. For general discussion of whether rights must be enforceable, see Kramer, Simmonds, and Steiner: 1998.

5. For a similar comment, see pp. 6 and 32 of *ASU*.

6. Nozick has some puzzling comments on the status of animals. He claims, in passing, that it is normally unjustified (wrong) for contemporary Americans to eat animals (p. 38). This is because higher animals morally count for something (p. 35). Indeed, higher animals have *claims* to certain treatment (p. 39). Presumably he holds that animals do not have any enforceable claims.

7. Thomson: 1981 argues against the view that all rights are absolute.

8. Davis: 1981, p. 346, suggests that there is a problem with the principle as formulated. Suppose we are all entitled to our holdings and then I steal *and destroy* some of your property. It seems that each person is still entitled to his holdings (since I no longer possess your property). This, however, is a mistake, if, as seems plausible, I owe you compensation for the harm. For then I am in possession of some property to which I am not entitled.

9. Purely procedural justice, in the sense used here, is different from what Rawls means by the same phrase (cf. Rawls: 1971, p. 86). He means that there is a procedure for which whatever it generates is just. He does not presuppose that the antecedent situation, in which the procedure is applied, was just.

10. Nozick presents his argument as being against end-state theories of justice (i.e., theories that do not recognize differential deserts or claims based on past actions) and patterned theories of justice (i.e., that call for certain distributions, such as equality or in proportion to desert). His distinctions, however, are somewhat confused and not very useful. His real target is theories that are not purely procedural.

11. Here and below, I draw on Becker: 1982 and Fried: 1995. See also Cohen: 1995 and 2009.

12. Scanlon: 1981 makes this point.

13. Nozick's implicit assumption that the initial rights and appropriated rights are full (unrestricted) rights of ownership is noted, for example, by Nagel: 1981; O'Neill: 1981; Ryan: 1981; and Cohen: 1995.

14. For more detailed discussion of the notion of full ownership, see Vallentyne, Steiner, and Otsuka: 2005. For a discussion of control ownership, see Christman: 1994.

15. For elaboration, see, for example, Vallentyne: 2007.

16. On p. 177, Nozick asks whether the situations of others is "worsened by a system allowing appropriation and permanent property," but this, I think, was just a slip on his part. The justice of actions on his view is based on their specific features and not on general features of some (perhaps non-existing) system.

17. For a defense of George's ideas against economic criticisms, see, for example, Gaffney and Harrison: 1994.

18. Steiner: 1994 defends equal share left-libertarianism, whereas Otsuka: 2003 and Vallentyne: 2009 defend equal opportunity for wellbeing left-libertarianism. For a collection of historical and contemporary writings on left-libertarianism, see Vallentyne and Steiner: 2000a and 2000b.

19. Here, I make the standard assumption that the proviso only applies to appropriation. Eric Roark: 2008, however, has plausibly argued that the proviso also applies to acts of mere use (without appropriation). Mack: 1995 rejects any special proviso on appropriation, but he agrees that there is a general (although weak) proviso on use.

20. Becker: 1982 clearly brings out the significance of the on-going nature of the proviso.

21. For further defense for the right of voluntary enslavement see: Nozick: 1974, p. 331; Feinberg: 1986, ch. 19; Steiner: 1994, pp. 232–234; Vallentyne: 1998 and 2000.

22. I here note one other problematic feature of Nozick's theory of justice in prevention and rectification. In his argument for the possible justness of the minimal state, he claims (see pp. 96–108) that the dominant protection agency does not violate rights of non-clients when it prohibits – and uses force to stop – them from using enforcement procedures against its clients that it deems unfair or unreliable (provided that it provides them appropriate compensation). This seems quite mistaken. If a client wrongfully attacks a non-client, what matters is whether the defense is in fact necessary and proportionate. What "procedure" is used and whether someone else deems it unfair or unreliable is irrelevant. For elaboration, see Vallentyne: 2006.

23. For helpful comments, I thank Ralf Bader, Xiaofei Liu, Eric Roark, Brandon Schmidly, Alan Tomhave, Patrick Tomlin, Jon Trerise, and the members of the audience at the 'Reappraising Anarchy, State, and Utopia' conference at King's College London.

7 Nozick's critique of Rawls: distribution, entitlement, and the assumptive world of *A Theory of Justice*

A Theory of Justice is a powerful, deep, subtle, wide-ranging, systematic work in political and moral philosophy which has not seen its like since the writings of John Stuart Mill, if then. It is a fountain of illuminating ideas, integrated together into a lovely whole. Political philosophers must now either work within Rawls's theory or explain why not ... It is impossible to read Rawls's book without incorporating much, perhaps transmuted, into one's own deepened view. And it is impossible to finish his book without a new and inspiring vision of what a moral theory may attempt to do and unite; of how *beautiful* a whole theory can be.

(p. 183)

Rawls's construction is incapable of yielding an entitlement or historical conception of distributive justice ... If historical-entitlement principles are fundamental, then Rawls's construction will yield approximations of them at best; it will produce the wrong sorts of reasons for them, and its derived results sometimes will conflict with the precisely correct principles. The whole procedure of persons choosing principles in Rawls's original position presupposes that no historical-entitlement conception of justice is correct.

(p. 202)

7.1 INTRODUCTION

The importance attached to Nozick's *Anarchy, State, and Utopia* (*ASU*) in contemporary political philosophy owes a great deal to the relationship between *ASU* and John Rawls's *A Theory of Justice* (*TJ*). *ASU* and *TJ* are often said to have framed the contemporary debate about the nature of justice by representing the two fundamental opposing views of what constitutes justice in the distribution of income and wealth (e.g., Fried: 2005; MacIntyre: 1985, ch. 17; Schmidtz: 2006, ch. 30).

While Nozick pays generous tribute to the brilliance of Rawls's philosophical construction, *ASU* also contains a fierce critique of Rawls's work. At the center of this critique is the entitlement theory of justice, which Nozick proposes as an alternative conception of justice to that advocated in *TJ*. The success or otherwise of Nozick's critique of Rawls is highly contested. This chapter will argue that Nozick's critique of Rawls is more telling than is commonly assumed: Nozick successfully shows that the concept of entitlement must play some part in any theory of justice, that the maintenance of any preferred pattern of distribution must involve continuous interference in people's lives that will violate their rights, and that Rawls's theory of justice is an artifact of the assumptions built into his philosophical construction of the original position.

The structure of this chapter is as follows: after this introduction, the second section will set out the critique of utilitarianism shared by *ASU* and *TJ* and founded upon the notion of the separateness of persons. The third and fourth sections will then show the very different theories of justice developed by Rawls and then Nozick from this common starting point. The fourth section will also consider a number of important critiques of Nozick's entitlement theory of justice. The following five sections will then set out Nozick's critique of the foundational assumptions of Rawls's work, beginning with the role of social cooperation in Rawls's theory, then Rawls's treatment of income and wealth as unowned manna from heaven, Rawls's rejection of the natural system of liberty as an institutional setting that allows arbitrary natural assets to determine the distribution of income and wealth, Rawls's focus on the basic structure of society rather than relationships between individuals, and finally Rawls's prioritization of the least advantaged. A short final section concludes.

7.2 THE SEPARATENESS OF PERSONS AND THE REJECTION OF UTILITARIANISM

Much scholarship on Rawls and Nozick properly focuses on the differences and disagreements between the two thinkers, but there are also important areas of accord. In particular, both *ASU* and *TJ* were intended to be critiques of and improvements upon utilitarian conceptions of ethics that had hitherto dominated liberal thinking.

The utilitarian approach, classically set out by Jeremy Bentham, James Mill, and John Stuart Mill, and formalized in the theorems of neoclassical welfare economics, is to calculate social welfare on the basis of the aggregate utility of the composite individuals within a given population. Policy proposals can then be judged on the basis of the net gains or losses in social welfare predicted to follow from different interventions. Hence, a policy proposal that anticipated a large loss of utility for one or two individuals but promised a small gain in utility for many thousands of people, such as the compulsory purchase of a small number of residential properties to facilitate the construction of a major road, is likely to be judged to produce a net social benefit according to a standard utilitarian calculus. Utilitarianism, then, justifies trade-offs between the utility of different individuals, allowing some individuals to be harmed (i.e., suffer a loss of welfare) in the name of the greater good (i.e., a positive gain in net social welfare). Utilitarianism in this seemingly crude form is more than an abstract model used by philosophers – it forms the basis of much contemporary policy evaluation (e.g., Nas: 1996; Weiss: 1998, ch. 10).

Rawls and Nozick both reject utilitarianism on the basis that, in the words of Rawls, it "does not take seriously the distinction between persons" (Rawls: 1999a, p. 24). It is argued that there is a qualitative difference between the welfare of society and the welfare of a single individual that an ethical theory that proposes trade-offs between the utility of different individuals in order to maximize social welfare fails to recognize – although individuals may make personal trade-offs in order to maximize their own utility, the same maximizing logic cannot be applied to justify trade-offs at the societal level. As Nozick put it:

[T]here is no social entity with a good that undergoes some sacrifice for its own good. There are only individual people, different individual people, with their own individual lives. Using one of these people for the benefit of others, uses him and benefits the others. Nothing more. What happens is that something is done to him for the sake of others ... To use a person in this way does not sufficiently respect and take account of the fact that he is a separate person, that his life is the only life he has. (pp. 32–33)

For Rawls and Nozick, a moral theory that serves to justify a reduction in the welfare of one individual in order to benefit other individuals is deeply flawed. Individuals are not, as Nozick puts it, "resources for others," but distinct entities with their own ends that must be respected (see p. 33). Both Rawls and Nozick draw upon Kantian ethics in their conceptualization of individuals as ends and not means and their consequent rejection of utilitarianism as a theory that proposes to harm some individuals in order to benefit others.

Nozick argues that the moral integrity and autonomy of each individual should lead to a conception of rights as side constraints: "In contrast to incorporating rights into the end state to be achieved, one might place them as side constraints upon the action to be done" (p. 29). For Nozick, individuals have rights and these rights act as side constraints on our actions, prohibiting people from doing things that violate the rights of others.

As Zwolinski has described, the puzzle that arises is to explain how two theories that both claim to treat the separateness of persons with appropriate seriousness can produce such dramatically different conclusions (see Zwolinski: 2008, p. 147). The solution to this puzzle lies in the different ways that Rawls and Nozick construct their theories of justice in the light of their shared view of the separateness of persons.

7.3 RAWLS'S THEORY OF JUSTICE

As is well known, Rawls's theory of justice is founded upon a particular model of the social contract in which individuals are assumed to enter an "original position," "the appropriate initial status quo," from which they will agree the institutional arrangements that will govern their closed society from the present time onward. The participants in the original position are required to assume a "veil of ignorance," whereby they have no knowledge of their social status or class, their natural abilities, aversion to risk, generational position or conception of the good (see Rawls: 1999a, esp. chs. 4 and 24). The veil of ignorance is said to mean that individuals "do not know how the various alternatives will affect their own particular case," so that, "they are obliged to evaluate principles solely on the basis of general considerations" (Rawls: 1999a, p. 118).

Individuals are assumed to be rational and self-interested, but because they do not know their future social or occupational position they cannot select arrangements that will favor their own personal interests, but must instead choose an outcome that will be acceptable to any individual irrespective of their personal character-istics or social position. It is assumed, therefore, that people in the original position under a veil of ignorance would not select institu-tional arrangements in which a majority of the population benefit at the expense of a minority because they do not know in which of the two groups they will reside – an individual who attempted to create exploitative arrangements might find him or herself one of the exploited (see Rawls: 1999a, pp. 120–121).

Taking the separateness of persons seriously means that in Rawls's model of the social contract set out in *TJ* each individual has a power of veto: "the requirement of unanimity [in constitutional agreement] is not out of place and the fact that it can be satisfied is of great importance. It enables us to say of the preferred conception of just-ice that it represents a genuine reconciliation of interests" (Rawls: 1999a, p. 122). Unanimous agreement of a social contract is believed to be possible because, according to Rawls, in the original position under a veil of ignorance everyone would select identical institu-tional arrangements – if everyone must come to the same conclusion then unanimous agreement is logically possible.[1] For Rawls, then, a social contract cannot be imposed upon unwilling individuals, even if such an imposition was believed to be of net social benefit.

Rawls argues that individuals in the original position will agree to organize society according to two basic principles (Rawls: 1999a, p. 266):

1.   Each person is to have an equal right to the most extensive system of equal basic liberties compatible with a similar system of liberty for all.
2.   Social and economic inequalities are to be arranged so that they are both:
     (a)   to the greatest benefit of the least advantaged, consist-ent with the just savings principle; and
     (b)   attached to offices and positions open to all under con-ditions of fair equality of opportunity.

These two principles have become known respectively as the lib-erty principle and the difference principle. The liberty principle sets out the basic rights that would be hypothetically agreed in the original position, while the difference principle sets out the basis upon which deviations from equality of income and wealth may be considered legitimate. Here, it is argued that economic inequalities may be tolerated only if they are to the benefit of the least advantaged group within society, who Rawls describes as those whose family and class origins are more disadvantaged than others, whose natural endowments permit to fare less well, or whose fortune and luck in the course of life turn out to be less happy. In practical terms, Rawls states that this could be assumed to mean that the least advantaged group consists of those individuals with less than half of median income (see Rawls: 1999a, pp. 83–84).

Rawls argues that absolute economic equality may not be to the benefit of the least advantaged because differential rewards may be needed to incentivize the most productive members of society to contribute to the generation of wealth. In the words of Rawls: "each society has a redistribution policy which if pushed beyond a certain point weakens incentives and thereby lowers production" (Rawls: 1999a, p. 142).

In the second part of *TJ* Rawls set outs the institutional framework required to implement the two principles of justice. This institutional framework involves an active role for government to protect the basic rights of individuals, maintain full employment, ensure the payment of a basic minimum income to all, preserve "justice in distributive shares" via taxation and adjustments in property rights, and ensure that those markets that exist are genuinely competitive, rather than controlled by monopolistic enterprises. What Rawls sets out is something akin to a traditional model of social democracy, in which market mechanisms are embedded in a governmental structure charged with maintaining certain allocative and distribution outcomes – in this case ensuring that economic inequalities exist only insofar as they benefit the least advantaged group. However, the primacy that Rawls gives to basic rights in his theory of justice means that his account has an important liberal dimension and therefore is not a straightforward example of social democracy. Rather, Rawls's theory may be more accurately characterized as a model of liberal egalitarianism.

7.4 NOZICK'S CRITIQUE OF DISTRIBUTIVE JUSTICE: WILT CHAMBERLAIN AND ENTITLEMENT

While the separateness of persons leads Rawls to develop a model of the social contract that sets out significant redistribution of income and wealth by the state, in *ASU* from what looks like the same starting point Nozick argues that any state more extensive than the minimal state must violate people's rights and therefore cannot be justified.

The first part of *ASU* contains Nozick's account of how the minimal state can arise without violating anyone's rights. The third part of the book aims to show how the minimal state can be an inspiring ideal within which people can pursue their many different conceptions of the good life. In the second part of *ASU*, and in particular in Chapter 7, by far the longest chapter of the book, Nozick presents his argument against the more-than-minimal state. The second half of Chapter 7 contains a direct critique of Rawls's position, while the first half presents a more general critique of standard theories of distributive justice that applies to Rawls's theory among others (see p. 150 n.).

Nozick seeks to critique standard accounts of distributive justice via comparison with his alternative entitlement theory of justice, which he considers to be more just. Nozick introduces his entitlement theory by noting that the very idea of "distributive justice" would seem to imply a deliberate allocation of resources: "Hearing the term 'distribution', most people presume that some thing or mechanism uses some principle or criterion to give out a supply of things," and that, "[i]nto this process of distributing shares some error may have crept" (p. 149). Distributive justice would seem to imply that someone or some group has deliberately decided what income and wealth each individual or family should receive and this outcome can then be evaluated as either just or unjust.

For Nozick, the basic error of this approach lies in the fact that in a market economy, "we are not in the position of children who have been given portions of pie by someone who now makes last minute adjustments to rectify careless cutting" (p. 149). The resources that would be reallocated in the name of social justice have not been created by a central authority that now distributes them, nor are they manna from heaven that has fallen unowned from the sky, but they are holdings that particular individuals are entitled to possess as a result of their actions in the creation of wealth and the exchange of goods and services (see pp. 149–150).

Nozick makes a distinction between time-slice or end-state and historical theories of justice. Time-slice/end-state theories are concerned with the distribution of resources at particular moments in time, whereas historical theories are only concerned with how a particular distribution came about (see pp. 153–155). Both time-slice/end-state and historical theories may also be patterned theories, in which distribution according to a particular pattern is desired, such as distribution according to desert, usefulness to society or IQ. For advocates of patterned theories the salient question is whether the distribution accords with the desired pattern, either at a particular moment in time in the case of time-slice/end-state theories or in terms of the repeated application of a particular principle in the case of a historical theory (see pp. 155–160).

Nozick proposes a historical conception of justice. He argues that the justice of any given distribution of income and wealth can be exhaustively covered by the repeated application of the three basic principles of justice in acquisition, justice in transfer, and rectification when the first two principles have been transgressed: "the holdings of a person are just if he is entitled to them by the principles of justice in acquisition and transfer, or by the principle of rectification of injustice (as specified by the first two principles). If each person's holdings are just, then the total set (distribution) of holdings is just" (p. 153).

These principles set out the entitlement theory of justice: people are entitled to holdings that are acquired via (repeated applications of) the principles of justice in acquisition and justice in transfer, or via rectification of transgression of those first two principles. Any inequalities of income and wealth that happen to arise as a result of legitimate acquisition and legitimate transfer are a matter of complete irrelevance when it comes to determining the justice or otherwise of a given distribution – the only relevant question concerns whether the holdings were legitimately acquired and/or legitimately transferred (see pp. 150–153).

Nozick does, however, add a proviso to his theory. Nozick's proviso is that a "process normally giving rise to a permanent bequeathable property right in a previously unowned thing will not do so if the position of others no longer at liberty to use that thing is thereby worsened" (p. 178). Nozick's proviso is intended to prevent someone appropriating the total supply of a necessity, such as all the drinkable water in the world. The proviso depends upon a narrow definition of "worsen," which does not include worsening others' position by leaving them less to appropriate, or appropriating materials in order to compete with other producers. The proviso not only limits what can be justly acquired, but also limits what can be legitimately transferred: "If the proviso excludes someone's appropriating all the drinkable water in the world, it also excludes his purchasing it all" (p. 179).

Nozick famously illustrated his entitlement theory of justice with the example of the wealth acquired by the basketball star Wilt Chamberlain in a fictional scenario. Taking as a starting point a distribution of resources that is considered just, which Nozick names D_1, Nozick supposes that large numbers of people are willing to pay 25 cents directly to Chamberlain (in addition to the standard ticket price) in order to watch him play basketball. Supposing that one million people come through the turnstiles during the course of a season, Chamberlain will acquire additional personal wealth of $250,000. As a result of the voluntary actions of a million basketball fans and Wilt Chamberlain, a new distribution of resources has emerged, which Nozick names D_2. In this new distribution one individual – Wilt Chamberlain – has amassed a sizeable personal fortune (see pp. 160–164).

For Nozick, the new distribution of resources (D_2) must be considered just because it meets the criteria of justice in acquisition and justice in transfer. The theoretical starting point of Nozick's example was a distribution of resources that was deemed to be just (it is left to the reader to imagine what such a distribution might be) and then people voluntarily transferred their justly held resources to Chamberlain in return for a service (watching him play) that they considered more valuable than the 25 cents that each paid. In neither case can an injustice be said to have occurred, and therefore Nozick argues that the new distribution that has emerged must logically be considered just: "If D_1 was a just distribution, and people voluntarily moved from it to D_2, transferring parts of their shares they were given under D_1 (what was it for if not to do something with?), isn't D_2 also just? If the people were entitled to dispose of the resources to which they were entitled (under D_1), didn't this also include their being entitled to give it to, or exchange it with, Wilt Chamberlain?" (p. 161).

On the face of it, Nozick's Wilt Chamberlain example would seem to portray a decisive argument against non-historical accounts of justice like Rawls's theory. The application of Nozick's theory to real world capitalist economies raises the thorny issue of the justice of acquisition within those societies, which Nozick seems to only partially address via his Lockean account of just acquisition (see pp. 174–178). But the application of Nozick's theory to an initial distribution agreed to be just and therefore meeting the criterion of justice in acquisition, such as the hypothetical distribution that would be derived from the application of Rawls's theory, would seem to be less problematic.

However, as Thomas Nagel has pointed out, the Wilt Chamberlain example appears to rely on the assumption that the entitlements to property that people have in D_I are absolute, but it is surely the case that "absolute entitlement to property is not what would be allocated to people under a partially egalitarian distribution" (Nagel: 1981, p. 201) of the kind imagined by Rawls. Rather, in a Rawlsian or similarly egalitarian distribution, "[p]ossession would confer the kind of qualified entitlement that exists in a system under which taxes and other conditions are arranged to preserve certain features of the distribution" (Nagel: 1981, p. 201).

Indeed, in *TJ* Rawls explicitly states that "the rights of property" agreed in the original position are not absolute, but are to be limited in accordance with the terms of the social contract (e.g., Rawls: 1999a, p. 245). Hence, if the parties in the original position agree to tax income at 25 percent in order to help the least advantaged members of society, for example, then Chamberlain would assume ownership of only 75 percent of the money paid to him by the spectators, with the remainder being transferred to the least advantaged via the tax and benefit system. Once holdings/entitlements/property rights are understood to be less than absolute, in Rawls's case as a result of the hypothetical unanimous agreement of all parties, then it is not clear on what basis the taxation and redistribution of part of Chamberlain's additional income in accordance with such an agreement could be considered unjust.

Even if the main thrust of Nagel's objection is accepted, however, Nozick's argument may still retain much of its force. Unless income is taxed at 100 percent and all actions that may increase or decrease the value of property are prohibited, then even taking into account the operation of a standard social democratic tax and benefit system, Nozick's argument shows that in any conceivable society there will be continuous deviations from any preferred or ideal time-slice/end-state distribution and there is no obvious basis for believing that the new distributions that emerge are unjust.

As Eric Mack has described, the challenge to those who would advocate an ideal time-slice/end-state distribution is that "[u]nless people are effectively prohibited from transforming and exchanging their holdings … there will always be many individuals who will find unexpected ways to enhance the value of their holdings by unilateral alteration of these holdings or by mutually agreeable exchange" (Mack: 2002, p. 87).

Indeed, as noted above, Nozick did not argue that property rights are absolute in all circumstances, but instead proposed a proviso that prevented people appropriating or transferring property that gave them a monopoly of something that was a necessity for life (see pp. 178–179). For this reason it seems clear that Nozick did not intend that his theory should rely upon a conception of absolute entitlement to property.

Nozick's argument in the first section of Chapter 7 of *ASU* seems to have shown that at least some element of entitlement must form part of any account of distributive justice. The fact that entitlements to property are not absolute does not mean that people do not have *any* entitlement to holdings or property acquired via just acquisition and just transfer. Rather, in the light of Nozick's theory the onus must lie with the critics of the entitlement theory to show that the fact that entitlements to property are not absolute means that entitlements have no role in a theory of justice in the distribution of income and wealth.

Nozick also appears to have successfully shown that "no end-state principle or distributional patterned principle of justice can be continuously realized without continuous interference with people's lives" (p. 163). The maintenance of a time-slice or end-state theory of distribution like that proposed by Rawls is possible only via continuous intervention to "correct" new distributions of income and wealth that emerge as a result of the actions of individuals in making, consuming, conserving, and exchanging things.

For Nozick, such interference is an infringement of people's rights as side constraints – rights that imply the ability to make choices about the disposal of one's resources in accordance with one's preferences (see pp. 164–166).

For Rawls, however, the level of interference implied by the difference principle does not violate people's rights so long the tax and benefit system is a clear part of the institutional framework within which people live and frame their expectations. As Rawls wrote in his restatement of his original theory of justice in *Justice as Fairness*:

Since the difference principle applies to institutions as public systems of rules, their requirements are foreseeable. They do not involve any more continuous or regular interference with individuals' plans and actions than do, say, familiar forms of taxation. Since the effects of those rules are foreseen, they are taken into account when citizens draw up their plans in the first place. Citizens understand that when they take part in social cooperation, their property and wealth, and their share of what they help to produce, are subject to the taxes, say, which background institutions are known to impose. (Rawls: 2001, pp. 51–52)

However, Rawls's theory of justice suggests that a process of collective deliberation and agreement – as in the agreement of the social contract in the original position – is required to legitimatize the redistribution of income and wealth via the tax and benefit system. The fact that contemporary welfare states redistribute income and wealth without having undertaken the kind of prior legitimizing process imagined by Rawls suggests that even on Rawlsian terms such intervention in people's lives may be considered a rights violation.

7.4.1 The entitlement theory and the consistency of ASU

A further objection to Nozick's entitlement theory based on the existence of alleged inconsistencies between Parts II and III of *ASU* has been set out by Barbara Fried (see Fried: 2005). Here it is argued that the redistribution of all or a portion of Chamberlain's income could conceivably be consistent with Nozick's "framework for utopia" set out in Part III of *ASU*. In the framework for utopia (discussed by Bader and by Kukathas in this collection) people may choose to live in any community they wish so long as they can convince sufficient others to join their association to make it viable and so long as everyone has a right to exit from the community.

Within this framework, Nozick recognized, it was at least conceivable that "if almost everyone wished to live in a communist community," the situation could arise where "there weren't any viable non-communist communities," so that those few individuals who did not wish to live in a communist association would have "no alternative but to conform" to life under communist principles. Such a situation would not, according to Nozick, violate the rights of an individual who had no feasible alternative but to live in a communist society even though communism was anathema to him: "the others do not force him to conform and his rights are not violated. He has no right that the others cooperate in making his nonconformity feasible" (p. 322).

If Wilt Chamberlain is placed in the position of the individual required to live in a communist community because there is no a feasible alternative, even though he has a nominal right of exit, then it must surely follow – on Nozick's own terms – that his income can be redistributed via taxation in accordance with the rules of this community without his rights being violated. It therefore may seem hard to resist Fried's conclusion that there is a significant tension between Nozick's framework for utopia, set out in Part III of *ASU*, and his argument for the minimal state in Part II of *ASU*: "Why does it not follow from the justificatory role of exit at the community level that *any* state, with *any* compulsory package of rights/restrictions/prohibitions, developed by *any* procedure whatsoever, is morally justified, as long as dissenters who do not like that particular package are permitted to exit?" (Fried: 2005, p. 224). Hence, following the logic of Nozick's own argument, it would seem that Wilt Chamberlain's rights cannot be said to be violated by the confiscation via taxation of all or a portion of the additional income paid by the spectators so long as he has the right to exit from such arrangements, even if there is no plausible alternative for him to exit to. According to Fried, if *ASU* is taken to advance a coherent, holistic argument then the argument of Part III would seem to render the argument of the first two parts of the book as moot.

Fried's argument is correct, however, *only* if Wilt Chamberlain lives within the context of institutional arrangements that have arisen via a process of voluntary agreement from which each individual has the freedom to exit. Rawls's model of political agreement, however, assumes "a closed system isolated from other societies" (Rawls: 1999a, p. 7), which would seem to imply a society from which exit is impossible. Hence, while Fried's work certainly raises important questions about the internal consistency of *ASU*, it is not clear that her argument is particularly damaging in terms of Nozick's critique of Rawls given the absence of an exit option from Rawls's theory.

In summary, Nozick's entitlement theory of justice and its application in the famous Wilt Chamberlain example make a strong case for believing that people's entitlement to justly acquired property should form at least part of any theory of justice in the distribution of income and wealth. Nozick also appears to successfully show that the maintenance of any preferred pattern of distribution can only be achieved via continuous interference in the lives of individual men and women that must violate those individuals' rights.

7.5 JUSTICE, DISTRIBUTION, AND SOCIAL COOPERATION

Nozick's critique of Rawls in the second section of Chapter 7 of *ASU* seeks to expose and challenge the assumptions that underlie Rawls's theory of justice. For Nozick, Rawls's contention that people in the original position will choose to arrange their society according to Rawls's principles of justice is an artifact of a series of unjustified and often implicit assumptions within Rawls's work.

Probably the most fundamental of Rawls's assumptions is that in the original position people will view income and wealth as a pattern of distribution that requires legitimization by political authority – thus creating the problem of distributive justice – rather than as individual holdings that owe their legitimacy to the process of acquisition and/or transfer via which they came about.

Rawls argues the distribution of income and wealth requires political legitimization on the grounds that the resources held by individuals in a society characterized by an advanced division of labour are in large part the creation of social cooperation rather than the result of the efforts or contributions of specific individuals. Rawls states: "social cooperation makes possible a better life for all than any would have if each were to live solely by his own efforts" and for this reason an appropriate task of a theory of justice is to "define the appropriate distribution of the benefits and burdens of social cooperation" (Rawls: 1999a, p. 4). The question of justice is said to be relevant to the distribution of income and wealth because the resources that are distributed depend upon widespread social cooperation for their creation.

Nozick, however, notes that Rawls's theory does not seem to take into account the fact that there must be some things that individuals would produce even in isolation and according to Rawls's formulation those things that are not the product of social cooperation should logically belong to the individuals who have created them. Hence, at the very least Rawls's theory would seem to imply a preliminary exercise of determining what things are the products of social cooperation and what things would be produced by individuals working alone that is absent from Rawls's enterprise (see pp. 183–185).

Nozick also questions why the existence of social cooperation should mean that the distribution of income and wealth requires legitimization by political authority? The most obvious answer, Nozick suggests, is that in an advanced division of labour it is impossible to "disentangle the contributions of distinct individuals who cooperate" given that "everything is everyone's joint product" and therefore income and wealth cannot be properly viewed as individual holdings resulting from straightforward historical processes of acquisition and/or transfer (p. 186).[2]

Nozick argues, however, that the assertion that individual contributions cannot be disentangled would seem to be empirically falsifiable. In reality, individual contributions "are easily identifiable" via reference to the prices and salaries that different goods, services and occupations command in the marketplace (p. 186). Hence, the bilateral transactions and exchanges that take place in a market economy reflect marginal individual contributions to the wider social product, providing the information required to isolate individual contributions in a meaningful way (see pp. 186–187).[3]

Indeed, in Chapter 8 of *ASU* Nozick notes that the argument that profits are a joint social product is rarely applied to losses. While many people feel entitled to claim a share of the profits when a venture is successful, very few people feel obliged to share the losses of an unsuccessful enterprise: "For example, croupiers at gambling casinos expect to be well-tipped by big winners, but they do not expect to be asked to help bear some of the losses of the losers" (p. 256). According to Nozick, then, an advanced economy should be understood as a vast matrix of interpersonal cooperation within which individual contributions are identifiable at the margin: "People cooperate in making things but they work separately; each person is a miniature firm" (p. 186).

Furthermore, Nozick argues that Rawls's central contention that absolute economic equality would not be to the benefit of the least advantaged because differential rewards are needed to incentivize the most productive members of society logically implies that different individuals do make different contributions and, moreover, that some individuals make a greater contribution than others that may have to be recognized and encouraged via the use of incentives (see pp. 187–189; Rawls: 1999a, p. 142).

In the words of Nozick, it is clear that, "Rawls is *not* imagining that inequalities are needed to fill positions that everyone can do equally well, or that the most drudgery-filled positions that require the least skill will command the highest income" (p. 188). The role of incentives in justifying the inequalities to be tolerated under the terms of Rawls's difference principle would seem to imply that the products of an advanced economy are not solely the collective products of completely interchangeable men and women, or that individual contributions are impossible to entangle, but would seem to suggest that the products of an advanced economy owe their existence to the unique contributions of particular individuals who may require personal incentives to ensure their maximal contribution.[4]

Nozick would seem to have made a good case for thinking that Rawls has not effectively proven his claim that because in an advanced economy income and wealth are the product of social cooperation rather than being attached to unique individual contributions, people in the original position will believe that the distribution of income and wealth requires legitimization by political authority and thereby creates the problem of distributive justice. Nozick further develops this critique of Rawls's foundational assumptions in his discussion of the absence of the notion of historical entitlement from Rawls's theory of justice.

7.6. DISTRIBUTION, ENTITLEMENT, AND MANNA
FROM HEAVEN

In the second section of Chapter 7 of *ASU* Nozick argues that Rawls's theory of justice is a prime example of the intellectual error of viewing income and wealth as unowned collective resources that exist independently of the actions of any individual men and women and can therefore be distributed by a political authority according to a deliberately chosen principle or pattern of distribution.

According to Nozick, Rawls's construction of the original position in which people have no knowledge of their history, abilities, or social and economic position effectively transforms all resources into manna from heaven; without an account of the historical processes via which resources were in fact produced income and wealth seem to have been created as if by magic: "For people meeting together behind a veil of ignorance to decide who gets what, knowing nothing about any special entitlements people may have, will treat anything to be distributed as manna from heaven" (p. 199).

Nozick employs one of his most striking examples to illustrate the error of Rawls's approach: suppose a class of students who have received examination grades between 0 and 100, of which they have not yet learned, are asked to allocate grades amongst themselves so that the total matches the sum of the grades they have actually been awarded. Nozick argues that "given sufficient restrictions on their ability to threaten each other, they probably would agree to each person receiving the same grade, to each person's grade being equal to the total divided by the number of people to be graded" (p. 199). Hence, if the students' grades were segments of a collective whole to be allocated deliberately in the absence of any historical knowledge about how those grades came about, then the agreement of a principle of equality would be the logical and fairest way to allocate the grades.

But in reality, Nozick contends, the grades are entitlements created by and intrinsically connected to the efforts and actions of individual students. Hence, Nozick continues: "Suppose next that there is posted on a bulletin board at their meeting a paper headed ENTITLEMENTS, which lists each person's name with a grade next to it, the listing being identical to the instructor's gradings" (p. 199). There is, Nozick contends, little chance of these grades matching those deliberately chosen by the students, or of the tutor's grades being agreed by the students in any deliberative process.

Nozick's argument, then, is that Rawls's theory of distributive justice is an artifact produced by the particular construction of the original position; by its very design the original position simply could not yield a historical or entitlement conception of justice: "Rawls' construction is incapable of yielding an entitlement or historical conception of distributive justice ... The whole procedure of persons choosing principles in Rawls' original position presupposes that no historical-entitlement conception of justice is correct" (p. 202).

It is inevitable, it is argued, that rational, self-interested individuals distributing income and wealth as if they are manna from heaven, without knowledge of any person's individual contribution to the creation of that income and wealth, will choose to distribute resources according to an egalitarian principle. But this approach neglects the fact that in the real world income and wealth are created by people's individual actions and contributions (informed by their diverse abilities and varied preferences). Hence, like the students' grades, income and wealth should be understood as holdings or entitlements, created by and intrinsically connected to the purposeful actions of individual men and women.

Rawls's difference principle may well be an appropriate criterion for distributing manna from heaven (if the distribution of that manna in some way influenced how much manna was produced so that incentives had to be taken into account), but Nozick makes a powerful case for believing that the creation of income and wealth in the real world via the actions of many different individuals considerably complicates matters and almost certainly creates entitlements that should not be dismissed by anyone seeking justice in the distribution of resources.

7.7 NATURAL ASSETS, ARBITRARINESS, AND DESERT

Although Rawls's theory of justice seems to be constructed in such a way so as to preclude the selection of a historical or entitlement theory of justice by those in the original position, Rawls does briefly consider what he calls "the natural system of liberty," which he describes as the implementation of the liberty principle combined with a free market economy. Rawls's objection to such an arrangement is that "prior distributions of natural assets – that is, natural talents and abilities" would exert a powerful influence over the distribution of income and wealth and it would be an "injustice" for "distributive shares to be improperly influenced by these factors so arbitrary from a moral point of view" (Rawls: 1999a, pp. 62–63).

A central argument of the second section of Chapter 7 of *ASU* is that Rawls does not provide a clear account of why it is wrong for the distribution of income and wealth to be determined by these morally arbitrary factors. Rawls writes: "There is no more reason to permit the distribution of income and wealth to be settled by the distribution of natural assets than by historical and social fortune" (Rawls: 1999a, p. 64). But this is simply question begging – it does not provide reasons for believing that distributional questions should not be determined by the distribution of natural assets or by historical and social fortune.

The longest part of Nozick's direct critique of Rawls concerns this dismissal of natural assets as a basis for distribution because of their moral arbitrariness. Nozick notes that Rawls's dismissal of natural assets as arbitrary would seem to have important implications for Rawls's own account of the separateness of persons discussed earlier in this chapter. By striking out natural assets as in some way disconnected from the individuals who (happen to) possess them, Nozick argues that Rawls seems to be "attributing *everything* noteworthy about the person completely to certain sorts of 'external' factors" (p. 214). What is important about individual people, Nozick argues, is what they may create and contribute via the development and application of their natural talents and assets. But Rawls appears to dismiss such creations and contributions as no more than the chance results of random allocations of mental and physical attributes combined with the good fortune (or otherwise) to develop those talents. Nozick argues that if people do not in some sense own their natural abilities and assets then it is hard to see what remains of the autonomy and dignity of persons that Rawls earlier placed at the center of his rejection of utilitarianism (see p. 214).

Nozick argues that Rawls does not provide an explanation as to *why* people in the original position would reject the natural system of liberty because natural assets may (at least in part) determine the distribution of income and wealth; why should rational individual men and women under a veil of ignorance decide that morally arbitrary factors should not exert at least some influence over the distribution of income and wealth? Nozick posits that there are two possible arguments that may be used to explain why those in the original position would not wish to allow morally arbitrary natural assets to determine the distribution of income and wealth. Nozick calls these arguments "the positive argument" and "the negative argument."

7.7.1 The positive argument: natural assets and arbitrariness

Nozick identifies four possible positive arguments that Rawls might employ to justify his claim that people in the original position would not want the arbitrary distribution of natural assets to determine the distribution of income and wealth. The first argument is that people should morally deserve the income and wealth they receive and therefore because natural assets are arbitrary they should not be allowed to determine the distribution of income and wealth. However, Nozick notes that "Rawls explicitly and emphatically *rejects* distribution according to moral desert" (p. 217), so Rawls cannot believe that those in the original position would not want natural assets to determine the distribution of income and wealth because they prefer distribution according to moral desert.

The second argument that Rawls might invoke is that income and wealth should be distributed according to a pattern that is not arbitrary from a moral point of view and therefore arbitrary natural assets should not be allowed to determine that distribution. However, Nozick points out that in a market economy income and wealth are *not* distributed according to natural assets – there is no calculation of people's natural assets which is then used to distribute resources. Rather, the distribution of income and wealth follows from people's use of their natural assets to serve others: "The principle of the system is *not* distribution in accordance with natural assets; but differences in natural assets will lead to differences in holdings under a system whose principle is distribution according to perceived service to others" (p. 218). Wilt Chamberlain, for example, is not allocated resources on the basis of his unique athletic abilities, but according to the extent to which he puts those abilities to the service of others by playing professional basketball as measured by the willingness of people to pay to see him play.

This objection, however, may give rise to a third positive argument that Rawls could invoke, which is that arbitrary factors – such as the distribution of natural assets – should not be allowed to affect the distribution of income and wealth, even if only indirectly or weakly. However, Nozick points out that this cannot be Rawls's argument against allowing natural assets to determine the distribution of resources because the distribution of natural assets clearly plays a weak or indirect role in distribution under the terms of Rawls's own theory: "The difference principle operates to give some persons larger distributive shares than others; which persons receive these larger shares will depend, at least partially, on differences between these persons and others, differences that are arbitrary from a moral point of view, for some persons with special natural assets will be offered larger shares as an incentive to use these assets in certain ways" (p. 219). Hence, the third possible argument against allowing natural assets to influence (though not wholly determine) the distribution of income and wealth would logically also apply to Rawls's difference principle, so it logically cannot be employed by Rawls as an argument against the natural system of liberty.

Nozick suggests that the final positive argument that Rawls might utilize in defense of his position is one that, like the difference principle, begins from the presumption of economic equality. Rawls might argue that the distribution of income and wealth ought to be equal unless there is a morally compelling reason for it not to be equal and given that natural assets are not distributed according to any moral criteria they cannot provide a morally compelling justification for inequality (see p. 222).

Nozick responds to this possible argument by questioning the validity of the presumption of equality. For Nozick, the assumption that people may legitimately require that other people treat one another equally is itself an assertion requiring philosophical justification. A person may favor a particular cinema, for example, and therefore choose to watch films at that one particular location, even though other cinemas exist. By so doing, that person treats the owner of the favored cinema unequally compared with other cinema owners. According to the presumption of equality, such unequal treatment should be prohibited, or, at the very least, the unequal distribution of income and wealth that follows should be corrected. For Nozick, then, the relevant question is: "Why must differences between persons be justified? Why think that we must change, or remedy, or compensate for any inequality which can be changed, remedied, or compensated for?" (p. 223). It is not clear that Rawls has provided an argument to show that people should not treat others differently if they wish to do so, perhaps because some people have particular natural assets that they have put to the service of others.

Nozick, then, considers four possible positive arguments that Rawls might employ in favor of ensuring that a principle other than the natural distribution of assets should determine the distribution of income and wealth. Nozick shows that in each case the possible argument that Rawls might utilize does not succeed. Nozick then attempts to see if Rawls could construct a negative argument that might form a compelling case against allowing natural assets to determine the distribution of income and wealth.

7.7.2 *The negative argument: desert and entitlement*

In *ASU* Nozick agrees with Rawls's argument that the arbitrariness of natural assets means a distribution of income and wealth that reflects people's natural abilities cannot be justified on the grounds that it allocates resources according to desert – people do not deserve their differential natural abilities and therefore cannot be said to deserve what follows from those differential abilities (see p. 224).

However, Nozick argues that this argument does not provide grounds for rejecting the natural system of liberty if the concept of entitlement replaces desert as the underlying justification for economic inequality within such a system. Hence, if people are entitled to their natural assets, and if they are entitled to something they are also entitled to whatever flows from it, then it logically follows that people are entitled to the unequal holdings that follow from their unequal natural assets (see pp. 224–225).

While the arbitrariness of natural assets does seem to provide Rawls with an effective argument against an unequal distribution of resources justified on the grounds of desert, Nozick does seem

to show that arbitrariness does not provide Rawls with an effective argument against an unequal distribution of resources justified on the grounds of entitlement. In Nozick's words: "Whether
or not people's natural assets are arbitrary from a moral point of
view, they are entitled to them, and to what flows from them"
(p. 226).

It is probably worth noting that classical liberal and libertarian advocates of a market economy have not tended to justify the
inequalities of income and wealth produced by the market on the
grounds of desert. Hayek, for example, rejected claims that the allocation of income and wealth within a market economy corresponded
to desert and also rejected weaker claims that distribution via the
market reflected the "value to society" of a person's contribution.
For Hayek, "[t]he remunerations which the individuals and groups
receive in the market are thus determined by what these services
are worth to those who receive them ... and not by some fictitious
'value to society'" (Hayek: 1976, p. 76).

Hayek believed that any attempt to attach moral significance to
the allocations of income and wealth that happened to be produced
by a market economy would lead to attempts to improve upon
that allocation by intervening to try to make it more accurately
reflect desert, value to society or whatever other moral criterion was
invoked. For Hayek, a market economy and individual liberty were
better served if their defenders resisted the temptation to attach
moral significance to the factors that determined the distribution
of resources in a market economy. Hayek, like Nozick, was concerned with the morality or justice of the overarching market *process* rather than the morality or justice of the specific determinants
of the distribution of income and wealth.[5]

Nozick, then, concludes that Rawls provides no explicit or implicit argument for believing that people in the original position will
decide that the arbitrariness of natural assets means that they should
not in whole or in part determine the distribution of income and
wealth: "We have found no cogent argument to (help) establish that
differences in holdings arising from differences in natural assets
should be eliminated or minimized" (p. 226). Rather, for Nozick,
Rawls's contention that the arbitrariness of natural assets provides
a decisive reason for rejecting the natural system of liberty is no
more than an unproven assumption.

7.8 THE BASIC STRUCTURE AND MICRO-SITUATIONS

A further foundational assumption of Rawls's theory of justice challenged by Nozick is the view that justice concerns the basic structure of society – the organization of the institutions of society – rather than the relationships and interactions between individual men and women. In *TJ* Rawls writes: "For us the primary subject of justice is the basic structure of society, or more exactly, the way in which major social institutions distribute fundamental rights and duties and determine the division of advantages from social cooperation" (Rawls: 1999a, p. 6).

For Rawls, the basic structure describes "the political constitution and the principal economic and social arrangements" that will determine much of the distribution of benefits and burdens in a given society (Rawls: 1999a, p. 6). Rawls, then, is not interested in the justice of (what we might call) micro-relationships between individuals, but in the justice of the meta-institutions that set the rules that govern those more personal interactions.

In Chapter 7 of *ASU* Nozick objects to Rawls's claim that justice only concerns the basic structure of society on two grounds. First, Nozick argues that there is an epistemological problem with the very notion of the basic structure: how are we to know in practical terms what constitutes the basic structure and how changes to this structure (however defined) will impact on the lives of individual men and women (see pp. 204–205)? Rawls acknowledges that "the concept of the basic structure is somewhat vague. It is not always clear which institutions or features thereof should be included" (Rawls: 1999a, p. 8). But this vagueness with regard to such an important tenet of Rawls's theory is never satisfactorily resolved, perhaps in part because Rawls's desire to construct a universal theory prohibits the use of specific examples that might facilitate clarification.

Second, Nozick challenges Rawls's claim that principles of justice do not apply to micro-situations. Nozick argues that this claim serves to inhibit our ability to evaluate Rawls's principles of justice. Evaluating whether or not specific principles of justice should apply on a societal basis seems an impossible task if we cannot analyse how those principles would apply at a more prosaic level: "Since we may have only a weak confidence in our intuitions and judgments about the justice of the whole structure of society, we may attempt to aid our judgment by focusing on microsituations that we do have a firm grasp of" (p. 204). For Nozick, analyzing a theory of justice exclusively at the meta-level is akin to evaluating the impact of a change in the rules of football on the basis of the standings of the different teams at the end of the season without observing how the rule change impacts on specific incidents within games. It seems a near impossibility to evaluate the justice of an overall outcome without knowledge of how the rules of the game impact at the micro-level.

Underlying these criticisms is Nozick's view, set out in the previous section, that Rawls's theory of justice has been constructed in such a way so as to rule out historical-entitlement principles of justice. If we cannot examine the micro-interactions between individuals that, for Nozick, create the historical trial of acquisition and transfer that leads different people to have different entitlements to income and wealth, and in so doing produce the overall societal distribution that is Rawls's principal concern, then again the adoption of a historical or entitlement theory of justice becomes a logical impossibility. Once again, Nozick's analysis illuminates the importance of a series of key assumptions to Rawls's framing of the question of justice and the theory of justice that he thereby derives.

7.9 THE PRIORITY OF THE LEAST ADVANTAGED

Rawls's difference principle is a prioritarian principle that gives priority to the least advantaged group in society; in the original position individuals are said to choose institutional arrangements in which inequalities may be justified only to the extent that they benefit the least advantaged group more than equality would do. As noted above, Rawls understands the least advantaged group to be those least advantaged in strict economic terms, so that "all persons with less than half of the median [income] may be regarded as the least advantaged segment" (Rawls: 1999a, p. 84).

In *ASU* Nozick identifies a number of difficulties raised by Rawls's prioritization of the least advantaged group. First, it is not clear "why individuals in the original position would choose a principle that focuses on groups, rather than individuals" (p. 190). Surely, Nozick contends, the logic of the original position is for people to be concerned with the position of the least fortunate *individual* rather than the least fortunate *group*, whose members could reflect a wide range of disadvantage and unhappiness.

Second, Rawls's understanding of what constitutes the least advantaged group would seem to be quite arbitrary. Why, Nozick asks, does Rawls's definition of the least advantaged "exclude the group of depressives or alcoholics or the representative paraplegic?" (p. 190). Indeed, as Schmidtz (2006, p. 188) has recently pointed out, Rawls defines the least advantaged so as to deliberately exclude those who are really the least advantaged when he assumes that amongst the least advantaged "everyone has physical needs and psychological capacities within the normal range, so that questions of healthcare and mental capacity do not arise" (Rawls: 1999a, pp. 83–84). Rawls simply removes those individuals with the greatest physical and psychological needs – who according to many criteria almost certainly are the least advantaged – from his theory in order to avoid the complications that they would present for the solution that he wishes to derive.

Third, notwithstanding the identity of the least advantaged, Nozick questions the notion that people in the original position would choose to give priority to this group. Given that Rawls's theory of justice is intended to form the basis of social cooperation, and in the light of Rawls's acknowledgment that the most able may have to be incentivized to ensure their full economic participation, Nozick argues that it seems incongruous that the terms of social cooperation should so favor the least advantaged. If we assume that the least advantaged gain the most from social cooperation and the most advantaged gain the least (surely it is logical to assume that the most advantaged would be the most productive individuals or group in the absence of more widespread social cooperation) then it is not clear why agreement must be secured on terms that give additional benefit to those who already stand to gain the most from social cooperation.

As Nozick puts it, "in the name of fairness, [Rawls places] constraints upon voluntary social cooperation (and the set of holdings that arise from it) so that those already benefiting most from this general cooperation benefit even more!" (pp. 194–195). It is not clear why those in the original position would choose Rawls's particular formulation as the basis of social cooperation given the relative benefits that the most and the least advantaged can be expected to gain from social cooperation prior to any redistributive agreement.

The priority of the least advantaged is a crucial component of Rawls's theory of justice, yet in Chapter 7 of *ASU* Nozick identifies a number of unanswered questions and unjustified assumptions in Rawls's proposition that individuals in the original position under a veil of ignorance would choose to prioritize this group as defined by Rawls.

7.10 CONCLUSION

Rawls's *TJ* and Nozick's *ASU* provide two of the most important contributions to contemporary debates about justice in the distribution of income and wealth. Nozick's entitlement theory of justice as exemplified in the Wilt Chamberlain example provides a striking counterpoint to Rawls's theory of justice as fairness derived from the hypothetical choices of people in the original position.

However, on Nozick's own terms redistribution of at least some of the income and wealth acquired by Chamberlain in Nozick's example may be justified if the entitlements to property that people possess at the starting point D_1 are not absolute. Given that Nozick invites the reader to imagine any distribution of income and wealth as constituting D_1 this must surely allow for an initial distribution in which entitlements to income and wealth are indeed limited, perhaps by Nozick's own proviso.

Nevertheless, Nozick does appear to have successfully demonstrated the following: (1) entitlement to justly acquired income and wealth should form at least part of any theory of justice in the distribution of income and wealth; and (2) the maintenance of any preferred pattern of distribution can only be achieved via continuous interference in the lives of individual men and women that constitutes a violation of those people's rights.

Nozick also effectively demonstrates that Rawls's theory of justice is the product of a series of assumptions that frame the question of justice in a way that produces Rawls's desired outcome. The assumptive world of Rawls's *TJ* is one from which only time-slice or end-result principles of justice of the kind preferred by Rawls could possibly emerge – historical or entitlement principles like those advocated by Nozick are precluded by Rawls's construction of the problem of distributive justice. Nozick's exposure of the assumptive world of Rawls's work would seem to weaken any claim Rawls might have to have provided a theory of justice that can serve as a blueprint for contemporary social organization. Instead, Rawls's contribution may lie in the construction of a thought experiment that shows how a particular set of assumptions leads to a particular conclusion.

Rawls is probably the most important philosophical defender of the contemporary social democratic welfare state in which income and wealth are continuously redistributed in accordance with egalitarian principles. Nozick's challenge to that model is certainly not the last word to be written on the subject of distributive justice, as Nozick himself recognized (see p. xii), but this chapter has attempted to show that it has provided a more powerful response to Rawls's work and other egalitarian theories of justice than is often recognized.

NOTES

I should like to thank Ralf Bader, Phil Parvin, and Mark Pennington for their written comments on an earlier version of this chapter. A much earlier version was presented at the 'Reappraising *Anarchy, State, and Utopia*' conference at King's College London on January 9, 2010 and I should like to thank those present for their comments. The usual caveat applies.

1. It should be stressed that Rawls believes that *unanimous* agreement of a social contract, and the reconciliation of interests that this implies, is only conceivable when contracting parties are under a veil of ignorance (see Rawls: 1999a, p. 122). In developing the notion of 'the overlapping consensus' in his later work (e.g., Rawls: 1996), Rawls seemed to move away from the idea that unanimous agreement should form the basis of legitimate political and social institutions.

2. This line of argument continues to motivate advocates of distributive justice: Anderson, for example, has relatively recently argued that it is appropriate to "regard every product of the economy as jointly produced by everyone working together," so that the economy should be regarded, "as a system of joint, cooperative production" (Anderson: 1999, p. 321).

3. More recently, Schmidtz has noted that it is understood that individual contributions are dependent upon the contributions of others, but that specific individuals do make a distinct and unique contribution to that joint production, so that individuals "contribute at the margin

(as an economist would put it) to the system of cooperative production, and, within limits, we are seen as owning our contributions, however humble they may be" (Schmidtz: 2002b, p. 255).

4. Rawls's argument for the necessity of incentives to ensure people's contribution to the social product was the subject of an extensive critique by G. A. Cohen: 2000c, ch. 8.

5. An alternative view from within the same intellectual tradition has been advanced by Schmidtz, who has argued that the notion of desert should be part of the moral justification of economic inequalities within a market economy (see Schmidtz: 2006, ch. 12). For Schmidtz, part of the moral case for the market is that the holdings people receive therein do in some sense reflect desert because people are free to pay others what they think they deserve on the basis of their performance or contribution. Hence, according to Schmidtz, *part* of the Wilt Chamberlain example is that the spectators who each paid 25 cents to see Chamberlain play believed that he deserved that extra income and were free to act accordingly. Schmidtz goes on to argue that if desert did not play some role in a market economy then the market would have few defenders. For Schmidtz, the judgment as to who deserves what is one that individuals make in their daily economic interactions, rather than one made by an overarching political authority. As such, Schmidtz seems to avoid the trap that Hayek foresaw, while highlighting an important moral dimension of a market economy.

8 The right to distribute

The examples in *Anarchy, State, and Utopia* (*ASU*) are among the most arresting ever constructed by a philosopher: the experience machine, Wilt Chamberlain, the distribution of mates, the distribution of grades, and pouring tomato juice in the ocean. Provocative though his examples have proven to be, they still strike me as somewhat underappreciated. This chapter reflects mainly on the second part of Nozick's book. There is some criticism here, and some extending to be sure, but my main purpose is simply to reconstruct some of Nozick's most important insights about justice.

8.1 RAWLS'S EXPERIENCE MACHINE

The agenda for contemporary philosophical works on justice was set in the 1970s by John Rawls and Robert Nozick. Nozick said: "Political philosophers now must either work within Rawls's theory or explain why not" (p. 183). There is truth in the compliment; yet when it came to explaining why not, no one did more than Nozick.

Rawls sought to model justice as a kind of fairness. Many sorts of things can be fair. Evaluations can be fair, or not. *Shares* can be fair, or not. As Rawls modeled the intuition behind his departure from strict egalitarianism, we initially assume we are entitled to an equal share of the pie, but realize we can make the pie bigger by encouraging each other to work harder. We encourage each other by rewarding efforts to make the pie bigger: offering more pie to those who do more work. In effect, we allow inequalities if and when doing so makes us better off. I call this the Precursor.

PRECURSOR: Inequalities are to be arranged to the advantage of everyone affected: everyone should get more than what *would have been* an equal share in a more equal but less productive scheme.[1]

What I call the precursor is "at best an incomplete principle for ordering distributions" (Rawls: 1999b, p. 135). It tells us that departures from equal shares are just only if they make everyone better off. However, "there are indefinitely many ways in which all may be advantaged when the initial arrangement of equality is taken as a benchmark. How then are we to choose among these possibilities?" (Rawls: 1971, p. 65). Rawls's way of completing the precursor is to target one position and maximize the prospects of persons in that position. Which position should be so favored? Some would pick those who bake the pie in the first place. Rawls picks the least advantaged – the group to which life has otherwise been least kind. Roughly, we make the smallest share as big as it can be. We thus arrive at the difference principle.

DIFFERENCE PRINCIPLE: Inequalities are to be arranged to the greatest advantage of the least advantaged.

8.1.1 The least advantaged class

Who are the least advantaged? First, Rawls is referring not to a least advantaged person but to a least advantaged class. Second, the class is identified by wealth and income, not by any other demographic.[2] In Rawls's theory, "least advantaged" refers in practice to unskilled laborers, typical representatives of the lowest income class, no more, no less.[3] Their disadvantages and needs are not unusual but are instead stipulated to be "within the normal range" (Rawls: 1999a, p. 83).

Why use a name like "least advantaged" to refer to people who are not literally the least advantaged? Rawls is trying to walk a fine line. He wants to articulate an ideal of justice that not only embodies compassion, but also reciprocity, thus separating his theory from utilitarianism. (He wants not only to say utilitarianism attaches too little weight to the least advantaged, but that it attaches weight for the wrong reason.) "The first problem of justice concerns the relations among those who in the everyday course of things are full and active participants in society" (Rawls: 1999a, p. 84). The least advantaged, as Rawls defines them, are least advantaged *workers*, not least advantaged *people*. They claim a share of the social product because they contribute, not because they need. "The least advantaged are not, if all goes well, the unfortunate and unlucky – objects of our charity and compassion, much less our pity – but those to whom reciprocity is owed" (Rawls: 2001, p. 139). So, I said above that some would treat the pie as belonging to those who baked it. As we see here, Rawls in some of his writings appears to be among them.

8.1.2 Strains of commitment

Is the least advantaged the only class that matters? Taken at face value, the difference principle says that (to borrow Rawls's example) if we can make the least advantaged better off in the amount of one penny, we must do so even when the cost to others is a billion dollars. To say the least, this "seems extraordinary" (Rawls: 1971, p. 157). However, Rawls says, "the difference principle is not intended to apply to such abstract possibilities" (Rawls: 1971, p. 157).[4] Whether the principle applies, though, has nothing to do with whether the possibility is abstract. For that matter, whether the principle applies has nothing to do with whether Rawls *intended* it to apply. Suppose Joe says: "There are no two-digit prime numbers." Jane asks: "What about eleven?" Joe responds: "The principle is not intended to apply to such abstract possibilities." Obviously, Joe has to do better. So does Rawls, but better answers are available.

First, Rawls did not intend to impose excessive "strains of commitment" (see Rawls: 2001, p. 104). We must not ask so much as to make compliance unlikely. Rawls mainly has in mind not asking too much of the less advantaged, but in any case what is most vital is that the system not ask too much of those whose contributions are most vital. Pushing them so hard that they emigrate – because we tried to take a billion, or because by the time the appropriation worked its way through various committees only a penny would have been left for less advantaged – would be bad for all, including the less advantaged.

Second, although the principle applies to "abstract" possibilities, it does not apply to case-by-case redistribution, but only to a choice of society's basic structure. Is this restriction ad hoc, as Rawls's critics often say?[5] No! Why not? Because applying the principle to every decision, as if Joe should never earn or spend a dollar until he can prove that doing so is to the greatest benefit of the least advantaged, would cripple an economy, hurting everyone, including the least advantaged. The difference principle rules out institutions that work to the detriment of the least advantaged, including institutions that overzealously *apply the difference principle* to the detriment of the least advantaged. Crucially, then, this constraint is not ad hoc. It derives straightforwardly from the difference principle itself.

8.1.3 The veil of ignorance

The core principles of Rawls's theory are these:

1. Each person is equally entitled to the most extensive sphere of liberty compatible with a like liberty for all.
2. Social and economic inequalities are to be arranged so that they are (a) to the greatest advantage of the least advantaged, and (b) attached to offices and positions open to all under conditions of fair equality of opportunity. (Rawls: 1971, p. 302)[6]

Rawls says the first principle takes precedence, where precedence "means that liberty can be restricted only for the sake of liberty itself" (Rawls: 1971, p. 244). Nozick does not quarrel with the first principle, and few do.[7] The controversy surrounds the second, particularly part (a), known as the difference principle.

It is easy to envision *skilled* workers objecting to the difference principle, saying: "You *imagine* us negotiating terms of cooperation, then conclude that *fairness* is about someone else getting *as much as possible*? We never asked you to see us as self-made Robinson Crusoes, only that you grant that our growing up in 'your' society does not affect our standing as separate persons, and by itself gives you no claim whatever to any skills we bring to the table." Rawls, in essence, has two replies.[8]

8.1.4 The lottery

First, Rawls argues, skilled workers are wrong to see themselves as mere means to the ends of the less advantaged. Workers make this mistake if they see their skills as part of them rather than as accidents that befell them. When skilled workers reconceive themselves as undeserving winners in a genetic and social lottery, they will see the distribution of skill as a common asset. They will not see themselves as bringing *anything* to the table, other than their interests. That turns Rawls's original position into an implicit answer to the question posed by Nozick's experience machine. Nozick asks us to imagine an experience machine (roughly, a "Matrix" is what we would call it today) that would lead us to believe we are living as good a life as a human being could live. Nozick asks us to reflect on whether we would hesitate to plug in, leaving aside any concerns about the machine functioning as advertised. Most of us would hesitate. What does that reveal about what we want out of life, aside from mere experience? Nozick's answer is that we want to be *agents*. We want to *do* things, not just experience them. The accent here is on our separateness as producers.

Rawls's original position hints at a different answer, because in a crucial way it treats people as if the important thing about them is what they experience; that is, the bundle of primary goods they take away from the table. What agents *bring* to the table – what they can do in the future and what they have so far – is deemed arbitrary from a moral point of view.[9] Although it may be no more than a difference of emphasis, the accent in Rawls, by contrast with Nozick, is on our separateness as consumers.

If we agree that principles of justice must respect what disadvantaged people *do*, we will be agreeing not only to respect what disadvantaged people do *from now on*, on the grounds that respecting them is in their interest. We will be choosing to respect what they have been doing all along. Otherwise, our attitude toward them is a patronizing and paternalistic simulation of respect, not the real thing.

8.1.5 In a just society, class structure is not rigid

A second reason to see the difference principle as less biased toward the least advantaged than it may appear is that "least advantaged" is a fluid category. If Joe starts as least advantaged, a system that serves him well eventually puts him in a better position than Jane, at which point the system turns to doing what it can for Jane, until she is sufficiently well off to make it someone else's turn, and so on.

Problem: is this fluidity real? Yes, or at least, it would be real in a society satisfying Rawls's difference principle. When Karl Marx was writing in the mid nineteenth century, Europe divided into rather rigid social classes, defined by birth. When Rawls began writing in the 1950s, Marxism was still influential among intellectuals, and Marxists tended to speak as if things had not changed. *If* we lived in a rigid caste society where sons of manual workers were fated to be manual workers (and their sisters were fated to be wives of manual workers), *then* their best bet would be to set a minimum wage as high as possible without going so far as to make it unprofitable to hire them.

Now suppose a worker has an alternative: emigrate to a fluid society where manual work pays less than it might, but where his sons and daughters can go to college and be upwardly mobile. Does he stay or go? Should what poor people want out of life affect our thinking about what is to their advantage?

Consider this: in a more fluid world, higher income classes can consist substantially of people who once were (or whose parents were) manual workers themselves. Higher income classes, accordingly, can consist substantially of people advantaged *because* they grew up in a world where people born poor – as they were – had a chance to move up.

In a vertically mobile society, there is a big difference between unskilled workers who have what it takes to move up and unskilled workers who, for whatever reason, do not. But note: this is a big difference *only* in vertically mobile societies. Behind the veil of ignorance, we have not yet chosen to create a vertically mobile society; within Rawls's framework, these subgroups have similar prospects *until we decide otherwise*. Behind the veil, we *decide* whether to tolerate talented young people being stopped cold by accidents of gender or class.

This fluidity is not what Rawls had in mind. Rawls was not envisioning a world where working-class Joe can acquire skills that will make him wealthy later in life. But *if* that fluid world is best for Joe, *then* (and only then) Rawls is right that what works for Joe works for every class. What would make Rawls right about that world is that higher income classes would contain large numbers of people who started (or whose parents started) as Joe did and made the most of the opportunity. If income mobility *is* to the benefit of younger people who earn less, then it *was* to the benefit of older people who once earned low wages themselves, then moved up. (Nozick's critics want to portray Nozick as defending the rich, but in his own mind Nozick, himself born poor, was defending the legitimacy of a poor person's dream of a better life.)

8.1.6 Fairness or security?

It comes down to a question: Are fairness and security the same thing? If not, which is the difference principle supposed to concern? If the answer is fairness, then if we ask which basic structure is best for the least advantaged, it *may* turn out to be one guaranteeing the highest minimum wage. Or the best system may, without guaranteeing much of anything, offer people the best chance to upgrade their skills and thereby earn more than they would in a system with higher minimum wages but less upward mobility. This is settled more by experience than by theorizing.

In the end, there also is something to say on behalf of Rawls's insistence that we talk of classes, not individuals. There is a cliché: a rising tide lifts all boats. This cliché, as Rawls knew, is not literally true, but the kind of society we want to live in is the kind of society that makes it roughly true. Rawls saw that even in the system he favors, people would fall through the cracks. The tide will never benefit literally every person, but good institutions can and do make it true that the tide lifts all income *classes*. (Even this is hard to guarantee, though. Rawls is being realistic when he says that even in his favored system, we could only "hope that an underclass will not exist; or, if there is a small such class, that it is the result of social conditions we do not know how to change" [Rawls: 2001, p. 140].) Even the least advantaged class shares in the tide of health benefits (life expectancy, safe water, immunizations) and wealth benefits (electricity, shoes) created by cooperation. If all goes well, that is, if Rawls's difference principle (or his precursor) is satisfied, whole classes will not be left behind by the tide people create when they contribute their talents to cooperative ventures in a free society.[10]

8.2 NOZICK'S PATTERN

Nozick distinguished historical from patterned principles of justice. The distinction is simple on the surface, but by the time we reach the end of Nozick's discussion, the two categories have become at least three, perhaps four, and not so easily kept separate. Some of Nozick's statements are hard to interpret, but the following is roughly what Nozick meant.

Current time-slice principles assess a distribution at a given moment. We look at an array of outcomes. It does not matter to whom those outcomes attach. For example, on an egalitarian time-slice principle, if the outcomes are unequal, that is all we need to know in order to know we have injustice. We do not need to know who got which outcome, or how they got it. History does not matter at all.

End-state principles say something similar, but without stipulating that the outcomes are time slices. So, for example, an egalitarian end-state principle could say we look at lifetime income; if lifetime incomes are unequal, that is all we need to know. The difference between time-slice and end-state principles is this. Suppose the Smiths and Joneses have the same jobs at the same factory, but the Joneses are three years older, started working three years earlier, and continually get pay raises in virtue of their seniority that the Smiths will not get for another three years. At no time are wages equal, yet lifetime income evens out. We have injustice by an egalitarian time-slice principle, but an end-state principle can look beyond time slices to conclude that the equality required by justice will be achieved.

Patterned principles include both of the above as subsets or examples, but within the broader class are patterns that are neither time-slice nor end-state. "Equal pay for equal work" is an example of an egalitarian principle that is patterned but neither end-state nor time-slice; it prescribes what outcomes should *track*, in this case the quality and/or quantity of labor inputs, but does not prescribe that outcomes be equal.

Historical principles say what matters is the process by which outcomes arise. Historical principles are complex because, notwithstanding Nozick's intended contrast, patterned principles can have a historical element, and vice versa. "Equal pay for equal work" is both patterned and historical; that is, it prescribes outcomes tracking a pattern of what people have done.

Nozick classifies Rawls's difference principle as patterned but not historical (it prescribes a distribution without asking who brought what to the table.) By contrast, what Nozick calls *entitlement theory* is historical but not patterned.

The problem with patterned principles is that, in Nozick's words, liberty upsets patterns. "No end-state principle or distributional patterned principle of justice can be continuously realized without continuous interference with people's lives" (p. 163). To illustrate, Nozick asks you to imagine that society achieves a pattern of perfect justice by the lights of whatever principle you prefer. Then someone offers Wilt Chamberlain 25 cents for the privilege of watching Wilt play basketball (see pp. 161–164).[11] Before we know it, thousands of people are paying Wilt 25 cents each, every time Wilt puts on a show. Wilt gets rich. The distribution is no longer equal, and no one complains. Moreover, we are all a bit like Wilt. Every time we earn a dollar, or spend one, we change the pattern. Nozick's question: If justice is a pattern, achievable at a given moment, what happens if you achieve perfection? Must you then prohibit everything – no further consuming, creating, trading, or even *giving* – so as not to upset the perfect pattern? Notice: Nozick neither argues nor presumes people can do whatever they want with their property. Nozick's point is, if there is *anything at all* people can do – even if the only thing they are free to do is give a coin to an entertainer – then even that tiniest of liberties will, over time, disturb the pattern (see pp. 161–164).[12] Entitlement principles recognize realms of choice that time-slice principles cannot recognize.[13] None of the resources governed by time-slice principles would ever be at a person's (or even a whole nation's) disposal (see p. 167).[14]

But not all patterned principles are prescriptions for time slices. There are passages where Nozick seems to assume that in arguing against end-state or time-slice principles, he is undermining patterned principles more generally. Not so. Not all patterns are the same, and not all require major interference. Nozick is right that if we focus on time slices, we focus on isolated moments, and take moments too seriously, when what matters is not the pattern of holdings at a moment but the pattern of how people treat each other over time. Even tiny liberties must upset the pattern of a static moment, but there is no reason why liberty must upset an ongoing pattern of fair treatment.

A moral principle forbidding racial discrimination, for example, prescribes no particular end state. Such a principle is what Nozick calls weakly patterned, sensitive to history as well as to pattern, and prescribing an ideal of how people should be treated without prescribing an end-state distribution (see p. 164). It *affects* the pattern (as would even a purely historical principle) without *prescribing* a pattern (or more precisely, without prescribing an end state). And if a principle forbidding racial discrimination works its way into a society via cultural progress rather than legal intervention, it need not involve any interference whatsoever.

If we achieve a society where Martin Luther King's dream comes true, and his children are judged not by the color of their skin but by the content of their character, what we achieve is a fluid, evolving pattern tracking merit rather than skin color. In the process, society comes to require far *less* intervention than the relentlessly coercive, segregated society from which it evolved. So, although Nozick sometimes speaks as if his critique applies to all patterns, we should take seriously his concession that "weak" patterns are compatible with liberty. Some may promote liberty, depending on how they are introduced and maintained. The problem is not with patterned principles in general but more specifically with end-state and especially time-slice principles.

A weakness in Nozick's critique of Rawls, then, is this. Nozick is right that time-slice principles license immense and constant interference with everyday life, the interference tends to distort exchange relationships and to require further layers of regulation that accumulate like barnacles, and progress eventually suffocates under the weight. But is Rawls defending such a view? To Rawls, the basic structure's job is not to make every transaction work to the working class's advantage, let alone each *member* of the class. Rawls was more realistic than that. Instead, it is the trend of a whole society over time that is supposed to benefit the working class *as a class*. To be sure, Rawls was a kind of egalitarian, but not a time-slice or even end-state egalitarian. The pattern Rawls meant to weave into the fabric of society was a pattern of equal status, applying not so much to a distribution as to an ongoing relationship.

It would be a mistake, though, to infer that Nozick's critique missed its target altogether. Nozick showed what an alternative theory might look like, portraying Wilt Chamberlain as a separate person in a more robust sense (unencumbered by nebulous debts to society) than Rawls could countenance. To Nozick, Wilt's advantages are not what Wilt *finds* on the table; they are what Wilt *brings* to the table. And respecting what Wilt brings to the table is the exact essence of respecting him and treating him as a separate person.

In part due to Nozick, today's egalitarians are acknowledging that any equality worthy of aspiration focuses less on justice as a property of a time-slice distribution and more on how people are treated: how workers are rewarded for their contributions and *enabled* over time (and inspired over time) to make contributions worth rewarding. This is progress.

8.3 THE ELEMENTS OF ENTITLEMENT

Nozick says an entitlement theory's principles fall into three categories. First, principles of *initial acquisition* explain how a person or group legitimately could acquire something that had no previous owner. Previously unclaimed land is a historically central example, as are inventions and other intellectual property. Second, principles of *transfer* explain how ownership legitimately is transferred from one person (or group) to another. Finally, principles of *rectification* specify what to do about cases of wrongful acquisition or transfer.

Nozick favors a version of entitlement theory, grounded in an ideal of voluntarism. Nozick says a distribution is just if it arises by just steps from a just initial position, where the paradigm of a just step is voluntary exchange. As an exemplar of the kind of society that would accord with his brand of entitlement theory, Nozick offers the ideal of a civil libertarian, free market society governed by a minimal state (roughly, a government that restricts itself to keeping the peace and defending its borders). In such a society, as people interact by consent and on mutually agreeable terms, there will be "strands" of patterns; people amass wealth in proportion to their ability to provide (more accurately, their actually providing) goods at prices that make their customers better off. Employees tend to get promotions when their talents and efforts merit promotion, and so on. However, although society will be meritocratic to that extent, that pattern will be only one among many. There will be inheritance and philanthropy, too, conferring goods on recipients who may have done nothing to deserve such gifts (see p. 158). Is that a problem? Not to Nozick. Nozick joins Rawls in denying that merit is a principle to which distributions (and transfers) must answer. The question, Nozick says, is simply whether people deal with each other in a peaceful, consensual way.[15]

Rawls says: "A distinctive feature of pure procedural justice is that the procedure for determining the just result must actually be carried out; for in these cases there is no independent criterion by reference to which a definite outcome can be known to be just" (Rawls: 1971, p. 86). By this definition, Rawls's is not a theory of pure procedural justice, but Nozick's is. To Nozick, the question is whether proper procedure was followed. So far as justice goes, that is it. There is no other question.[16]

Nozick's theory in a nutshell is that we need not preordain an outcome. We need not know what pattern will emerge from voluntary exchange. What arises from a just distribution by just steps is just. If people want to pay Wilt Chamberlain just to watch him play basketball, and if this leads to Wilt having more than others, so be it.

One thing we might say in support of Wilt having a right to live as he does, and our having a right to pay him for doing so, is that Wilt, like us, is a self-owner. After all, it is not for no reason that we speak of people's talents as *their* talents. One way or another, someone makes the call regarding how to use Wilt's athletic skill. Who, if not Wilt, has the right to make that call?

According to G. A. Cohen, liberalism's essence is that people are self-owners. Their lives are theirs; they can live as they please so long as they live in peace. As Cohen defines the terms, right-wing liberals like Nozick believe people can acquire similar rights in external objects, whereas left-wing liberals do not. How should we classify Rawls? Cohen says:

Rawls and Dworkin are commonly accounted liberals, but here they must be called something else, such as social democrats, for they are not liberals in the traditional sense just defined, since they deny self-ownership in one important way. They say that because it is a matter of brute luck that people have the talents they do, their talents do not, morally speaking, belong to them, but are, properly regarded, resources over which society as a whole may legitimately dispose. (Cohen: 2000a, p. 252)[17]

Rawls and Nozick each saw a gap between (1) saying Jane owns her talents and (2) saying Jane owns the cash value of what she produces when she puts her talent to use. Yet, Nozick thought, to take Jane seriously as a separate person is to presuppose her right to make and execute plans of her own, including plans involving the external world. To say Jane can do what she wants, needing our permission *only* if she wants to alter the external world – say, by giving a coin to an entertainer – would be to make a joke of self-ownership. So, where Rawls *embraced* the gap between (1) and (2), Nozick was struggling to *bridge* the gap when he gestured at a Lockean theory that we acquire bits of otherwise unowned external world by working on them.[18] I say "gestured" because Nozick is unsure how the theory works at the edges. Must labor add value? Must labor be strenuous? If I pour my tomato juice into the ocean, why do I not thereby come to own the ocean?[19]

With similar candor, Nozick admits he is unsure what to say about a case where, through no one's fault, a town has only one remaining water source, and Joe is the sole owner of it. If the result came about via a process that violated no one's rights, would that make the result okay?[20] At first, Joe could sell his water for whatever his customers were willing to pay. After Joe accidentally becomes a monopolist, though, Nozick is less sure. We cannot take any simple concept of property for granted here. We must ask what a community is for, how property rights (and specific ways of establishing legal title, including more or less ritualistic forms of labor-mixing) enable a community to serve its purpose, and whether the role of property rights in serving that purpose is ever superceded. Part of the point is that neither in Robert Nozick's work nor in any classical liberal's is there any suggestion that the right to property implies a correlative duty to roll over and die rather than trespass on someone's land. For the system to be stable enough to last, respecting the property system has to be a good option for just about everyone, including those who arrive too late to be part of the wave of first appropriators. And for respecting the system to be a good option for just about everyone, it has to be true that just about everyone has good options regarding how to make a living within the system. As Nozick himself acknowledges in his discussion of the last waterhole, there are strands of patterns at work here, carrying more weight than Nozick's simple story suggests.

8.3.1 *Regarding initial acquisition*

When Nozick drew our attention to a problem with what he called the Lockean Proviso, philosophical critics of private property jumped on the bandwagon. Property's critics were seduced by the Proviso because it seemingly cannot be satisfied, and thus (private) property in land cannot be justified along Lockean lines. As Judith Thomson (not herself a critic) put it, if "the first labor-mixer must literally leave as much and as good for others who come along later, then no one can come to own anything, for there are only finitely many things in the world so that every taking leaves less for others" (Thomson: 1990, p. 330). Thomson was not alone:

"We leave enough and as good for others only when what we take is not scarce" (Fried: 1995, p. 230 fn.).

"The Lockean Proviso, in the contemporary world of overpopulation and scarce resources, can almost never be met" (Held: 1980, p. 6).

"Every acquisition worsens the lot of others – and worsens their lot in relevant ways" (Bogart: 1985, p. 834).

"The condition that there be enough and as good left for others could not of course be literally satisfied by any system of private property rights" (Sartorius: 1984, p. 210).

"If the 'enough and as good' clause were a necessary condition on appropriation, it would follow that, in these circumstances, the only legitimate course for the inhabitants would be death by starvation ... since *no* appropriation would leave enough and as good in common for others" (Waldron: 1976, p. 325).

And so on. If we take something out of the cookie jar, we *must* be leaving less for others. This appears self-evident. It has to be right.

But it isn't right, for two reasons. First, it is hardly impossible – certainly not logically impossible – for a taking to leave as much for others. We can at least imagine a logically possible world of magic cookie jars in which, every time you take out one cookie, more and better cookies take its place. Second, the logically possible world I just imagined is the sort of world we actually live in. Philosophers writing about original appropriation tend to speak as if people who arrive first are luckier than those who come later. The truth is, first appropriators begin the process of resource creation; latecomers get most of the benefits. Consider America's first permanent English settlement, the Jamestown colony of 1607. (Or, if you prefer, imagine the lifestyles of people crossing the Bering Strait from Asia twelve thousand years ago. It does not affect the point at hand.) Was their situation better than ours? How so? They were never caught in rush-hour traffic jams, of course. For that matter, they never worried about being overcharged for car repairs. They never awoke in the middle of the night to the sound of noisy refrigerators, leaky faucets, or even flushing toilets. They never wasted a minute at airports waiting for delayed flights. They never had to change a light bulb. They never agonized over the choice among cellular telephone companies. They never faced the prospect of a dentist's drill. Life was simple.

Philosophers are taught to say, in effect, that original appropriators got the good stuff for free. We have to pay for ugly leftovers. But in truth, original appropriation benefits latecomers far more than it benefits original appropriators. Original appropriation is a cornucopia of wealth, but mainly for latecomers. The people who got here first literally could not even have imagined what we latecomers take for granted. Our life expectancies exceed theirs by several *decades*.

Original appropriation diminishes the stock of what can be originally appropriated, at least in the case of land, but that is not the same thing as diminishing the stock of what can be owned.[21] On the contrary, in taking control of resources and thereby removing those particular resources from the stock of goods that can be acquired by original appropriation, people typically generate massive increases in the stock of goods that can be acquired by trade. The lesson is that appropriation typically is not a zero-sum but a positive-sum game. As Locke himself stressed, it creates the possibility of mutual benefit on a massive scale. It creates the possibility of society as a cooperative venture.

The point is not merely that enough is produced in appropriation's aftermath to compensate latecomers who lost out in the race to appropriate. The point is that being an original appropriator is not the prize. The prize is prosperity, and latecomers win big, courtesy of those who arrived first. If anyone had a right to be compensated, it would be the first appropriators.

So, for twenty years following the publication of *Anarchy, State, and Utopia*, critics celebrated this seemingly gaping hole in Lockean property theory (a hole to which Nozick drew our attention). But the hole got filled, informed critics stopped talking about it, and this is another place where we have made progress.

8.3.2 Regarding transfer

In Nozick's theory, rights are trumps or side constraints, not merely weights to balance against other considerations. So, what justifies side constraints? Nozick sometimes is accused of having no foundation, of merely assuming what he needs to prove. For better or worse, Nozick borrowed Rawls's foundation, accepting Rawls's premise about the separateness and inviolability of persons, saying, the "root idea, namely, that there are different individuals with separate lives and so no one may be sacrificed for others, underlies the existence of moral side constraints" (p. 33; also see Lacey: 2001, p. 25ff.). If this is not a foundation, then Rawls has no foundation either.

Another answer (to the question of what justifies side constraints) is that some rights are prerequisites of a society being a cooperative venture for mutual advantage, partly because some rights enable people to know what to expect from each other, and to plan their lives accordingly.[22] On this view, what gives rights their *foundation* also limits their scope. Why do we have rights? Answer: because we cannot live well together unless we treat each other as having rights. Why do we have *limited* rights? Answer: because we cannot live well together unless we treat our rights as limited. That is how we know Wilt's right to enjoy his property in peace does not include a right to build biological weapons in his garage in an otherwise ordinary neighborhood.[23]

That also is how we know Wilt's right to buy a sports car does not include a right to drive through school zones as fast as he pleases (see p. 171). At some point, a community, guided by a principle that drivers must be able to get where they need to go so long as they do not impose undue risk on pedestrians, concludes that ten to twenty miles per hour is within reason, then picks something in that range. After a community posts a limit, such as fifteen miles per hour, drivers no longer have a right to judge for themselves whether twenty is within reason. From that point, pedestrians have a *right* that drivers observe the posted limit.

Such a right is a straightforward exemplar of a side constraint, and the story is an exemplar of how side constraints emerge and what they come to mean in a given society. Ordinary drivers in normal circumstances have no right to judge for themselves whether the constraint is outweighed. When the constraint applies, it applies decisively. It may, however, have limited scope. For example, the community may decide that the law does not apply to ambulances. If an ordinary driver has an emergency, such as getting his wife to the hospital, and is willing to break laws to get her there sooner, he is liable for the penalty that goes with breaking the law, although courts may at their mercy waive the penalty. If the driver was driving an ambulance, by contrast, he does not need the court's mercy. If the law does not apply to ambulances, then he was within his rights.

Nozick's version of entitlement theory embraces an ideal of voluntarism: a distribution is just if it arises by just steps (paradigmatically, voluntary exchange) from a just initial position.

I am not sure Nozick should have said that. It sets the bar high: what can a historical theory say about a world where few titles have an unblemished history? Or perhaps that is how it is; like it or not, there is no path from here to a world where distributions are just. Either way, Nozick may have been mistaken in seeing himself as addressing distributive justice per se, since his theory wants to go in a different direction: his theory is about justice as how we treat each other, not justice as cleansing the world's distributions of original sin.

In other words, the core of Nozick's theory is not as previously stated. Nozick's real claim should not be that a distribution is just if it arises by just steps from a just initial position. When Nozick said this, he obscured his real contribution. In truth, Nozick has a theory of just *transfer*, not a theory of just *distribution*: roughly, a transfer from one person to another is thoroughly just if thoroughly voluntary. The theory ultimately is not so simple, but this is its true essence.

Voluntary transfer cannot cleanse a tainted title of original sin, but any injustice in the result will have been pre-existing, not *created* by the transfer. We are fated to live in a world of background injustice, all of us descended from both victims and victimizers, so it is a virtue of Nozick's theory that it does not pretend we might achieve perfect justice if only we can "even the score." Still, it remains possible for moral agents, living ordinary lives, to abide by Nozick's principle of just transfer, and to that imperfect extent to have clean hands.

Nozick says the question, contra patterned principles, is whether a distribution results from peaceful cooperation. More accurately, to avoid encouraging our self-destructive tendency to dwell on histories of injustice, Nozick might have said the question is whether ongoing *changes* in distributions result from peaceful cooperation.

8.3.3 Regarding rectification

G. A. Cohen sees a problem for anyone who, like Nozick, believes in property rights on the grounds that they embody a commitment to peaceful cooperation. First I will explain the problem, and then explain what Cohen's insight tells us about the limits of our right to rectify historical injustice.

Cohen's view is that enforcing property rights is as coercive as robbery. Property rights require us not to initiate force. Governments back that requirement with a threat of force, but that very threat is itself an initiation of force.

"I want, let us say, to pitch a tent in your large back garden, perhaps just in order to annoy you, or perhaps for the more substantial reason that I have nowhere to live and no land of my own, but I have got hold of a tent, legitimately or otherwise. If I now do this thing that I want to do, the chances are that the state will intervene on your behalf. If it does, I shall suffer a constraint on my freedom" (Cohen: 1995, p. 56).

To Cohen: "The banal truth is that, if the state prevents me from doing something that I want to do, then it places a restriction on my freedom" (Cohen: 1995, p. 55). His "general point is that incursions against private property which *reduce* owners' freedom by transferring rights over resources to non-owners thereby *increase* the latter's freedom. In advance of further argument, the net effect on freedom of the resource transfer is indeterminate" (Cohen: 1995, p. 57).

There is no denying Cohen's basic point: even when the state is trying to protect our freedom, its methods are coercive. We would be wrong to infer from this, though, that the net amount of freedom does not change, or even that we will have a problem discerning a change. Cohen's example concerns your garden. What if he were asking not about control of your garden but of your body – about me enslaving you? Would my enslaving you make me more and you less free, with indeterminate net effect?[24] Cohen might agree, the answer is no, but then remind us he was talking about your garden, not your body. Moreover, he never said there is no net effect, only that we would need further argument to discern a net effect. So, if we suppose Cohen's point covers only external goods, such as your title to your garden, what further argument would make the net effect on freedom easier to discern?

Here is a suggestion. What if we treat Cohen's claim not as a conceptual analysis but as a testable empirical hypothesis, then compare countries where property titles are stable with countries where they are not? In Zimbabwe (at the time of writing), Robert Mugabe and his army have been pitching tents wherever they please, and anyone unlucky enough to find Mr. Mugabe in his or her back garden would rather be elsewhere. No one who knows the unfolding catastrophe that is Zimbabwe could believe that as Zimbabwe's property rights crumble, it merely trades one freedom for another, with indeterminate net effect.

Closer to home, my freedom to drive through a green light comes at a cost of your freedom to drive through a red. Is anything indeterminate about the net effect? Not at all. And property rights manage traffic on our possessions roughly as traffic lights manage traffic on our roads.[25] Both systems help us to form expectations about other people's behavior, and to plan accordingly. A good system of traffic regulation makes everyone more free to go where they wish, even those who currently face red lights. Of course, the red light that some face must turn green from time to time. Further, those who wait must be alert enough to notice when lights turn green. If people are asked to wait forever, or even think they are, the system will break down.

Traffic laws help us to stay out of each other's way. Property laws let us do more; they also help us to engage in trade, with the result that our traffic (our trucking and bartering) leaves fellow travelers not only unimpeded but enriched. The traffic of a healthy economy is something to celebrate, not merely tolerate.

Cohen says lack of money is lack of freedom (see Cohen: 1995, p. 58). Cohen also says having money is like having a ticket one can exchange for various things. And, he adds, having such a ticket is a freedom. Let us be clear, though, that on Cohen's analysis, freedom is access to *real* wealth, not merely to pieces of paper offered as a symbol of stored value. A government cannot create more seats in a stadium just by printing more tickets, and likewise cannot create more wealth just by printing more currency. Work creates wealth, and this is not merely a theoretical possibility but is instead our actual history, wherever property rights are stable. If Cohen is right to equate wealth with freedom (and if Cohen is not entirely right about this, he is not entirely wrong either), then a world of stable property rights is not zero-sum. Where property rights are treated with respect, we find that nearly all are wealthier – which is to say, more free in Cohen's sense – than their grandparents were.[26]

It is in the context of rectification that Cohen's claim (that protecting property is coercive) has great practical relevance. When victims and victimizers are long dead, and nothing can be done short of transferring property from one innocent descendent to another, that is when enforcing rights by rectifying an ancient history of unjust transfers really does start to look like an initiation of force.

Cohen did not intend his point to apply most especially to this aspect of rights enforcement; yet this is its most poignant and plausible application. Should we enforce property rights of long dead victims at the expense of people who have not themselves initiated force, and who themselves will turn out to descend from victims if we go back far enough?[27]

Richard Epstein says: "Any system of property looks backward to determine the 'chain of title' that gives rise to present holdings. But this is not because of any fetish with the past but chiefly from the profound sense that stability in transactions is necessary for sensible forward-looking planning" (Epstein: 2003, p. 130). Dwelling too much on the past is wrong for the same reason that ignoring the past altogether is wrong: excess in *either* direction reduces stability in transactions, thus making it harder to go forward in peace. A routine title search when buying a house (to verify that the seller's holding of the deed is in fact uncontested) is one thing; going back as many centuries as the land has been occupied is another.

If we must return a wallet seized from a previous owner, must we also make sure the previous owner did not seize the wallet in turn? Nozick envisions a civil libertarian society where we carry on from where we are, in peace. Yet we cannot carry on in peace unless there is a limit on our obligation to undo the past. There are places where people have been "evening the score" for centuries, and the cycle of mutual destruction will not stop until people *aim* to leave the past behind. The point is to make amends, but for making amends to work, there has to be uptake: victims and their descendents, for their own sakes, have to embrace the aim of achieving closure. Descendants of victims, for their own sakes, must accept that guilt is not a weapon to be used against a perpetrator's descendents forever.

8.4 ARBITRARY

Nozick thought a bias against respecting separate persons lurks in the very idea of *distributive* justice. The idea leads people to see goods as having been distributed by a mechanism for which we are responsible. Nozick believes there generally is no such mechanism and no such responsibility. "There is no more a distributing or distribution of shares than there is a distributing of mates in a society in which persons choose whom they shall marry" (p. 150).[28]

The lesson: If we have a license to distribute X, then we ought to distribute X fairly, and Rawls gave us a theory about how to do that. However, we lack a license to distribute mates. Therefore, we have no right to distribute mates unfairly, and neither do we have a right to distribute mates *fairly*. They are not ours to distribute.

More generally, to show that I have a right to distribute X according to a given plan, we may at some stage need to show that my plan is fair, but before that, we need to show that X's distribution falls within my jurisdiction. In effect, Rawls's principles do not start at the start. Rawls's principles tell us how to distribute X (inequalities), given that X's distribution is our business. But the latter is not a given.

Rawls speaks of mitigating the arbitrary effects of luck in the natural lottery (see Rawls: 1971, pp. 74–75). Is there a difference between a lottery Jane wins by luck of the draw, and a lottery rigged to make sure Jane wins? Is there a difference between Joe turning out to be less skilled than Jane, versus a situation where Joe deliberately is held back so as to *make sure* Jane will be more skilled? As one way of motivating his two principles, Rawls says, "[o]nce we decide to look for a conception of justice that *nullifies* the accidents of natural endowment and the contingencies of social circumstance ... we are led to these principles. They express the result of leaving aside those aspects of the social world that seem arbitrary" (Rawls: 1971, p. 15, emphasis added).

Arbitrary? The word has two meanings. Natural distributions can be arbitrary, meaning *random*. Or choices can be arbitrary, meaning *capricious*. In one case, no choice is made. In the other, an unprincipled choice is made.[29] There is a difference. In fair lotteries, winners are chosen at random. A *rigged* lottery is unfair because it *fails* to be arbitrary in the benign sense. It is by *failing* to be arbitrary in the benign sense that it *counts* as arbitrary in the bad sense. What of the natural lottery, then? The natural lottery is arbitrary in the benign sense, but how does that connect to being unfair in the way capricious choice is unfair?

It doesn't. Rawls says: "Intuitively, the most obvious injustice of the system of natural liberty is that it permits distributive shares to be improperly influenced by these factors so arbitrary from a moral point of view" (Rawls: 1971, p. 72). However, when "arbitrary" means random, as it does in this passage, there is no connection between being arbitrary and being improper. Capricious choice wears impropriety on its sleeve; the natural lottery does not. Had Joe's mother assigned Jane all the talent, deliberately leaving Joe with none, we might at least wonder why. In fact, though, Joe's mother did not assign him less talent. It just happened. It was chance, not caprice.

Put it this way: life is about playing the hand you are dealt. Being dealt a bad hand is not the same as facing a stacked deck. A deck is stacked only if a dealer deliberately stacks it, declining to leave the matter to chance.

8.4.1 The natural lottery

Rawls says: "We are led to the difference principle if we wish to arrange the basic social structure so that no one gains (or loses) from his luck in the natural lottery of talent and ability, or from his initial place in society without giving (or receiving) compensating advantages in return" (Rawls: 1999a, p. 140).[30] Interestingly, Rawls took the trouble to put "or loses" in parentheses, signaling that in his mind gaining is a problem all by itself, and may even be the main problem. But if a life-extending mutation appears in a population, should we arrange basic structure so no one gains from the mutation? No! Gaining is good. There is a problem if Jane gains at Joe's expense, but then the problem is still with the losing, not the gaining.

To Rawls, "it is not just that some should have less *in order* that others may prosper" (Rawls: 1971, p. 15, emphasis added). I agree. Yet, as noted, a natural lottery is not a stacked deck but a random shuffle. No one is dealt a bad hand in order that others may prosper. On the other hand, if someone *had* stacked the deck, deliberately assigning to Joe a lazy character and no talent, we would want to know why, but in any case the reason would not be so "others may prosper." Joe's being untalented is no help to others. On the contrary, if we sought to assign to Joe a talent level that would help others prosper, we would need to assign to Joe *more* talent, not less. Making Joe a provider of high-quality services would help others prosper, and that is what would give us a real reason to compensate him.

One way (the only way I know of) to rationalize the idea that *Jane's* being more talented entitles *Joe* to compensation is to suppose that life is like a zero-sum poker game in which the more talented Jane is, the less chance Joe has of winning. If Jane is more talented, Jane captures more pie, and captures more at Joe's expense. However, this is not what Rawls is imagining. It is Rawls's point, after all, that society is not a zero-sum card game, but a cooperative venture in which the pie's size is variable. Almost everyone can have a better life than they could have had on their own, and the reason is simple: other people's talents make all of us better off. Talented bakers don't *capture* the pie. They *make* it.[31] The rest of us have more pie, not less, when talented people put their talent to work.

The natural lottery is not zero-sum. When a baby is born with a cleft palate, it is not "in order that others may prosper." When the next baby is born healthy, needing no special care, the second baby's health does not come at the first baby's expense.[32] Rawls says it is unjust that some should have less so that others may prosper, but the first baby does not have a cleft palate so that the second baby may prosper.

Rawls says: "The natural distribution is neither just nor unjust; nor is it unjust that persons are born into society at some particular position. These are simply natural facts. What is just and unjust is the way that institutions deal with these facts" (Rawls: 1971, p. 102). If Rawls is right, then when institutions "deal with natural facts," they are not undoing wrongs.

A distribution of talent per se is not a problem, solvable or otherwise. But even if, as Rawls says, there is no injustice in a natural distribution, there may yet be a problem. Being born with a cleft palate is a problem. The problem is not that a cleft palate is unjust but that it is bad. Its badness gives us some reason to intervene so as to fix the problem.

But note the real issue: we are not trying to fix an *improper distribution* of cleft palates. We are trying to fix cleft palates.

8.5 DEBTS TO SOCIETY AND THE PROBLEM OF DOUBLE COUNTING

We are better off with society than without it. We also are better off with the sun than without it. What does that imply? Is the sun doing us a favor? Is society? Beyond the simple fact of our being vastly better off living together than we would be living apart, what else would have to be true in order for us to have an unpaid debt to society?

Needless to say, in addition to benefits we receive from specific trades, we all benefit from living in a productive, prosperous society. Is our living in such a society somehow an extra benefit, on top of what we receive from each other in trade? Would that mean we have some unpaid debt? If so, what would repay it? Have we already repaid by participating in the same trades through which our partners receive – at the same time as they, like you, help to create – those very same background benefits? Might we still have some amorphous duty to repay society even after every member of society has (like us) been paid in full for services rendered?

My point is not that answers to these questions are obvious. Rather, I am saying that however we answer these questions, in search of foundations for obligations to society, we need to be careful not to double count. It is not as if a worker who shows up for work every day and does the best she can has so far only been *taking*. We need to keep in mind that, just as the trade of millions of people adds value to our lives, so too does our trade add value to millions of lives in return. It would be a mistake to discount either side of this equation. Wilt's discounting what others contribute to his life is bad, but no worse than our discounting what

Wilt contributes to the lives of others in return; both are instances of the same mistake.

We sometimes speak as if the only way to "give back" to society is by paying taxes, but any decent mechanic does more for society by fixing cars than by paying taxes. If that is not obvious, consider Thomas Edison. There is no amount that Edison could have paid in taxes that would have begun to compare with what Edison contributed to society when he gave us the light bulb. We gave Edison a vast fortune, but what we gave Edison was nothing compared with what Edison gave us.

8.5.1 If it is your talent, should you get all the benefits?

Why should talented people get *all* the benefits that accrue from exercising their talents?

The question is a moot point, based on a false premise, because competitive markets ensure that people do not get all the benefits. Competitive markets give people a better option: the option of cooperating, thereby setting in motion far-reaching ripples of mutual benefit. Life expectancy nearly *doubled* in the course of a single, tragedy-filled, yet technologically (and in some ways culturally) progressive century, and for all we know may continue to rise in the century to come. Free societies make progress. They do not make progress without people like Thomas Edison (whose light bulbs surely contributed to the increase in life expectancy) but on the other hand, free societies tend to produce people like Edison.

Wilt normally has to bring something to the market before he can take anything away. Not everyone likes this fact about markets, but it would be inconsistent to note this fact and then go on to say Wilt ought to give something back, as if he had not already given. This is not to say Edison would be mistaken to think about his legacy, and thus about how he might give back even more. The mistake would lie in thinking that if Edison is better off, he must not yet have done his share.[33]

That *Edison* is better off for participating in society is not what determines whether he is in debt. Whether he is in debt depends on whether *society* is better off in turn. If Edison participates in networks of mutual benefit, then by that very fact, he is more or less doing his share to constitute and sustain those networks.

8.6 CONCLUSION

Nozick meant to treat voluntarism as grounding a theory of just transfer. He gestured at how to get unowned resources into the realm of what can be voluntarily transferred. He also gestured at the idea that some part of justice is concerned with undoing wrongful transfers. However, to Nozick, the point of undoing wrongful transfers is simply to undo wrongful transfers, and not to make current holdings match a favored pattern.

For example, sometimes justice is about returning a stolen wallet to the person from whom it was stolen. Why return the wallet to that person? Not to restore a previously fair pattern but to restore the wallet to the person from whom it was stolen. Sometimes, justice is about *returning* the wallet, not *distributing* it. The wallet's history trumps any thoughts about how it might best be distributed.

NOTES

This essay is a major revision of Part 6 of my *Elements of Justice*. I also borrow in minor ways from "Institution of Property" in my *Person, Polis, Planet*, and from my essay "Introductions" in *Robert Nozick*. I wish to thank Ralf Bader, Martin Cox, Barbara Fried, Chandran Kukathas, Eric Mack, John Meadowcroft, Michael Otsuka, Patrick Tomlin, and Peter Vallentyne for helpful feedback.

1. See Rawls: 1971, pp. 60 and 62. In addition to entering Rawls's argument as the difference principle's logical precursor, what I call the precursor was temporally prior too, appearing in Rawls's writing as early as 1958. Amazingly, in his first published statement of the two principles of justice, the second principle is not the difference principle! It is closer to what I call the precursor. Here is the passage: "The conception of justice which I want to develop may be stated in the form of two principles as follows: first, each person participating in a practice, or affected by it, has an equal right to the most extensive liberty compatible with a like liberty for all; and second, inequalities are arbitrary unless it is reasonable to expect that they will work out for everyone's advantage, and provided the positions and offices to which they attach, or from which they may be gained, are open to all."

See Rawls's "Justice as Fairness" (Rawls: 1999b, p. 48; 1st pub. 1958).
See also "Constitutional Liberty and the Concept of Justice" (Rawls: 1999b, p. 76; 1st pub. 1963).

2. This assumes basic rights are secure for all. For example, no class is disadvantaged in virtue of being enslaved (see Rawls: 2001, p. 59 n.).

3. Cf. Rawls: 1999b, p. 139; Rawls: 1971, p. 98; Rawls: 2001, p. 59.

4. Rawls offers two further answers. First, the difference principle is prevented from applying to such questions by lexically prior principles of justice. Second, the problem tends not to arise in practice because "in a competitive economy (with or without private ownership) with an open class system excessive inequalities will not be the rule ... Great disparities will not long persist" (Rawls: 1971, p. 86).

5. Most prominently, see Cohen: 2000c.

6. Rawls sometimes adds to part (a) a qualification that the difference principle must be consistent with a principle of just savings.

7. In a little-noted passage, Rawls retracts the idea that his first principle has "lexical" priority: "While it seems clear that, in general, a lexical order cannot be strictly correct, it may be an illuminating approximation under certain special though significant conditions" (Rawls: 1971, p. 45). Rawls likewise retracts the claim that the first principle calls literally for a "most extensive" system of liberty, indeed going so far as to say: "No priority is assigned to liberty as such, as if the exercise of something called 'liberty' has a preeminent value " (Rawls: 1996, p. 291). See also Rawls: 2001, p. 42. For a critique of Rawls's retreat from the original maximalist formulation, see Lomasky: 2005.

8. The initial technical move here is a device for helping us to imagine what it would be like for an arrangement to be fair, that is, leaving no one with grounds for complaint. Suppose Jane assesses alternative distributions from behind a *veil of ignorance,* not knowing which position in the distribution she will occupy. If Jane has no idea whether she is a manual worker or a mid-level manager, she will not try to bias the arrangement in favor of managers. She will seek an option that is good for all. The idea is that Rawls imagines her picking is what anyone would imagine themselves picking.

In a later essay, Rawls took a different approach, saying the contractarian thought experiment was a dispensable heuristic for envisioning what it would be like (in Kantian terms) to strip away our contingent phenomenal characteristics and choose as pure noumenal selves. Since our noumenal selves are identical – mere tokens of the essence of rationality – negotiation is superfluous, and the veil of ignorance now models how a single noumenal self would choose. This avoids problems with hypothetical bargaining but abandons the contractarian commitment to explicitly building respect for the separateness of persons into the theory's foundation. See "Kantian Constructivism in Moral Theory" in Rawls: 1999b, 1st pub. 1980.

9. Rawls would defend himself here by insisting that what agents do of course matters in some sense, but not in a sense that bears on grounding principles of distributive justice.

10. We can imagine Rawls saying nation Y is just only if its government officially dedicates itself to satisfying Rawls's principles. (Rawls comes close to saying this in Rawls: 2001, pp. 137 and 162. See also Brennan: 2007.) But this would be refuted by the same argument by which Rawls refutes strict egalitarianism: namely, if X were better for all, rational agents would choose X over Y regardless of whether system X is less equal, makes fewer promises, or has a different declared aim.

Meadowcroft says: "even though the unequal distribution of income and wealth produced by a market economy bears no relation to need or desert, and is not combined with equality of opportunity, it should nevertheless be considered just because it meets the only relevant moral criterion: procedural justice" (Meadowcroft: 2005, p. 56). I suppose that Meadowcroft is not speaking literally when he says market outcomes bear no relation to need or desert. What he means is that market outcomes are not guaranteed to bear any relation. If workers did not as a matter of fact tend to get what they need, the market would have virtually no defenders. If workers did not tend to get what they deserve – for example, if their employers did not tend to pay workers what they agreed to pay – the market would have virtually no defenders. Indeed, even to suppose such failures is to imagine something that flies in the face of the very concept of a market – that is, a place where people go to acquire things they need, and a place where people go to offer products that they think their customers need, in the confident expectation that their customers will reward them for having done so. If that is not what people are doing in a given place, we probably would not call that place a market. On the topic of desert, see Schmidtz: 2002a or Part II of Schmidtz: 2006. See also Olsaretti: 2004. Regarding questions about what forms of equality an egalitarian should want, see Part IV of Schmidtz: 2006. For a contrast between my conception of justice and Brian Barry's, see Schmidtz: 2007.

Nozick's question about how grades ought to be distributed is relevant and illuminating here. If one is not trying to distribute grades according to desert as manifested in students' performance – if one is taking into account anything but one's assessments of the students' actual performance, and perhaps what one knows about a given student's overall pattern of performance – then one is failing to take grading and the responsibility that goes with being a grader seriously.

11. Wilt Chamberlain was the dominant basketball player of his era, once (in 1962) scoring a hundred points in a single game.

12. See also Feser: 2004; Fried: 1995; and Fried: 2005.

13. Nozick uneasily suggests that rights do not stop us from doing what it takes to avoid catastrophic moral horror. Where, then, is the line between overriding rights so as to avoid catastrophe, and ignoring rights so as to promote efficiency?

14. Rawls's reply: "The objection that the difference principle enjoins continuous corrections of particular distributions and capricious interference with private transactions is based on a misunderstanding." On the next page, Rawls clarifies: "even if everyone acts fairly as defined by the rules that it is both reasonable and practicable to impose on individuals, the upshot of many separate transactions will eventually undermine background justice. This is obvious once we view society, as we must, as involving cooperation over generations. Thus, even in a well-ordered society, adjustments in the basic structure are always necessary" (Rawls: 1996, pp. 283–284). The clarification makes it hard to see what Nozick misunderstood. (I thank Tom Palmer for this point.) In any case, one challenge in constructing a constitutional democracy is to limit "necessary adjustments" that signal to citizens that their income is a political football and they are to that extent governed by men, not law.

15. Nozick sees forming attachments and working to make the world a better place as parts of what we always have done to make life meaningful. Nozick also thinks we need not compel high-mindedness; people left in peace have a history of freely contributing to their communities. Is Nozick right? Under what conditions? What if we are unsure? Nozick may be right: our neighbors may be as high-minded as Nozick hopes. There are no guarantees, though. As a matter of fact, we are unsure. What, if anything, does our uncertainty entitle us to do to each other?

16. Meadowcroft likewise interprets Nozick as offering a theory of procedural justice (cf. Meadowcroft: 2005, p. 58). I would add only that procedural justice need not be purely historical. It too can exhibit what Nozick calls "weak" patterns.

17. Is this far-fetched? Rawls rejects a "liberal equality" interpretation of the difference principle in favor of a "democratic equality" interpretation (Rawls: 1971, p. 73ff.). Rawls also says "it is persons themselves who own their endowments," which sounds liberal, but then his next remark is: "What is to be regarded as a common asset, then, is the

distribution of native endowments, that is, the differences among persons. These differences consist not only in the variation of talents of the same kind (variation in strength and imagination, and so on) but in the variety of talents of different kinds" (Rawls: 2001, pp. 75–76). *Liberal* self-ownership, as Cohen might correctly insist, includes the aspects of our selves that distinguish us.

18. Nozick borrows the theory from John Locke: 1960, ch. 5.
19. Cohen says: "the claim people can make to the fruits of their own labor is the strongest basis for inequality of distribution, and the claim is difficult to reject so long as self-ownership is not denied" (Cohen: 2000a, p. 253). In effect, Cohen says, left-liberalism is not viable. Either we deny self-ownership, abandoning left-liberalism in favor of socialism, or embrace inequalities resulting from people freely employing unequal talents, thereby abandoning left-liberalism in favor of right-liberalism. See also Cohen: 2000b, pp. 273–274.
20. Nozick himself eventually came to think, "not necessarily." He told me once (it was the only time I met him, and it was the first thing he said as we sat down to dinner) that the extent of his departure from libertarianism had been greatly exaggerated. When I replied that it was he who had trumpeted his departure, Nozick said his only real departure was that he came to believe there was something wrong with some kinds of voluntary trade, namely the kind in which people literally sold themselves into slavery. Nozick's reasoning was that a society not only allows some things and forbids others. A society also *stands* for something, and a society that stands for liberty cannot tolerate slavery in its midst, even when slavery is a result of voluntary contracting.

Interestingly, concern for symbolic value has parallels in American law. As the twentieth century dawned, American blacks had made few advances since the end of Reconstruction. The ruling of *Plessy* v. *Ferguson* in 1896 asserted the right to segregate streetcars, and effectively made the Jim Crow era constitutional. It upheld the constitutionality of segregation on the grounds that separate public facilities could still be equal facilities, and so segregation did not entail inequality before the law. In 1911, thirty out of thirty-nine owners in a St. Louis neighborhood signed a covenant barring the sale of their parcels to non-whites. In 1945, the owner of one such parcel sold to Shelley, an African American family. Neighbors sued to stop Shelley from taking possession. Shelley counter-sued, saying the covenant did indeed violate the Constitution's fourteenth amendment, which guarantees to each citizen "equal protection of the laws." *Shelley* v. *Kraemer* went to the Supreme Court, which ruled in 1948 that private racist covenants are constitutional, but *public enforcement* is not. Private covenants per se do not implicate the state, but public enforcement of private covenants does.

Shelley terminated half a century of segregation via covenant. Today people have a right to enter covenants or exchange easements with neighbors, but they cannot bind future generations by creating racist covenants that *run with the land*. Being a racist is one thing; binding future owners to uphold a racist covenant is another. If a covenant is designed to run with the land, the issue is no longer just one of contract. It has become a property issue. In property law, *limiting doctrines* prevent idiosyncratic wishes of previous owners from running with the land. Contractors can agree to whatever they want, but when restrictions meant to run with the land are challenged, those who wish to retain them must make a case that such restrictions aim at making the community a better place and are reasonably expected to be of value to subsequent owners. Could racist covenants be good for subsequent white owners? Perhaps, but suppose a court agrees that a community would be better for unspecified subsequent owners by virtue of enforced legal covenants that exclude blacks. The state would be enforcing covenants prejudicial to black citizens on the supposition that excluding blacks is a way of making communities better. This is precisely what the fourteenth amendment's 'equal protection' clause forbids.

21. Is it fair for latecomers to be excluded from acquiring property by rules allowing original appropriation? Sanders notes that latecomers "are *not* excluded from acquiring property by these rules. They are, instead, excluded from being the first to own what has not been owned previously. Is *that* unfair?" (Sanders: 1987, p. 385)

22. A utilitarian theory needs to treat some topics as beyond the reach of utilitarian calculation. Rights can trump (not merely outweigh) utilitarian calculation even from a broadly consequentialist perspective. Why? Because, there is enormous utility in being able to treat certain parameters as beyond the reach of utilitarian calculation. Unconstrained maximizers, by definition, aim (do we want to say that by definition, they succeed?) to optimally use any resources to which they have access, including their neighbors' organs. To get good results in the real world, though, we need to be surrounded not by unconstrained maximizers but by people who respect rights, which enables us to trust each other enough to count on each other's peaceful cooperation. When we cannot count on others to treat us as rights-bearers with separate lives, we are living in a world of lesser potential.

All optimizing is done relative to a set of constraints and opportunities. Some of our constraints may be brute facts about the external world, but most will be to some extent self-imposed; some will reflect our beliefs about what morality requires. (See Schmidtz: 1992 or Schmidtz: 1995.) If other people can count on us not to murder them, new possibilities open up – opportunities people would not otherwise have. When doctors embrace a prohibition against harvesting organs of healthy but unconsenting patients so as to save larger numbers of patients in critical need, doctors give up opportunities to optimize – to save as many lives as possible – but *patients* gain opportunities to visit doctors safely. They gain a world with a higher ceiling. Such utility comes from doctors refusing even to ask whether murdering a patient would be optimal. (See Otsuka, this volume.)

23. Why can't our neighbors build biological weapons in their garages? Why can't they drive drunk? Not because they are hurting us, exactly, but because they are putting us at risk. They are doing the *kind* of thing that *tends* to hurt people. Of course, driving within speed limits also imposes risk. The difference is that risks imposed by speeders and drunk drivers are too much, or too pointless. At one extreme, we imagine saying it is okay to shoot at people so long as you do not hit them. At the other extreme, we imagine saying we cannot risk selling hot coffee to people who might spill it on themselves. Few believe either extreme, but where do we draw the line? Should we expect to be able to draw lines with principles of justice? Are principles (as opposed to custom, common law, or evolving community norms) always the right tool for drawing lines?

24. Cohen sometimes seems to use the word 'free' to refer to (1) an absence of external impediments. This is fine, but there are other kinds of freedom: freedom as (2) an absence of impediments *caused* by other persons; (3) an absence of impediments *deliberately* caused by other persons; (4) an absence of *removable* impediments: that is, impediments not caused by others, but which others have the power to remove; (5) an absence of self-imposed baggage (for example, having made no promises, and being correspondingly free to choose how to spend the rest of one's life). Philosophers argue about which of these is "real" freedom, but the truth is that different senses fit different purposes. See Schmidtz and Brennan: 2010.

25. Ralf Bader explains Nozick's theory of rights as side constraints (see Bader: 2010, p. 16). It is essentially the same idea, without the trappings of the traffic metaphor.

26. Perhaps I have read Cohen too literally. Perhaps he was not really talking about the indeterminate net effect of the *police* not preventing you from seizing my back garden for purposes of your own. Perhaps he was talking about an alternative *system* that legalizes or even administers such seizures. Would he have insisted that his favored system, backed by the threat of force, would be as coercive as robbery? I do not know.

27. Chandran Kukathas says people are not responsible for injustices committed before they were born. Neither are societies responsible.

Societies do not choose or act, so are not the kind of entity that can be at fault. Yet, rejecting all accountability for the past comes close to rejecting justice itself. So, Kukathas argues, we need a third option, and we have one. Even if people now living are blameless, associations to which some of them belong may be held responsible because *they did the deeds.* "Without going into the details of Aboriginal history since settlement, it is enough to note that there is more than sufficient evidence to confirm that many injustices were committed by the governments of the various states of Australia. To a lesser extent, the sins of the church are also on the record. In these circumstances, the attribution of responsibility for past injustice is not a problem: it can be laid plainly at the door of those associations, still in existence, which committed them" (Kukathas: 2003, p. 183).

28. I thank Jerry Gaus for reminding me of the following remark by David Gauthier: "If there were a distributor of natural assets, or if the distribution of factor endowments resulted from a social choice, then we might reasonably suppose that in so far as possible shares should be equal, and that a larger than equal share could be justified only as a necessary means to everyone's benefit ... In agreeing with Rawls that society is a cooperative venture for mutual advantage, we must disagree with his view that natural talents are to be considered a common asset. The two views offer antithetical conceptions of both the individual human being and society" (Gauthier: 1986, pp. 220–221).

29. When we call a choice arbitrary, we imply not only that it is unjustified, not only that it is wrong, but that it exhibits a certain arrogance. For example, a person's attitude might be "I can do what I want."

30. Strictly, this consideration leads only to the precursor. We get the difference principle only after deciding to "complete" the theory, then rejecting other ways of completing it.

31. Needless to say, even the most self-reliant bakers get help.

32. If others do complain, then as Cohen says about appropriating water in a world of plenty, "your powerful reply is to say that no one has any reason to complain about your appropriation of the water, since no one has been adversely affected by it" (Cohen: 1995, p. 75).

33. Actually, Jane can enjoy some goods – public goods – without bringing anything to market, but these too are cases where if we get specific about what to count as Jane's share, Jane may have already done it. If Jane's neighbors put up Christmas decorations, Jane is enriched. But if Jane already put up comparable decorations, then she already did her share.

9 Does Nozick have a theory of property rights?

9.1 INTRODUCTION

Surely the most famous statement in *Anarchy, State, and Utopia* (*ASU*) is the manifesto with which it opens: "Individuals have rights, and there are things no person or group may do to them (without violating their rights). So strong and far-reaching are these rights that they raise the question of what, if anything, the state and its officials may do."

In Part II of *ASU*, Nozick elaborates that view as follows:

No one has a right to something whose realization requires certain uses of things and activities that other people have rights and entitlements over. Other people's rights and entitlements to *particular things* (*that* pencil, *their* body, and so on) and how they choose to exercise these rights and entitlements fix the external environment of any given individual and the means that will be available to him. If his goal requires the use of means which others have rights over, he must enlist their voluntary cooperation ... No rights exist in conflict with this substructure of particular rights. Since no neatly contoured right to achieve a goal will avoid incompatibility with this substructure, no such rights exist. The particular rights over things fill the space of rights, leaving no room for general rights to be in a certain material condition. (p. 238)

From these and other statements throughout Part II, one can glean the essential features of Nozickian property rights:

(1) They are absolute: if you are the owner of X, you control it absolutely.

(2) One of the key rights of control you possess over X by virtue of owning it is the right not to have your interests in X interfered with or altered in any way without your consent.

> As a corollary, whatever price you can negotiate for your agreeing to an alteration is just: "[A]n entitlement theorist would find acceptable whatever distribution resulted from the party's voluntary exchanges" (p. 188).

Even self-styled libertarians generally accept the need to interfere with an owner's rights of enjoyment to some extent. Some of those limitations are innocently packaged in the classic common-law adage, "sic utere tuo ut alienum non laedas" (use your property so as not to wrong others). Others arise from a recognition that the state must deploy some coercive powers to solve collective action problems for the good of all. Among libertarians, Nozick stakes out a position pretty far at the end of "no interference" in Part II of *ASU*. The heart of that position is that, in general, "people have a right not to be forced to do" things they do not want to do with themselves or their property, subject only to the right of the nightwatchman state to use force, if necessary, to protect the like rights of others.

This prohibition holds, even if (in others' view or even your own) you would be left better off as a result. Thus, for example, compulsory redistributive taxation is impermissible in a Nozickian world, even if everyone supports helping the poor and coordinated giving to the needy is (by hypothesis) more efficient than uncoordinated individual action because of collective action problems (see p. 268). If everyone would really prefer compulsory coordinated giving, says Nozick, then get their consent. If you cannot get everyone's consent because there are dissenters, hold-outs, or the transactions costs of getting consent are too high, tough. That is what it means to have a historical rather than end-state theory. "[I]t would violate moral constraints to compel people who are entitled to their holdings to contribute against their will" (p. 268).

(3)   Consent means explicit consent. As Nozick famously put it, "tacit consent isn't worth the paper it's not written on" (p. 287). You may not imply consent to a rights waiver from the fact that an owner has voluntarily continued to reside physically in the jurisdiction that strips her of that right. (To put it another way, individuals have a right of internal exit: they can stay put in a jurisdiction but refuse to abide by individual laws if they deem those laws unjust from a libertarian perspective.)[1] And (pace Herbert Hart) you also may

not imply consent to pay for benefits received from the state (see pp. 90–93).

(4)   Natural rights are straightforwardly derivable from libertarian premises: "A line (or hyper-plane) circumscribes an area in moral space around an individual. Locke holds that this line is determined by an individual's natural rights, which limit the action of others" (p. 57). Moreover, the rights derived from libertarian premises are not just vague abstractions, like self-ownership. They are "particular rights over particular things" (p. 238).

(5)   The boundaries around individual rights are non-overlapping. To put it in Nozick's terms, "[i]ndividual rights are co-possible" (p. 166).

(6)   Rights occupy most of the space of social interaction, drastically limiting the domain of collective choice. "The exercise of … rights fixes some features of the world. Within the constraints of these fixed features, a choice may be made by a social choice mechanism based upon a social ordering" (p. 166). But, warns Nozick, "[a]fter we exclude from consideration the decisions which others have a right to make, and the actions which would aggress against me, steal from me, and so on, and hence violate *my* (Lockean) rights, it is not clear that there are *any decisions* remaining about which even to raise the question of whether I have a right to a say in those that importantly affect me. Certainly, *if* there are any left to speak about, they are not significant enough a portion to provide a case for a different sort of [that is, a more extensive] state" (p. 270).

Over the past forty years, this conception of rights has been subject to vigorous criticism on a number of fronts, in particular its analytic indeterminacy and normative underpinnings. I agree with many of these criticisms, and have voiced some of them myself (see Fried: 1995; 2003; 2005). But with the exception of criticisms going to points (4) and (6) above, I do not want to press them here. Instead, I want to suggest that when one reads the three parts of the book together, it is not clear that Nozick has any theory of property rights at all. More precisely, he has at least three mutually inconsistent theories: utilitarianism; Lockean libertarianism; and anything goes, provided that citizens have some unspecified level of choice among legal regimes. Insofar as one can detect any predominant theory, it is not libertarian, or even liberal, but utilitarian.

Some of the inconsistencies in Nozick's treatment of property rights are doubtless explained by the book's origins. As others have pointed out, the three parts of *ASU* started out as three unconnected essays, and in many ways that is where they ended up. Other inconsistencies can be written off to the analytically casual nature of Nozick's enterprise. If that were the end of the story, Nozick's own inconstancy to his professed libertarian commitments would be of limited philosophical interest. But my own view is that many of Nozick's lapses are symptomatic of the problems deontologists of all stripes encounter in translating abstract statements of rights into concrete rules. One way of putting the difficulty is, when the going gets tough, rights theorists tend to turn utilitarian. To that extent, there are lessons to be learned for rights theory more generally from a close reading of *ASU*.

I will consider Nozick's treatment of property rights in Parts I and III of *ASU*, then return to reconsider Part II, and conclude with some speculations about how best to understand Nozick's inconstancy.

9.2 ANARCHY

The task Nozick sets for himself in Part I of *ASU* is to show that the minimal state could have come about from the state of nature (SON) through a series of uncoordinated, private transactions, none of which violates any individual's rights.[2] If some of the hypotheticals he tests libertarian property rights against in Part II are not exactly taxing (e.g., ruling out forcible eyeball transfer from the two-eyed to the blind), he has gone to the other extreme here.

Nozick starts out with an imaginary SON populated with multiple independent protective associations (IPAs) in close proximity to each other. Each of the IPAs is pursuing the identical, prima facie legitimate end (protecting its own members from wrongful transgressions by non-members). In the course of pursuing that end, each imposes identical risks on non-members by virtue of its unavoidably error-prone enforcement procedures.

Being able to show that "individual rights are [at least roughly] co-possible" (point [5] above) is essential to any theory of rights. If there is an absolute right to do X, but A's doing X entails B's not doing X, or not doing it to the same extent as A, then we need some meta-principle to adjudicate the conflict between A's and B's asserted right to do X. The consequence of that meta-principle will be to leave A, B, or both with a less than absolute right to do X.

If one steps back from the details of Nozick's baroque thought experiment, there would seem to be only three places to which a good (Nozickian) libertarian could go from his starting point.

The first is to get the unanimous, explicit consent of the members of all IPAs to give up their rights to their own IPA in return for the benefits of a minimal state. Nozick rejects this possibility on the grounds of implausibility. Some people may prefer to remain independent; others may hold out in negotiations for strategic reasons. Finally, even if all are willing to cooperate, such agreements are often prohibitively costly to reach.

But, of course, these are just the typical problems that make unanimous consent to collective action, practically speaking, unattainable. The way around that problem that most social contractarians have adopted is some version of implied consent. Nozick, however, rejects that solution as not consent at all. (See point [3] above.) It is tantamount, says Nozick, to giving someone a book and grabbing money from him to pay for it, on the grounds he has "nothing better to spend the money on" (and by implication also would have valued having the book at least at its cost). The fact that we are "social products," says Nozick, "does not create in us a floating debt which the current society can collect and use as it will" (p. 95).

The second alternative is to decide that individuals do not, after all, have a right to their own IPAs in the SON – to decide, that is, that in the SON, might makes right, and moralized Lockean rights arise only after a state comes into being by whatever means necessary. This strategy, however, renders Part 1 of the book irrelevant, and Nozick ostensibly rejects it out of hand. ("Our explanation does not assume or claim that this makes right") (p. 118).

The third alternative is to give up on the idea of a minimal state and make one's peace with anarchy. It is true that doing so requires one to forego the social gains a minimal state makes possible. But that is the price you pay for being a strict libertarian with a strong notion of consent: it can (and in situations requiring collective action often will) lead to suboptimal results for everyone. If that bothers you enough to dispense with consent, then you are a consequentialist, not a libertarian – a conclusion Nozick inevitably invites in rejecting this third alternative as well.

Instead, Nozick opts for a fourth alternative, which is a complicated amalgam of alternative (2) and the implied consent version of alternative (1). His solution takes on board all the objectionable features of both of those alternatives, from the perspective of a strict libertarian, and adds a few of its own. Here are the essential moves.

9.2.1 Doing away with consent

In Nozick's "invisible hand" tale, the minimal state emerges from the anarchic SON when the dominant protective association (DPA) unilaterally forces all non-members to give up their IPAs and join the DPA. Thus, in place of actual or implied consent, Nozick does away with consent entirely. (The door to this solution is opened with surprising insouciance. After asserting, famously, that "[a] line (or hyperplane) circumscribes an area in moral space around an individual," determined for Lockeans by an individual's natural rights, Nozick opines that that principle raises the following question: *"Are others forbidden to perform actions that transgress the boundary or encroach upon the circumscribed area, or are they permitted to perform such actions provided that they compensate the person whose boundary has been crossed?"* Unravelling this question, says Nozick, "will occupy us for much of this chapter" (p. 57). But no libertarian should need thirty pages to answer that question. Three words should suffice: they are forbidden. That is what consent means.

Presumably the IPAs are free to leave the territory now ruled by the DPA-turned-ultraminimal-state if they wish. But if they stay put, they will be deemed to have relinquished any independent right of self-protection. That is to say, there is no right of internal exit for dissenting IPA members. That result is arguably even more objectionable from a libertarian perspective than implying consent to pay for benefits, pursuant to something like Herbert Hart's "principle of fairness." Hart is responding to a situation where holdouts are happily enjoying the benefits of membership but refusing to pay for them. They are, in short, free riders. In Nozick's ultraminimal state, dissenters do not want to be free riders; they want to remain completely independent, but have been denied that option.

In the section on "Prohibition, Compensation and Risk," Nozick tries to reconcile the coercion he licenses here with a strong consent version of libertarianism by arguing that what the IPAs lost involuntarily – an absolute right to self-defense – they never had to begin with, because in exercising that "right," the IPAs unavoidably jeopardized the rights of others through their unreliable enforcement procedures.[3] Hence what the DPA took from the losing IPAs without their consent (the right to act in a way that puts the rights of others at risk) was never "theirs" to begin with.

This strategy might seem promising at first, but it is hopeless, for reasons that go to the heart of the problems rights theorists face in translating abstract rights claims into operationalizable rules about "particular rights over particular things."

9.2.2 What is the rights violation here?

The face-off between identical interests that are not co-possible sets any rights-based argument on an obvious collision course between incompatible intuitions about who is the wronger and who the wronged. When the DPA forbids other IPAs from protecting their own members, who is the (would be) victim here? The DPA, which is protecting its members from the risky conduct of all the other IPAs (albeit at the same time imposing an identical risk on those other IPAs)? Or the other IPAs, which have lost the right to protect themselves, merely because doing so imposes some risks on others – a loss that arguably is incompatible with a free society?[4] And whichever side we deem to have the entitlement to protect itself from harm, how is that right to be enforced? By a property rule, which gives them the right to retain the entitlement without paying any compensation? By a liability rule, which allows the other side to trample that entitlement provided it pays compensation?

Rather than trying to reconcile warring intuitions about these two questions in some fashion, Nozick simply embraces them in seriatim. The result is an analytic train wreck, in which Nozick flips between three of the four possible combinations of answers to the two questions: who gets the entitlement; and is it protected by property or liability rule?

(1) Nozick initially assigns the entitlement to the IPAs (in assuming they have a right to defend their members), which

entitlement he protects by a property rule (the IPAs have a right to enjoin the DPA from interfering with their activities, which right the DPA would have to negotiate to buy out from the IPAs in a voluntary transaction).

(2)   He then switches the entitlement to the DPA (to be free from IPAs' risky enforcement activities), and protects that entitlement by a property rule (the DPA may enjoin the IPAs from any enforcement activities).

(3)   Then, pursuant to the Principle of Compensation, he abruptly shifts the entitlement back to the IPAs, but concludes that the entitlement should be protected not by a property rule (which would permit the IPAs to continue to defend themselves) but by a liability rule (which permits the DPA to enjoin such activities, but requires it to compensate the IPA in an amount equal to the diminution in the IPA members' welfare as a result of the injunction).

Again, it is easy to write this mess off to the casual nature of Nozick's enterprise. But there is a deeper cautionary tale here for rights theories concerning the indeterminate content of rights derivable from the key libertarian principle, "you may do whatever you wish with yourself and what you own, provided you do not harm others." Traditionally, the deontological literature on harm to others has treated this proviso as more or less self-executing: it is presumptively violated whenever one party harms another (without justification or excuse). Since the popularization of Coase's "The Problem of Social Cost" (Coase: 1960) in the 1970s, it has been widely recognized in legal circles that the presence of harm-in-fact resolves nothing. All disputes between two or more parties involve conflicting desires about how to deploy scarce resources; however we decide the dispute, one side will be "harmed" as a matter of fact, in the sense that it will no longer be able to do as it wishes with impunity. As a result, the question of who is *wronging* whom cannot be resolved by an unmoralized (factual) determination of who is *harming* whom. It can be resolved only on the basis of some normative commitments (implicit or explicit) that lead us to favor one side's interests over the other's.

In the typical hypotheticals that populate the deontological literature, it is easy to miss this analytic truth, because we have clear and widely shared intuitions about whose interests deserve protection, and those intuitions frequently track the more visible and violent forms of harm-in-fact (in Nozick's words, acts involving "primarily, physical aggressing" against others [p. 32]). We all know who will win the dispute between the two-eyed and the blind over forcible eyeball transfers, or the able-bodied and the society that wishes to harvest his organs to save ten lives (see p. 206), just as we all know who will win as between A, who wishes to stick her knife into B's back just for the hell of it, and B, who would prefer that A not do so (see pp. 170 and 282). Because the conclusion in these – to borrow Nozick's characterization – "slightly hysterical" (p. 206) examples is never in doubt, the reasons adduced in support of it tend to go unscrutinized, in particular, the assumption that the mere presence of harm-in-fact to the "victim" resolves the question.

In contrast, the conflict that the Nozickian SON sets in motion forces the Coasean problem front and center, both because all of the IPAs are engaged in identical conduct (self-defense) that imposes an identical risk of harm to others (inadvertent boundary crossings), and because that conduct is of the sort we regard as prima facie socially productive. Nozick, understandably lacking any clear moral intuition how to resolve this stand-off – whether to regard the imposition of risk as a right or an incursion on others' rights, and how to break the tie between identically positioned parties – just cycles among the various possibilities.

9.2.3 The set of "rights" that emerge from Nozick's "invisible hand" procedure are not co-possible

The conclusion that the rights that emerge from the invisible-hand procedure described in Part 1 are not co-possible follows directly from the fact that all the IPAs are identically situated at the start. Given that symmetry, the only way to get from multiple IPAs to a minimal state without favoring one IPA over another is to endow all IPAs with equal prerogatives, and let them work it out among themselves – by force, in a Hobbesian SON, by explicit agreement in a Lockean one.[5] As noted above, Nozick rejects both of these alternatives. Instead, he gives one of the IPAs (the DPA) the prerogative to extinguish all other IPAs, relegating the members of the other IPAs to the lesser right to be compensated for their involuntary loss. Whatever else this is, it is not an example of co-possible rights.

9.2.4 *Measuring compensation for the losers*

In the chapter on "Prohibition, Compensation and Risk," Nozick considers three possible measures of compensation for the loser IPAs. The first, market compensation, is "that price that would have been arrived at had a prior negotiation for permission [to extinguish the loser PAs' right of self-defense] taken place" (p. 65). The second, confusingly termed "full compensation," is equal to the minimal amount the loser PAs would have settled for to give up their rights voluntarily (see p. 63). In normal economic parlance, this would be equal to their minimum reservation price. The meaning of the third, "compensation for disadvantages," is a bit elusive. At one point, Nozick defines it as the diminution in preference-satisfaction suffered by the prohibited individual "as compared to the normal situation" (p. 82). This appears to refer to the situation of others (see pp. 82–83), but it is unclear what others and how we are to calculate the value of their "normal situation." At various points, Nozick states unambiguously that compensation for disadvantages is lower than "full compensation" (see pp. 87 and 145–146). At other points, however, he defines it in a manner that appears indistinguishable from "full compensation."[6] I will assume for present purposes that it entails something less than full compensation.

For a libertarian, the choice among these three measures should be clear. The second-best alternative to requiring the DPA to get the loser IPAs' consent to extinguish their right to self-protection would be to make the DPA pay the IPAs whatever price the loser IPAs could have extracted in arm's length negotiations to give up that right – in Nozick's parlance, "market compensation." Indeed, in another context Nozick himself goes even further, requiring a penalty to be levied on top of compensatory damages for unconsented-to boundary crossings (p. 57).

Instead, Nozick relegates the loser IPAs to either "full compensation" or "compensation for disadvantages." As Nozick notes, the effect of full compensation is to give to the DPA *all* of the joint gains from achieving one state with a monopoly on power, a result that he himself describes as "unfair and arbitrary" (p. 64). A fortiori, "compensation for disadvantages," which leaves the loser IPAs with even less, is even less defensible. Why, then, choose either measure, rather than market compensation? Nozick's answer is that partial compensation is a fair resolution to "risk of harm" cases, because both sides have some legitimate claim of right: the DPA, to protect itself from the loser IPAs' risky procedures; the loser IPAs, to protect themselves via procedures that *might not ever* result in harm to the DPA (see pp. 82–82, 84, 145–146).[7]

But the DPA and the loser IPAs do not just have offsetting claims of right; they have *identical* claims of right. Given that, Nozick's solution seems like adding *insult* to the loser IPAs' injury. The loser IPAs not only must forego the right to the protective agency of their choice; they also get no share in the surplus value generated by the forcible creation of a monopoly state, and indeed, under the "compensation for disadvantages" measure, are likely to find themselves in a worse position than they were in the SON.

Worse yet, in conceding that both sides have legitimate claims, Nozick threatens to win the battle but lose the war for libertarianism, as that concession exposes the wholesale inability of libertarian principles to delineate "particular rights over particular things." I return to this point in subsection 9.2.6.

9.2.5 *Might makes right*

While Nozick goes to much trouble to present the minimal state as an outcome of a non-rights-violating "invisible hand" procedure, in the end, might makes right in Nozick's SON.[8] The procedure that produces Nozick's minimal state is "invisible" only in the very limited sense that it does not result from any explicit social choice mechanism. Otherwise, it lacks the two key attributes of the Smithian invisible hand: *voluntary*, private transactions that produce an optimal outcome (here, the minimal state) *without any one trying to produce it*. What it does is to replace the "visible hand" of collective action with the "visible hand" of one dictatorial PA that conquers and absorbs all the others by force. The fact that might makes right in Nozick's tale would seem to doom the enterprise from the start, rendering the rest of the argument in Part I of *ASU* superfluous.

At the end of the day, then, the "invisible hand" process that Nozick imagines will ferry us from anarchy to the minimal state without any rights violations violates virtually every tenet of libertarian rights. The DPA gains a monopoly on coercive force by forcefully extinguishing every other IPA's natural right to self-defense.

The loser IPAs are relegated to compensation (under the Principle of Compensation) equal at best to their minimal reservation price for giving up their own PA. If the losers are unhappy with that outcome, they are left with exactly the choice that Nozick denounces in Part II of *ASU* as no choice at all: If you don't like it, leave the territory; if you stay put, you will be deemed to have consented to the legitimacy of the resulting state. Indeed, the losers in Part I are arguably worse off than the losers in the more-than-minimal, redistributive, state imagined in Part II. The latter at least can console themselves that they lost pursuant to a majority (or supermajority) vote, in which their vote counted as much as everyone else's.[9] In contrast, the losers in Part I were vanquished solely by force.

And what justification does Nozick offer for this rout of libertarian rights? At first, he asserts that it is the *only* way to get us to "civil government," which alone can remedy (in Locke's words) the "inconveniences of the state of nature" – that is, its suboptimality (p. 10). He then extends that argument to any case in which obtaining consent would cost more than it would be worth, and still further to any case in which force would be the "efficient" solution because "the transactions costs of reaching a prior agreement are greater, even by a bit, than the costs of the posterior compensation process," provided that the benefits of the act are "great enough" (p. 73). That position seems vanishingly close to straight utilitarianism.[10]

Indeed, Nozick reveals his true utilitarian colors from the start of Part I, when he declares that one could justify the state *either* by showing it "would arise by a process involving no morally impermissible steps, *or* would be an improvement if it arose," and then conditions the first route on being able to show that it too would lead to improvements rather than deterioration. (p. 5 and fn. *, emphasis added). If we are to take Nozick at his word here – and the rest of Part I certainly suggests we should – then the entire historical (invisible hand) justification can be dispensed with, in favor of a comparison of the goodness or badness of the end states of anarchy and the minimal state.[11] But of course this is exactly the instrumental justification for coercive collective action that Nozick repudiates in Part II of *ASU*, on the ground that, even if collective action would benefit everyone, including the dissenters, one may never "compel people who are entitled to their holdings to contribute against their will" (p. 268).[12]

9.2.6 What is left of libertarian rights?

Nozick intermittently recognizes that his willingness to dispense with consent if there are significant enough welfare gains from doing so leaves libertarian rights in a shambles. But he tries to contain the damage by suggesting that we may jettison rights for a utilitarian calculus, provided compensation is paid to the losers, *only* when we "act in self-protection in order to increase [our] own security" from potential harm resulting from the actions of others, and those actions "might actually have turned out to be harmless" (p. 114). In short, the conduct must "risk crossing another's boundary," with a probability less than 1.0 (see p. 74).[13]

The unstated assumption here is that deontological principles can handle cases of certainty in either direction straightforwardly. If a given act is certain to result in harm to others, it is wrongful and may be prohibited without compensation; if it is certain not to result in harm to others, it is permissible, and hence any waiver of that right must be negotiated.[14] Only where the action might or might not turn out to be harmful do deontological principles run out. In such cases, says Nozick, "it is difficult to imagine a principled way in which the natural-rights tradition can draw the line" between acceptable and unacceptable risks imposed on others. "This means that it is difficult to see how, in these cases, the natural-rights tradition draws the boundaries it focuses upon" (p. 75).[15]

In fact Nozick does not limit the Principle of Compensation to conduct that presents merely a risk of harm.[16] More importantly, the category of conduct that merely risks harm to others is not small. It encompasses virtually everything we do, including conduct that we routinely prohibit without requiring compensation (e.g., driving 100 m.p.h. through crowded city streets) and conduct that we permit people to engage in with impunity (e.g., driving prudently down a crowded city street, knowing that doing so imposes some irreducible risk of harm to pedestrians), as well as conduct that we permit people to engage in provided that they compensate victims for any harm that results (so-called strict liability rules). If, as Nozick suggests, we should assign risky conduct to one of these three categories based not on the natural rights of the actor but on the social utility of the conduct (judged both by the value of the activity to society at large, and its value to the would-be actor), he has effectively conceded the regulation of most human conduct to welfarist principles. That means that rights, rather than occupying most of the space of social interaction, occupy almost none. The bulk of that space is to be governed by "a social choice mechanism based upon a social ordering" (p. 166).

9.3 UTOPIA

Nozick's Utopia is a Tieboutian paradise, in which every imaginable sort of community is on offer: ones to satisfy the preferences of "[v]isionaries and crackpots, maniacs and saints, ... capitalists and communists and participatory democrats," Nozick and Rawls, you name it (p. 316). In this utopia, individual consent operates at the level of choice of which community to join rather than the design of any given community. "[I]n a free society people may contract into various restrictions which the government may not legitimately impose upon them. Though the framework is libertarian and laissez faire, *individual communities within it need not be*, and perhaps no community within it would choose to be so" (p. 320). If Swedenville wants to run itself on social-democratic principles, god bless it. If you don't like it, don't join Swedenville.

So, the best of all possible worlds that Nozick can imagine is one in which we are given a choice among a reasonably diverse range of communities and then told, with respect to each of them, take it or leave it. But to the naive observer, that arrangement sounds a lot like the position of citizens in many countries of the world. If American citizens do not like the laws adopted by their fellow countrymen by majority rule (indeed, by any procedure), they are free to leave. If they would prefer a more socialist-democratic alternative, there is Canada and Western Europe. If they would prefer something closer to the libertarian ideal of unregulated capitalism, there is the Cayman Islands.[17]

The Nozick of Part II of *ASU*, however, explicitly rejects the Tieboutian justification for permitting a hundred flowers to bloom at the national level: "The minimal state is the most extensive state that can be justified. Any state more extensive violates people's rights" (p. 149). Nozick would allow a very narrow exception, when every citizen explicitly consents to a given deviation from the minimal state (see p. 293). But this exception – if it is even an exception – is a null set, since one could never get unanimous consent to any term of governance.

Is it possible to reconcile Nozick's vision of Utopia at the community level in Part III of *ASU* with his vision of the just (minimal) state in Part II? To a libertarian sensibility, the problems with the "let-a-hundred-flowers-bloom" solution in Part III are clear, and well rehearsed in the literature on Tieboutian sorting. Even in (ideal) theory, there will never be enough communities on offer for any person to realize all of her preferences about political arrangements; in order to assemble a critical mass of co-citizens, everyone will have to make compromises. In the real world, the choice of political community is further constrained by a host of non-political considerations (job opportunities, financial constraints, proximity to friends and family) that for many people are determinative, thereby forcing further compromises with respect to political arrangements. And once located in a given community (by choice or by birth), the costs of exit for many people become prohibitively high.

Thus, inevitably, people will happily opt into a particular community (say, Swedenville) because the total package of social, economic and political benefits on offer is better than in any other community (or at least not so much worse that it is worth the costs of exit), but want to opt out of particular Swedenville laws that are unjust from a libertarian perspective (say, its steeply progressive income tax or its socialized medical care). As noted above, the Nozick of Part II concludes that the state is morally required to give its citizens the right to opt out of particular laws at the national level. But faced with the same hypothetical demand at the local level, the Nozick of Part III concludes otherwise. It is enough, he argues, that you are given a diverse range of choices – which choices need not include a libertarian option (see p. 320). Once you have chosen Swedenville, you are bound by all of its laws, whatever they are. You may leave any time if you wish, but you have no right to stay put and pick which of its laws you wish to comply with.[18] Nor does it matter whether you disagree with a particular law as a matter of mere preference or because it violates (libertarian) rights: "A nation or protective agency may not compel redistribution between one community and another, yet a community such as a kibbutz may redistribute within itself (or give to another community or outside individuals)" (p. 321).

What explains this radical disjunction in the legitimate reach of collective action at the local and the national level? Nozick considers and rejects what is surely the most obvious and plausible explanation: for most people, it is simply more feasible to move from Massachusetts to New Hampshire than from the United States to the Cayman Islands to obtain the tax-and-expenditure package they prefer.[19] Given the greater feasibility of exit from local communities, we need not be as solicitous of their demands for accommodation if they stay put.

Having so much turn on the practical feasibility of exit is not without its dangers for libertarians. It opens them up to demands more generally to evaluate freedom on functional rather than formal grounds, demands they rightly perceive will be their undoing.[20] In addition, even within the narrow confines of political exit options, it plunges them into a normative and empirical morass it is not easy to climb out of.[21] On the other hand, concern with meaningfulness of choice at least sounds in values (liberty, self-determination) that are congenial to libertarianism.

Nozick, however, refuses to distinguish the local and national cases on this basis:

Even if almost everyone wished to live in a communist community, so that there weren't any viable noncommunist communities, no particular community need also ... allow a resident individual to opt out of their sharing arrangement. The recalcitrant individual has no alternative but to conform. Still, the others do not force him to conform, and his rights are not violated. He has no right that the others cooperate in making his non-conformity feasible. (p. 322)

Instead, he suggests the cases should be distinguished on the following ground. Many people will be offended by the knowledge that their fellow community members have refused to comply with some of the (duly adopted) laws of the community. Such offense constitutes a harm, which is itself a rights violation, *but only if one has one's face rubbed in it daily*. That will be the case with respect to dissenters with whom one must interact face-to-face on a daily basis, but not dissenters in far-flung regions of the country (see p. 322).

The distinction Nozick urges here is an empirical one, and it may well be wrong. In the world of mass media, we often have much more intimate knowledge of events in far-flung places than we glean from casual contact with our neighbors. But even granting the truth of Nozick's empirical assertion, surely it is stunning that any libertarian would think that thwarting others' nosy preferences about how you live your life might constitute a cognizable harm that trumps your right to live as you wish.[22] And should it turn out that Nozick's empirical hunch is wrong, and the offense we take at how others live knows no geographical bounds within a given country, does that mean that our conception of Lockean rights in the minimal state must be reconfigured to accommodate this newly cognizable harm?

9.4 THE MINIMAL STATE RECONSIDERED

Up until now, I have implicitly treated the libertarian credentials of Nozick of Part II as impeccable. But in fact, many of the same problems that dog the Nozick of Parts I and III arise in Part II as well. The only reason they are not more prominent in Part II is that, with a very few exceptions, Nozick never spells out the "particular rights over particular things" implied by libertarian principles, relying instead on (in his words) "placeholders for [those] conventional details" (p. 150). The exceptions tend to be the easy cases: acts of physical aggression in which our universally shared intuitions (and most policy arguments) clearly favor the victim. Because they are easy cases whatever normative premises one starts with, they do not put libertarian (or any other) principles to a serious test.

Since *ASU* was published, numerous commentators have observed that, depending on how the details are filled in, Nozick's three principles (Justice in Acquisition, Justice in Transfer, and Rectification) could house virtually any distributive scheme of "particular rights over particular things," from requiring us to give the United States back to the Native Americans, to Rawlsianism, to something approximating Nozickian libertarianism. I want to make a different point here: that whatever scheme ultimately emerges, it cannot be derived straightforwardly from libertarian principles. What Nozick dismisses as merely "conventional details" emerge from thousands of micro decisions about how to balance conflicting but prima facie legitimate interests, and libertarian principles – which do not admit of the need to compromise – cannot tell us how to make them.

Nozick acknowledges as much with respect to the Principle of Rectification, which requires us to "balanc[e] the conflicting considerations" that argue in favor of the wrongly deprived (or their successors in interest) on the one hand, and the settled expectations of third party beneficiaries of that unjust acquisition on the other (see p. 173). And, one could argue, he implicitly acknowledges it in the countless questions he raises but never answers throughout Part ii of *ASU*.

But equally difficult choices have to be made at almost every juncture in fleshing out Nozick's three principles, once one gets beyond the easy cases. Consider for example income taxation, the one genuinely hard case that Nozick tackles in Part ii. Famously equating income taxation with forced labor, Nozick concludes it is clearly impermissible under the libertarian principle of self-ownership (see p. 172). Nozick's target in making this argument is taxation used to finance the redistribution of wealth. But his argument applies with equal force to taxes used to finance the operations of the minimal state. Nozick of Part i avoids confronting the permissibility of such taxation by assuming away the public goods nature of the "protective services" the minimal state would provide. If (as he assumes) individual residents could be excluded from the benefits of protective services if they chose not to pay for them, then compulsory taxation would be unnecessary; such services could be financed through voluntary (market) transactions (see pp. 110–115). And Nozick of Part ii ignores entirely how we are to finance the minimal state.

But given the public goods nature of many of the functions performed by the minimal state, its operations cannot be financed by a voluntary market model. At some point coercive taxation will be required. If coercive taxation violates libertarian rights when the proceeds are used for redistributive purposes, why does it not equally violate them when used to finance the minimal state? There are a number of possible answers (including H. L. A. Hart's "benefit" principle, which as noted above Nozick rejects), but they all require adopting a much more qualified notion of consent than Justice in Transfer gestures towards. Those qualifications, whatever they are, are *not* going to come from any of Nozick's three principles, or indeed any other libertarian principles.

Finally, the one "particular right over a particular thing" that Nozick deals with in detail in Part II of *ASU* – our right to appropriate things out of the commons – he resolves the same way he derives the minimal state in Part I: by doing away with consent, and requiring only that we compensate those who were deprived of "enough and as good" without their consent. As in Part I, the compensation required under this "weak" reading of the Lockean proviso is set at a level sufficient to return the expropriated to the same place on the indifference curve they would have occupied in the absence of private property (see p. 178). As Nozick plausibly concludes, this is functionally equivalent to giving an unfettered right of appropriation that can be overridden in the case of "catastrophe," since "the baseline for comparison is so low as compared to the productiveness of a society with private appropriation that the question of the Lockean proviso being violated arises only in the case of catastrophe (or a desert-island situation)" (p. 181). At a minimum, all of the surplus value generated by converting the commons to private property goes to the expropriators themselves. And as in Part I of *ASU*, Nozick's motivation for doing away with consent is the immense utilitarian benefits to be derived from allowing private appropriation out of the commons (see p. 177). Again, the point is not to criticize that resolution; it is to insist that it cannot be derived from libertarian premises.

9.5 CONCLUSION

What are we to make of Nozick's inconstancy to libertarian principles? I am not sure, but here are some possibilities.

(a) Nozick is a fair weather libertarian. When the going gets tough – meaning when it does not give him the answer he wants – he ditches it, usually for utilitarianism.

(b) Nozick is not a libertarian. The only distinctly libertarian thing he really cares about is blocking income redistribution. All the rest of the trappings are there to justify that result in terms that seem to have broader philosophical interest.

(c) Nozick is a libertarian; the concessions he has made in Parts I and III are either minor or unnecessary.

Alternative (c) may describe some of the concessions Nozick has made, but it does not describe most. The problems that Nozick the libertarian founders on are problems that any liberal rights theory has difficulty handling: What background options are required to make consent morally significant? What should we do about collective action problems that cannot be solved by unanimous consent? And can we really derive "particular rights over particular things" from broad and vague libertarian principles like self-ownership, the rights to the fruits of one's labor, the rights to transfer what one owns, etc.? In Nozick's optimistic view, once we exclude the clear cases where I have an unfettered right to do X and the equally clear cases where I have no right to do X, almost no details remain to be filled in (see p. 270). But in reality almost everything remains to be filled in. The details fill volumes and volumes of civil-law statutes and court decisions in contracts, torts, real property, intellectual property, trusts and estates, civil procedure, corporations, debtor/creditor law, environmental law – the list goes on and on. Many of these problems would arise under a minimal or maximal state. For the most part, they cannot be resolved by libertarian principles – that is why they are not clear cases. And what is true of law is true of morality as well.

Many (indeed, most) deontologists have done a more careful job filling in the details of their proposed scheme of rights than Nozick does in *ASU*. But in the end, none has shown that broad principles such as "we own ourselves and the products of our labor" can generate answers to the everyday problems we actually face, without an illicit assist from ad hoc intuitionism, naked self-interest, or (I believe) most often welfarism manqué, snuck in through terms like fault, due care, negligence, and definitions of what constitutes a boundary crossing. Which brings us to the last possibility:

(d)   Libertarianism, and indeed all rights theory, is in some significant trouble, once it gets beyond a relatively limited set of clear-cut cases that everyone agrees on.

My own view is that this – if anything – is the overarching lesson to be learned from *ASU* at thirty-five years' distance.

NOTES

1. For Nozick's insistence that only such a right of internal exit could legitimize the more-than-minimal state, see pp. 173–174; 292–293.
2. "I argue that a state would arise from anarchy (as represented by Locke's state of nature) ... by a process which need not violate anyone's rights"

(p. xi). In particular, he believes that he has shown that the "transition from a state of nature to an ultraminimal state (the monopoly element) was morally legitimate and violated no one's rights and that the transition from an ultraminimal to a minimal state (the 'redistributive' element) also was morally legitimate and violated no one's rights" (p. 113).

3. Cf. pp. 108 and 114. Nozick is ambiguous as to whether the "unreliability" is procedural ("fair" substantive rules applied in an imperfect fashion) or substantive (rules substantively unfair to the members of the other IPAs). He seems to lean toward the former, raising a further question: why should we assume that the many imperfections of a given IPA's procedure would systematically disadvantage the members of the other IPAs, as compared with the IPA's own members, such that the former is entitled to some sort of special protection?

4. "Since an enormous number of actions do increase risks to others, a society which prohibited such ... actions would ill fit a picture of a free society as one embodying a presumption in favor of liberty, under which people permissibly could perform actions so long as they didn't harm others in specified ways" (p. 78).

5. Nozick himself raises this objection but never answers it: "It might be thought that moral considerations require allowing another to do whatever you do; since the situation is symmetrical some symmetrical solution must be found ... What moral right does [one party] have to *impose* this asymmetry, to *force* others not to behave as he does?" (p. 125)

6. Nozick states that compensation should be set at "one extremity of the contract curve," which he (correctly) equates with "full compensation" (p. 84).

7. What Nozick actually argues is that "compensation for disadvantages" is a fair compromise between full compensation and no compensation (see p. 146). But the real question for a libertarian is not whether to compromise from *full* compensation but whether to compromise from *market* compensation.

8. Although all IPAs may act to protect their members against other IPAs' unfair procedures by seeking to prohibit the use of those unfair procedures, "only the DPA will be able to do so with impunity," because the DPA "occup[ies] a unique position by virtue of its power," and as a consequence "alone is in a position to act solely by its own lights" [pp. 108–109]. Nozick explicitly denies that this argument amounts to "might makes right" (p. 118). But it is hard to see what else explains it, as the disavowal itself goes on to concede inadvertently: "Our explanation does not assume or claim that might makes right. But might does make enforced prohibitions, even if no one thinks the mighty have a

special entitlement to have realized in the world their own view of which prohibitions are correctly enforced" (pp. 118–119). It is hard to see how to construe these two sentences, other than as saying: I am not saying might makes right; I am simply saying might makes might.

9. Nozick famously asks in Part II, what rationale yields the result that a person is free to emigrate to escape any obligation to help the poor, but cannot stay put and opt out of that compulsory scheme? (See p. 173.) The rationale, of course, is democracy.

10. It is not clear that requiring there to be significant benefits from overriding rights meaningfully differentiates Nozick's proposal from conventional utilitarianism, as circumventing the market for gains anticipated to be small is unlikely to be optimal from a utilitarian perspective in any event. Statements casually embracing a utilitarian cost/benefit calculus are sprinkled throughout Part I. See for example Nozick's discussion of how to decide what forms of pollution to allow: *"Presumably [society] should permit those polluting activities whose benefits are greater than their costs,"* which should be determined via the Kaldor/Hicks criterion (p. 79).

11. Indeed, one could argue *must* be dispensed with, as – to quote the Nozick of Part II – "Contract arguments embody the assumption that anything that emerges from a certain process is just. Upon the force of this fundamental assumption rests the force of a contract argument" (p. 208).

12. Nozick seems to suggest at the very end of Part II that he might waive consent even for the more-than-minimal state, judging the justness of resulting societies instead by the extent to which they embody and protect the moral side constraints of individual rights. Indeed, Nozick goes even further down the consequentialist road, to suggest that consent is neither necessary nor sufficient to validate the society it produces: A society that protects individual rights but arose unjustly is much preferable, says Nozick, to one that arose justly but fails to protect individual rights (see p. 294, last paragraph). In short, the end-states justify the means.

13. See also p. 110: enjoined IPAs must be compensated only where "it is perfectly possible that the independents' activities including self-help enforcement could proceed without anyone's rights being violated."

14. I do not believe that articulated libertarian premises can resolve cases of certain harm either, without an assist from other unstated normative premises that often turn out to be welfarist manqué. But we need not reach that further problem here.

15. See also p. 101: "The natural-rights tradition offers little guidance on … how principles specifying how one is to act have knowledge built into their various clauses."

16. He applies it, for example, to polluting activities without regard to whether harm is certain to result or merely possible.

17. One might legitimately question how much that right of exit is worth in a world in which rights of entry are severely limited. But as suggested below, libertarian principles do not lend themselves well to a functional interpretation of rights. More importantly, if closed borders are the problem, that suggests a very different solution from the one proposed by the Nozick of Part II: not that we pressure any given country to reconfigure its political arrangements along libertarian (or any other) lines but that we pressure all countries of the world to open their borders.

18. "[F]ounders and members of a small community may, quite properly, refuse to allow anyone to opt out of equal sharing, even though it would be possible to arrange this" (p. 321).

19. Nozick considers and rejects another possible defense – that nations can more easily accommodate internal exit than can communities – as empirically unproved (see p. 322). To a true libertarian, however, the ease of accommodating rights should be irrelevant to whether we are obliged to accommodate them.

20. For Nozick's insistence on a bright-line rule turning on the legality of the constraining factors, see: "If facts of nature [limit one's alternatives], the actions are voluntary ... Other people's actions place limits on one's available opportunities. Whether this makes one's resulting action non-voluntary depends upon whether these others had the right to act as they did" (p. 262).

21. For more on this, see Fried: 2003.

22. Just to remind Nozick what a libertarian would say about this argument: "Others have no right to a say in those decisions which importantly affect them that someone else ... has a right to make" (p. 270).

Part IV **Utopia**

10 The framework for utopia

10.1 INTRODUCTION

Having argued in Parts I and II of *Anarchy, State, and Utopia* (*ASU*) that a minimal state is justified and that no state more extensive than the minimal state is legitimate, Nozick attempts to establish in Part III that the minimal state is an inspiring meta-utopia which we should strive to realize. Nozick's discussion of utopia and his argument to the effect that the minimal state is a framework for utopia is important for three overarching reasons. First, it constitutes a fascinating and underappreciated investigation into utopian theorizing. Second, it provides us with an account of the features that a Nozickian society is likely to exhibit, thereby enhancing our understanding of the positive vision underlying Nozick's project. Third, it is meant to constitute an independent argument for the minimal state that does not rely on any moral considerations, in particular an argument that does not rely on Nozick's controversial theory of individual rights (see p. 309 fn. and p. 333). The results of the different parts of *ASU* are meant to converge from different starting points on the same end point, namely a minimal state. This means that even if Nozick's libertarianism should turn out to be lacking a solid moral foundation, as has frequently been raised as an objection, his argument that the minimal state is a meta-utopia would still have to be reckoned with, which means that it is not possible to circumvent Nozick's defense of the minimal state by simply rejecting his theory of individual rights.

This chapter identifies and critically examines three arguments in favor of the minimal state that can be found in Nozick's discussion of the framework for utopia, namely:

1.   the minimal state is inspiring because it is a meta-utopia that counts as a realization of Nozick's possible-worlds model of utopia;

2.   the minimal state is the common ground of all possible utopian conceptions and as such can be universally endorsed; and

3.   the minimal state is the best means for approximating or realizing utopia.

While constituting fascinating lines of inquiry, all arguments are found to be wanting. Although they establish interesting and important results, they do not yield the conclusions that Nozick intended to establish.

10.2 MODELING UTOPIA

Nozick begins his discussion by noting that the minimal state is primarily conceived of in negative terms. Advocates of the minimal state are concerned with placing restrictions on the state, rather than identifying an inspiring positive role that the state is meant to fulfill. Given this negative portrayal, the minimal state seems too lack lustre. In order to find out what exactly it is that the minimal state is lacking, Nozick proceeds to investigate the notion of utopia and examine what features utopias have that make them inspiring and attractive.

Utopia is the best possible world. Utopia is the best imaginable world. It is the world that is such that no better world can be imagined. Nozick takes this characterization at face value and provides a possible-worlds model to capture this notion. The model is based on the idea of individuals having the power to create worlds as well as their inhabitants by imagining them, whereby each person has the same powers of imagination.[1] This gives rise to a process in which worlds are generated by being imagined. The inhabitants of a world can then either remain within that world or use their powers of imagination to create new worlds.

The question then arises whether any worlds will be stable, that is, whether any worlds will be such that their members decide to remain in these worlds rather than creating new worlds. If this should be the case, then these worlds will have the important property of being such that none of their members can imagine any other world they believe to be stable and of which they would rather be a member.[2] The notion of a stable world consequently captures the idea of a world that is judged to be the best possible world by all of its members, a world that is such that no better world can be imagined by its inhabitants. This means that within this possible-worlds model stable worlds are utopian worlds.

STABILITY$_W$: Stable worlds have the property of being such that none of their inhabitants can imagine any world they consider to be stable and of which they would rather be an inhabitant.

Nozick's possible-worlds model thus allows us to identify a structural condition that worlds must satisfy to classify as utopian, namely that they be stable worlds. Being stable turns out to be a necessary and sufficient condition for a world to have the utopian property. A world that satisfies this condition is a world that is such that none of its members can imagine a better world, a world they would rather be in.[3]

UTOPIA$_W$: A world w is a utopian world iff w is stable.

An important corollary of this result is that there will be different best possible worlds, different utopias for different people. Utopia is manifold and not unitary. No world counts as the best possible world simpliciter. The betterness ordering is determined by the criteria of bestness and these criteria vary from individual to individual. There is no world that is best according to all possible criteria. There are only worlds that are best according to particular criteria. This means that people who differ in terms of the worlds they classify as the best cannot co-inhabit the same utopia since any world that they co-inhabit will at best be utopian for some of them, but not for each of them. However, they can each have their own best possible world, their own utopia (shared with people who have compatible betterness orderings). This means that there is no world that is the best possible world for everyone. A world can only be best for each of its inhabitants. The model thus translates differences in values as well as differences in weightings of shared values into differences in utopias. To accommodate the diversity of preferences of people we need many utopias and not one.

Nozick's possible-worlds model provides us with an operationalization of the notion of a best possible world that turns the notion of utopia into a theoretically fruitful notion by identifying informative and clearly specifiable conditions that a world must satisfy to classify as utopian. This operationalization requires us to specify what the criterion for judging bestness is and what is understood by a possible world:

I. BEST FOR WHOM?

Nozick notes that what is best for me need not be best for you (see p. 298). Yet utopia should be the best possible world in a comprehensive and all-encompassing sense. It should not simply be best for a particular individual or group, but should be best for each of us.

Utopia is the best possible world for each person living in that world.

2. BEST ACCORDING TO WHICH STANDARDS?

An informative operationalization requires us to appeal to internal rather than external standards. This means that a world is utopian if it is the best possible world in the eyes of those living in that world. We do not assess whether a world is the best according to some objective and external criterion of bestness, but assess whether the people in the world judge the world to be best according to the standards that they endorse. We assess whether they wish to remain in the world or whether they can imagine a world that they would judge to be better.

Appealing to internal standards implies that we do not have to adopt a substantive conception of the good in order to assess for bestness. This allows us to give an account of utopia that does not presuppose any conception of the good and hence does not favor any particular utopian conception from the outset, which is a requisite criterion for an informative operationalization.

Utopia is the best possible world according to the standards of its inhabitants.

3. WHICH ASPECTS OF A WORLD ARE ASSESSED?

Since we are concerned with political philosophy, what we are assessing are institutional features. The operationalization is meant to provide or identify criteria that institutional structures must meet in order to qualify as utopian.

Restricting our focus to institutional features implies that a world that satisfies these criteria can be a miserable world if its non-institutional aspects should turn out to be miserable. Utopian worlds understood in this way need not be good in all respects but need only be best with respect to those features that are the subject of political philosophy. Put differently, the utopian theorizing with which we are concerned deals with questions of institutional design and evaluation and not with assessments of all features and aspects of life.

Additionally, this restriction implies that the inhabitants of a utopian world can differ widely in terms of their preferences regarding non-institutional features. For the world to be utopian, that is, best for each of them, it is only required that their preferences regarding institutional features agree in what counts as best.[4] Accordingly, utopian worlds need not be homogeneous and uniform and do not require that the preferences of their inhabitants coincide. All that is needed for utopia to be possible, is that there be homogeneity with respect to bestness judgments of the assessed features, that is, of institutional features.

Utopia is the best possible world in terms of its institutional structure.

4.   WHAT NOTION OF POSSIBILITY IS AT ISSUE?

Given that we are assessing institutional structures, we need to hold non-institutional factors fixed when assessing for what the best possible world is. Put differently, we are concerned with the question of what the best possible institutions are in a particular context of non-institutional circumstances.

This is important because different circumstances will require different institutions. What is best in one context need not be best in another context. From this it follows that there is no such thing as the best institutional structure simpliciter. Instead, certain institutional arrangements can only be considered to be the best possible arrangements for a certain range of circumstances. Hence, in order to make meaningful comparisons as to which institutions are better, we need to hold the context fixed. Otherwise, we would not get a total ordering and the notion of a best possible world would not be applicable.

In particular, preferences need to be held fixed. Otherwise it would not be possible to adequately operationalize the notion of bestness by appealing to internal standards. This is because a failure to hold preferences fixed would imply that the standards of bestness would themselves vary. Such shifting standards would not yield a determinate verdict as to which institutional arrangements are the best and we would not end up with a proper betterness ordering.

This feature of the operationalization has important implications for our understanding of the relation between stability and utopia. According to traditional utopian theorizing, utopias exhibit a distinct absence of change and are standardly depicted as conforming to a static end state. This is because any change in utopia is seen to either lead to a deterioration or at best have a neutral impact. No improvements are possible in utopia since *ex hypothesi* the world is already the best possible world. Nozick retains this insight insofar as the notion of stability is used by him to capture the idea that a world classifies as the best world and that no improvements are possible.[5] Yet, at the same time, Nozick's account allows for change and does not commit us to a static and rigid understanding of utopia. A dynamic conception of utopia is possible because bestness is defined relative to a set of parameters that can undergo changes. Rather than fixing in detail what utopian worlds have to be like, Nozick provides a structural condition that worlds have to satisfy to be utopian, whereby this condition is specified in terms of the preferences of the inhabitants of the worlds. This implies that as the preferences change the nature of the worlds satisfying the structural condition also changes. This means that Nozick's framework allows for but does not require change. It thereby reconciles a dynamic and flexible conception of society with the idea that a utopian society is in equilibrium and cannot be improved upon.

Utopia is the best possible world given the non-institutional circumstances.

Thus, the relevant notion of utopia is that of the best possible institutional structure (given a context in which certain non-institutional factors are being held fixed), whereby this structure has to be the best for each of us according to our own standards. In short, every member of the world must judge it to be the best possible world. If this condition is satisfied, then the world is stable and has the utopian property.

10.3 APPLYING THE MODEL

Nozick's possible-worlds model can be transferred to the real world by looking at associations rather than worlds and by considering the process of creating and joining associations rather than the process of imagining worlds. Instead of having different people create new worlds by their powers of imagination until stable worlds emerge, in the real world we have different people forming communities and associations until stable associations emerge. Put differently, associations fulfill a role in the actual world that is analogous to that of worlds in the possible-worlds model.

Although there are disanalogies between the model and the actual world, the analogies are sufficiently strong to ensure that the model is of relevance and has explanatory power. In particular, we can transfer the insight that stable worlds are utopian worlds to the idea that stable communities are utopian communities. That is, we can transfer the insight that stability is the structural condition that must be satisfied for something to have the utopian property (where stability is again understood relative to certain parameters that are being held fixed).

STABILITY$_A$: Stable associations have the property of being such that none of their members can imagine any association they consider to be stable and of which they would rather be a member.

Accordingly, we can understand a utopian community as a community that is such that none of its members would rather belong to any other community (that they believe would be stable). This means that they judge their community to be the best possible community. Within the actual world being stable is a necessary and sufficient condition for an association to have the utopian property.

UTOPIA$_A$: An association x is a utopian association iff x is stable.

As in the case of the model, we will again end up with a plurality of utopias. There will be different best possible associations for different people. Utopia will consist of many utopias. If all associations will be stable, then there will be a diverse set of utopian communities, each of which exemplifies the utopian property. This account is in stark contrast with traditional utopian theories which identify a unique way of life, a unique community that is taken to constitute the ideal.

It is important to note that diversity per se does not matter. A diverse collection of associations is not what counts as such. Diversity is not the goal that is to be achieved. What matters is that associations have the utopian property. This means that diversity of associations matters only insofar as we have a diversity of preferences. In particular, a diverse set of associations matters only if (1) people differ in the values they hold and/or (2) people differ in the weightings they assign to the values that they share, given that trade-offs need to be made and that it is not possible to realize all values simultaneously (see p. 297). That is, for one community to count as the best possible community for certain people, it is not enough that these people share the same values. They must also give the same weightings to these values. Otherwise, different combinations of these values will be ordered differently by them.

Specifying utopia in terms of the preferences of individuals implies that we can translate a diversity of preferences into a diversity of associations, thereby ensuring that all associations can have the utopian property. The extent to which diversity of communities is to be valued is fixed by the extent of the diversity of preferences. In case preferences should turn out to be uniform, having a diverse set of associations would be sub-optimal and a single homogeneous community would be required instead. What Nozick objects to is not the possibility of a homogeneous utopian society, but rather the *essential* homogeneity and uniformity of traditional utopias. Nozick is simply making the claim that as a matter of fact people differ significantly and that a plurality of associations is required to cater for these different preferences if utopia is to be achieved. In short, the framework allows for but does not require diversity.

There are various disanalogies between the model and the real world that require us to make some modifications. We will focus on two disanalogies.

I.   TRANSACTION COSTS: While imagining worlds involves minimal costs, creating and switching associations can be highly costly.

As soon as transaction costs are involved we can end up with multiple equilibria. The problem then is to avoid sub-optimal equilibria that result from transaction costs. In the presence of transaction costs, stability per se does not suffice for the utopian property. When in a sub-optimal equilibrium, the reason why people do not switch associations is not because they consider the association they are in to be the best possible association. Instead, they do not switch because the process of switching to an association they consider to be better would be too costly to make it worthwhile. The stability that obtains in such a situation is simply the result of transaction costs and not the result of utopia, that is, the absence of possible improvements. Stability has to be due to the absence of possible improvements, not due to possible improvements being too costly. Only in the absence of transaction costs are we justified in making the inference from an association's being stable to its being a utopian association. Accordingly, we need to look at stability under no transaction costs if stability is to be a sufficient and not only a necessary condition for possession of the utopian property.

2.   COERCION: While possible worlds are isolated, associations impinge on each other.

We need to avoid sub-optimal equilibria that result from coercion. In the presence of coercion, stability per se does not suffice for the utopian property. A stable association classifies as utopian if its stability is due to its members voluntarily deciding to remain in it on the basis that they consider it to be the best possible association. The members of an association must remain in that association because they take it to be the best possible association, not because they are coerced to remain in it. Accordingly, we need to look at stability in the absence of coercion if we are to be justified in making the inference from an association's being stable to its being a utopian association. Stability has to be due to the absence of possible improvements, not due to people being coerced to remain in their associations. In short, stability must be the result of voluntary choice.

Taking these disanalogies into account, the result of transferring the possible-worlds model to the real world is that non-coerced stability in the absence of transaction costs is a necessary and sufficient condition for an association to have the utopian property.

10.4 THE FRAMEWORK

Nozick specifies that the framework for utopia is an institutional arrangement "in which utopian experimentation can be tried, different styles of life can be lived, and alternative visions of the good can be individually or jointly pursued" (p. 307). He then claims that this institutional arrangement amounts to the minimal state.

The minimal state is a meta-association. It is a framework within which associations operate. The framework itself is not a utopia, but is the institutional setting within which particular utopias can be realized. While associations have the utopian property if they are stable, we can say that a framework has the meta-utopian property if all the associations that operate within it have the utopian property.

META-UTOPIA: A framework x is a meta-utopia iff all associations that operate in x are utopian associations.

Unfortunately, Nozick does not tell us how exactly he considers these considerations to support the minimal state. In particular, he neither tell us why it matters that the minimal state classifies as a framework for utopia, nor whether he thinks that the minimal state is the only state that satisfies the description of the framework. Given that Part III is meant to establish the claim that the minimal state is inspiring, we can take Nozick's first utopian argument to go roughly as follows:

The minimal state is the real-world analogue of the possible-worlds model of utopia. It is an institutional framework that replicates the relevant structural features of the model within the actual world and can consequently be considered as a realization of the model. Given that the model gives rise to a process that generates utopian worlds and given that such worlds are inspiring, the minimal state should also be inspiring since within it utopian associations are generated that should be considered to be equally inspiring.

This kind of argument faces two significant problems:

I.   WHAT NOTION OF 'INSPIRING' IS AT ISSUE?
      There is some ambivalence in Nozick's description of the virtues of the framework. At times it seems that Nozick considers a society evolved within the framework to be

inspiring because of the diversity that it is likely to exhibit. However, in order for the argument to not rely on any particular conception of the good or set of such conceptions, Nozick has to argue that such a society is inspiring because it satisfies the structural condition required for counting as a meta-utopia. If the framework is meant to be in principle inspiring, then its inspiringness cannot be linked to any particular conception of the good. The framework should accordingly be inspiring even to those who adhere to a conception of the good that explicitly rejects diversity.

While it is clear why the particular utopian associations are inspiring to their members, it is not at all clear why the meta-association should be considered to be inspiring. A society evolved within the framework will be inspiring to someone who wants it to be the case that people can live their lives the way that they choose and that they can freely pursue their utopian ambitions, but it is not clear if there is any sense in which such a society will be inspiring to someone who rejects those views. Similarly, the fact that the framework is likely to exhibit diversity constitutes a reason to support the framework for those people who attach value to diversity. Yet, this does not hold in the case of those people who do not value diversity. The problem is that every aspect of the framework that might be considered to be inspiring will only be inspiring to people adhering to a particular conception of the good. Every ascription of inspiringness seems to have its source in a substantive conception of the good and consequently does not generalize to people who do not share the relevant values. Accordingly, these explanations cannot form the basis for claiming that the framework is in principle inspiring. Thus, Nozick seems to be committed to saying that satisfaction of the structural condition somehow constitutes a sufficient reason on its own for the framework to classify as being inspiring. Yet, how satisfying this structural condition can be considered to be inspiring is not clear.[6]

2. WHAT IMPORT DOES THIS ARGUMENT HAVE?

Being inspiring does not in any way single out the minimal state and does not allow us to identify the features such a state should have. If the claim that the minimal state is inspiring in virtue of being a meta-utopia is meant to be an argument in favor of the minimal state, then it needs to be shown that such a state is more inspiring or at least more likely to be more inspiring than its alternatives. However, no such argument has been put forward by Nozick and no such argument seems to be forthcoming since many states satisfy the relevant description.

Whilst not being an independent argument, it can nonetheless play some role in Nozick's project since it can be considered as providing independent support for the minimal state by rebutting the charge that the minimal state lacks lustre and fails to be inspiring. This requires us to look at the inspiringness argument in the context of the preceding part. While Part II of *ASU* tells us what the minimal state looks like, Part III can then tell us that such a state corresponds to the possible-worlds model, that it is the real-world analogue of the model. Such considerations can thus play a limited role in Nozick's overall argument. They can be used to show that the minimal state is inspiring, even though they do not show that it is uniquely or maximally inspiring. For the inspiringness argument to play this limited role, the minimal state must satisfy the description of the framework (and the framework must be considered to be inspiring), but it is not required that all those states that satisfy this description be minimal states.

Accordingly, we can grant Nozick that there is something about the minimal state that is in some sense inspiring to at least some of us. It is not in the first place the minimal state itself that is inspiring. It, after all, is not a utopia but only a meta-utopia. Rather, it is that which happens within the confines of the minimal state that can be considered to be inspiring. It is the associations that develop and operate within it that are inspiring to their members.[7] They can all have the utopian property, thereby making the minimal state into a meta-utopia, something that will be inspiring to all those who value that people can pursue their utopian dreams and can live whichever way they consider to be best. This is not an independent argument for the minimal state, but nonetheless provides some independent support for the minimal state.

10.5 THE COMMON GROUND

A more promising argument for the minimal state can be identified by focusing on the fact that the minimal state not only is an institutional framework "in which utopian experimentation can be tried, different styles of life can be lived, and alternative visions of the good can be individually or jointly pursued" (p. 307) but that it is a framework in which all possible visions of the good can be pursued. Put differently, while many more-than-minimal states allow for utopian experimentation, the minimal state has the distinguishing characteristic of being a framework that does not exclude or rule out any associations and is accordingly compatible with all utopian conceptions. Given this characteristic, the minimal state can be considered to be the common ground of all possible utopian conceptions and can consequently be universally endorsed.

Thus, if we understand utopia as a situation in which all associations have the utopian property, then this implies that the minimal state is the maximal institutional structure that is in principle compatible with utopia. No matter what preferences people should have, no matter what utopian conceptions they should adhere to, the minimal state allows them to pursue their utopian ambitions and is compatible with a situation in which all of these people belong to associations that have the utopian property. Put differently, the minimal state can have the meta-utopian property no matter what utopian conceptions people should hold. That is, if we distinguish between institutional structures that are in principle compatible with a situation in which all associations have the utopian property and those that only accidentally allow for such a situation, then we can see that the minimal state is the maximal institutional structure that can in principle have the meta-utopian property.

COMMON GROUND 1: The minimal state is the maximal institutional structure that is in principle compatible with utopia.

Any institutional structure that is more extensive than the minimal state will fail to be neutral and will privilege certain views of utopia. Any restrictions on what associations can be like will ensure that there will be some people who do not consider their association to be the best possible association, but would rather be members of an association that would not be subject to those restrictions. This means that any more extensive state cannot in principle be the best for each of us but can only be the best for those adhering to the utopias that are thus privileged. More-than-minimal states will thus only be accidentally compatible with utopia, namely only in those situations in which no one should wish to be a member of an association that is subject to the restrictions of a more-than-minimal state.

An important corollary of this result is that if a state happens to be accidentally compatible with utopia in a certain situation, then it will not perform any functions in that situation that go beyond those of the minimal state. In other words, all the non-minimal features of a more-than-minimal state will be ineffective in utopia. All the restrictions it imposes on what associations can be like will be inoperative in utopia since ex hypothesi no one will want to belong to such an association. Put differently, if a state is merely accidentally compatible with utopia, then it coincides with the minimal state in utopia and any differences between them will not be operative in these circumstances.

COROLLARY: The functions performed by any state in utopia will coincide with those of the minimal state.

This in turn implies that the minimal state can be universally endorsed. While any state more extensive than a minimal state will privilege certain conceptions of the good, thereby precluding the possibility of having a system that can in principle be endorsed by everyone, the minimal state is compatible with all utopian conception. Accordingly, everyone should hold that the minimal state would at least be an adequate institutional structure in utopia. There should consequently be no in principle opposition to the minimal state. Anyone opposed to the minimal state should at most be contingently opposed to it and should hold that a more extensive state is only required because people happen to have the wrong preferences. At most, people should oppose the minimal state on the grounds that we are not ready for it yet, that utopia has not yet been reached. As Nozick notes, everyone should hold that the framework is an adequate institutional structure for a society of good men (see p. 319).

10.6 IMPERIALISTS

We have just seen that the minimal state is the maximal institutional structure that in principle allows for a situation in which everyone is a member of a utopian association. Within the framework of the minimal state everyone can belong to an association that has the utopian property, no matter what utopian conception they should hold. To this it might be objected that the minimal state excludes what Nozick calls imperialistic conceptions of utopia and accordingly fails to be neutral after all.

Nozick distinguishes between existentialist, missionary and imperialist conceptions of utopia (see pp. 319–320). While existentialists hold a neutral stance with respect to the views held by others, and while missionaries want others to adopt their views but require that this adoption be voluntary, imperialists condone the use of force in getting other people to subscribe to their views. Since utopia is incompatible with coercion, it is incompatible with imperialistic behavior. This incompatibility gives rise to a need to impose restrictions on behavior and regulate the interactions between different communities. In particular, the framework is required to rule out coercion. Accordingly, the framework appears to be non-neutral and appears to privilege non-coercive conceptions of utopia over coercive ones.

While the framework rules out coercion, it nonetheless does not exclude imperialistic associations. Instead of excluding imperialistic communities, the framework only excludes imperialistic behavior.[8] Imperialists can form associations and govern their associations according to their preferred principles. The framework simply makes it the case that they cannot impose their preferences on others. Put differently, it is perfectly acceptable for there to be an imperialistic community that has imperialistic ambitions but does not act upon them. As a result, the framework can provide imperialists with associations that have the utopian property. This means that imperialists can be members of associations that are such that there is no other association of which they would rather be members, since their current association is governed according to their own ideal principles. Accordingly, the framework can be a meta-utopia even if some or all people should adhere to imperialistic conceptions of utopia. Everyone can be in an association that has the utopian property. In other words, despite ruling out coercion, the framework still classifies as being the common ground of all possible utopian conceptions since it is compatible with the existence of imperialistic communities and only rules out the use of force in establishing such communities.

Since the meta-utopian property is had by a framework if all associations operating within it have the utopian property, that is, are

such that none of their members would rather be in any other association that they consider to be stable, it is instantiated in situations in
which everyone's self-regarding first-order preferences are satisfied.
Put differently, when focusing on the meta-utopian property we only
look at whether the people within the framework are all members
of utopian associations. We do not look at whether their preferences
regarding other people or their preferences regarding the meta-
association are satisfied. Thus, the result that the minimal state is
the maximal institutional structure that can in principle have the
meta-utopian property amounts to the result that the minimal state
is the maximal institutional structure that is in principle compatible
with a situation in which everyone's self-regarding first-order preferences are satisfied.

COMMON GROUND 2: The minimal state is the maximal institutional structure that is in principle compatible with the complete satisfaction of everyone's self-regarding first-order preferences.

While the framework allows everyone to be in an association with
the utopian property, that is, everyone's preferences regarding what
kind of association they wish to be a member of can be satisfied, it is
not the case that other kinds of preferences can always be satisfied.
In particular, other-regarding preferences and preferences regarding
meta-associations will not always be satisfied.[9] For instance, unless
everyone should be in favor of the minimal state, it will not be the
case that everyone's preferences concerning meta-associations will
be satisfied by the framework. As Fowler notes, "in the eyes of the
communities the minimal state is forcing *its* ideals on them" (Fowler:
1980, p. 559). The framework allows people to choose their ideal association, but it does not allow them to choose their meta-association.
Every meta-association will impose its ideals on those people who prefer a different meta-association.[10] The minimal state is not an exception in this regard. What makes the minimal state special is that its
ideals are compatible with all self-regarding first-order preferences.

The restriction to first-order self-regarding preferences is
required if utopia is to be in principle possible. That is, if we understand utopia as in some way involving the complete satisfaction
of preferences (here preferences regarding institutional matters),
then the maximal non-arbitrary set of preferences that are in principle co-satisfiable are preferences that are self-regarding and first-

order. Put differently, a situation in which everyone's preferences are satisfied is in principle only possible if we restrict our focus to self-regarding first-order preferences, that is, preferences about the association of which one is a member.[11] Other-regarding preferences as well as preferences about meta-associations must be excluded since they are not in principle co-satisfiable, that is, these preferences are such that satisfaction of one of them precludes satisfaction of many others.

COMMON GROUND 3: The minimal state is the maximal institutional structure that is in principle compatible with the complete satisfaction of the maximal non-arbitrary set of preferences that are in principle co-satisfiable.

The need for this restriction is nicely illustrated by imperialists since their preferences are essentially such that, as long as anyone holds views that differ from theirs, they will not be satisfied unless not everyone is satisfied.[12] Since it is impossible in principle to satisfy all preferences of all people, the best that can be achieved is for a restricted range of preferences to be satisfied. The maximal non-arbitrary set of preferences that are in principle co-satisfiable are first-order self-regarding preferences. Thus, to the extent to which the idea of utopia is in principle possible, it can only consist in every association having the utopian property, that is, a situation in which everyone's first-order self-regarding preferences are satisfied, and the maximal institutional structure that is compatible with such a situation is the minimal state.

Although the minimal state is the common ground of all utopian conceptions, the fact that other-regarding preferences and preferences concerning meta-associations will at best be accidentally satisfied implies that imperialists will oppose, or at least not fully endorse, the framework. This is because the framework does not allow them to use what they consider to be adequate means, namely coercive means, for realizing their utopian visions. Imperialists will consequently see themselves as being restricted by the framework. Even though they would not rather belong to any other association, they would prefer for their association to be embedded in a different framework, namely one that would not restrict their coercive behavior. Accordingly, while allowing imperialists to be members of associations that have the utopian property, the framework cannot in principle provide them with a world that has the utopian property; that is, there are worlds that are such that they would rather have their association be a part of those worlds, namely worlds in which they can implement their imperialistic ambitions or worlds in which everyone adheres to their views. It can, of course, happen that a particular imperialistic utopian vision is fully realized, in which case the imperialists will no longer oppose the framework. As Nozick notes, they "will oppose the framework so long as some others do not agree with them" (p. 320), but if everyone should agree with them, then they will no longer oppose the framework. Similarly, missionaries will not be fully satisfied with the framework as long as others should hold differing views since they would prefer to be in a world where everyone adhered to their utopian conception. This means that the opposition to or lack of full endorsement of the framework on the part of imperialists and missionaries is not a principled opposition, but is contingent on what preferences other people happen to have.

Nozick has frequently been criticized on the basis that he needs to smuggle in moral considerations to deal with imperialists (cf. Hailwood: 1996 and Mack: 1975, p. 10). We can now see that these criticisms are misplaced. There is no need to appeal to moral considerations in order to rule out imperialistic behavior. The impropriety of imperialistic behavior simply follows from utopia being the best possible world for each of us. Imperialistic behavior is ruled out because this is a presupposition of achieving a meta-utopian situation, that is, a situation in which all associations have the utopian property. More precisely, it is necessary that no one be coerced to live in a particular way, that is, that no one be subjected to imperialistic behavior, if it is to be possible that everyone is to be a member of an association with the utopian property. In this way we can have a situation in which all self-regarding preferences are satisfied, that is, all preferences regarding the community of which one is a member. This, though, leaves the other-regarding preferences of imperialists (as well as of missionaries) unsatisfied. It might now be asked why we privilege the self-regarding preferences of non-imperialists over the other-regarding preferences of imperialists. The reason why other-regarding preferences are excluded is that their inclusion would contravene the co-satisfiability criterion, a criterion that follows from utopia being best for each of us. If only some people's preferences are satisfied, then the world will only be the best possible world for those people and not for each of us. This means that the preferences that must be satisfied for a situation to be utopian must be co-satisfiable. As we have seen, the maximal non-arbitrary set of in principle co-satisfiable preferences is the set of first-order self-regarding preferences. Accordingly, for utopia to be possible, for a situation that is best for each of us to be possible, imperialistic behavior has to be ruled out.

10.7 THE FRAMEWORK AND THE MINIMAL STATE

Nozick claims that the framework is to be identified with the minimal state and that Part III of *ASU* constitutes an independent argument for the theory defended in the prior parts. It is, however, questionable to what extent a meta-association that satisfies the condition of not placing any restrictions on the non-imperialistic pursuit of utopian conceptions should be identified with a Nozickian minimal state. In particular, the argument that the minimal state is the maximal institutional structure that is in principle compatible with utopia provides at best partial confirmation or corroboration for the results established in Parts I and II and to some extent even seems to be in conflict with those results. (1–5 focus on partial confirmation, while 6 establishes a direct conflict.)

1. The compatibility argument only establishes an upper bound, insofar as the minimal state is the maximal institutional structure that is compatible with all possible utopian conceptions, and no lower bound. The argument shows that no state more extensive than the minimal state is in principle compatible with utopia, but this leaves open the possibility that it would be preferable to have a less-than-minimal state (such as Nozick's ultra-minimal state) or no state at all.

2. Nozick states that the major role of the central authority "would be to enforce the operation of the framework – for example, to prevent some communities from invading and seizing others, their persons or assets" (p. 329). However, he does not tell us how to understand assets. For this we need

an account of property rights, but no such account straight-forwardly follows from the compatibility argument. Put differently, the framework argument does not yield any clear account of property rights, yet property rights play a crucial role in the conception of the minimal state developed in Parts I and II.

3. The framework rules out coercion since coerced stability does not give rise to the utopian property.[13] However, the framework argument lacks sufficient resources to rule out killing. The reason why the argument does not result in a prohibition on killing is that utopia is specified by means of a structural condition that only applies to those people that do exist at a particular time. This means that stability can be achieved by eliminating all those people that are dissatisfied, that is, those that are such that they can imagine associations of which they would rather be a member.[14] The structural condition looks only at those people that do exist and not at those that have been killed.[15]

4. All that matters is that everyone be in an association that has the utopian property. It does not matter how we get to such a stable situation. In particular, people can be coerced into utopia. The fact that people were coerced to enter an association in no way undermines the utopian character of an association, as long as all its members wish to remain in the association. Put differently, we can be coerced to do that what we would have chosen anyway, or what we would have chosen in the absence of akrasia. This means that choice per se is irrelevant and drops out of the picture. All that matters is that our preferences be adequately aligned with the associations to which we belong. Relatedly, being prohibited from leaving an association is unproblematic as long as one does not desire to leave that association, that is, as long as that association retains its utopian character. Only once one no longer wishes to remain in an association does a prohibition on leaving it give rise to a sub-optimal and hence non-utopian situation.

5. The structural and non-historical nature of the characterization of utopia also has untoward consequences when looking at preference formation. What matters is that at each time

associations be aligned with preferences. How preferences are formed or how they change is irrelevant from the point of view of the framework argument. This means that it is possible to attain utopia by changing people's preferences. In particular, stability can be achieved by changing the preferences of all those people who are dissatisfied in such a way that they will come to judge the associations of which they are members as being utopian according to their new preferences. This implies that a situation in which everyone considers the association of which he or she is a member to be the best possible association is a utopian situation, independently of whether it has been achieved by brainwashing or in some other way.[16]

6. Nozick suggests that joining an association can bring with it commitments regarding the conditions under which the association can be exited (see pp. 330–331). For instance, if someone signs a contract to the effect that he or she will remain in a particular association, then that person will not be allowed to leave while the contract is in force even if that person's preferences should change and the person should no longer regard that association as the best possible association. According to Nozick's moral philosophy, the person can be forced to remain in that association and such a use of force would not count as coercion, given that Nozick is dealing with a moralized conception of coercion. The framework argument, on the contrary, does classify such a use of force as coercion since it is based on a non-moralized conception and implies that this kind of coercion gives rise to a suboptimal equilibrium that needs to be avoided if utopia is to be achieved. If someone's preferences change, then a meta-utopian situation is not restored until that person switches to an association that conforms to the modified preferences. Prior commitments, contracts, or promises to the previous association seem to be irrelevant from this point of view and completely drop out of the picture. Put differently, the exit option flowing from the framework argument is entirely unrestricted, whilst the exit option resulting from Nozick's moral argument is limited since it requires that commitments and obligations be met.[17] The difference between the

moralized and non-moralized conceptions of coercion thus implies that Parts I and II rule out certain actions as being impermissible, such as breaking a contractual agreement in order to exit a sub-optimal association and switch to a utopian association, while Part III classifies them not only as permissible but as required for achieving utopia.

Thus, we can see that the argument that the minimal state is a framework for utopia only partially confirms the results established in the previous parts of *ASU* and to some extent is even in conflict with those results. The differences and conflicts result, on the one hand, from a clash between a moralized and non-moralized understanding of coercion and, on the other, from a clash between a procedural account of morality and a structural account of utopia.

10.8 EXTERNAL STANDARDS

So far, being utopian has been understood as being the best in the sense of being judged to be the best by the members of the association or the inhabitants of the world. The operationalization has appealed to internal standards of bestness, to the judgments and preferences of the members or inhabitants. On the basis of this understanding, it has been argued that the minimal state is a real-world analogue of Nozick's possible-worlds model of utopia and that the minimal state is the maximal institutional structure that is in principle compatible with utopia.

This conception of utopia can be rejected. Instead, it can be insisted that utopia consists in conformity to certain objective and external standards.[18] This raises the question how Nozick can respond to someone who rejects the operationalization and argues that we should appeal to external rather than internal standards. Three strategies suggest themselves, namely to (1) strengthen the case for internal standards, (2) find ways to connect external to internal standards in such a way as to ensure that the results are still valid, and (3) identify arguments in favor of the minimal state that hold even in the context of external standards.

I.   INFORMATIVE OPERATIONALIZATION: Those who reject an operationalization in terms of internal standards and instead appeal to external standards to specify the notion of utopia are not able to accord a substantive and theoretically interesting role to this notion. Disagreements will then not be directly about utopia but will concern the underlying conception of the good. All debates can accordingly proceed in terms of the more fundamental questions about value and the good. On such a view, "utopia" will simply be a label attached to certain situations singled out by one's value theory. The notion of utopia will consequently only be a convenient shorthand that is dispensable in moral and political theorizing. Yet, if one wants to grant a distinctive role to the notion of utopia and wants to allow that there is an interesting characterization of utopia on which people can agree even if they adhere to different conceptions of the good, then one needs to provide a non-trivial and non-question-begging operationalization of this notion. Whilst a direct specification of utopia that derives from a particular conception of the good simply consists in attaching a label, an operationalization in terms of internal standards allows us to give an informative indirect specification of utopia. Such an operationalization allows one to have substantive debates about this notion and discover interesting results.

An operationalization via internal standards not only provides us with a theoretically interesting and fruitful notion, it also gives us a plausible and well-grounded understanding of what utopia amounts to. Rather than resulting from an arbitrary and ad hoc stipulation, we are led to this characterization by a natural chain of reasoning that proceeds from (1) utopia is the best possible world, to (2) utopia is the best imaginable world, to (3) utopia is the world that is such that none of its members can imagine a better world. Defenders of external standards have to reject this natural chain of reasoning.

2. ENDORSEMENT CONSTRAINT: We can connect external to internal standards by imposing a condition that requires that utopia not only consist in conformity to certain objective and external standards, but that these standards also be endorsed by the members of the association, that is, requiring that external and internal standards coincide in utopia. Imposing such a condition can be motivated by noting that

utopia is supposed to be the best society for its members, which suggests that they should recognize and judge it to be the best. What is objectively best should ideally not be completely disconnected from what the subjects take to be best. The endorsement condition allows us to retain the previously established results in the context of external standards. In particular, we can retain the result that in utopia more-than-minimal states will not do anything that would exceed the functions of the minimal state; that is, in utopia the state will at most exert the functions of a minimal state. Accordingly, we can also retain the result that there should be no in principle opposition to the minimal state.[19]

It should be noted that connecting external standards to internal standards by means of an endorsement condition only leads to interesting results in contexts where there are different best lives for different people. If we have complete homogeneity, then we will end up with a unique best association. The framework will then become completely irrelevant and ineffective. Put differently, the framework only plays a significant role if there is a plurality of associations, which requires that there be different best lives for different people (i.e., different values or different weightings of shared values, where trade-offs need to be made).

3.   INSTRUMENTAL CONSIDERATIONS: Once external standards are brought in, epistemic worries arise. While one might reasonably hold that there is an objectively best society, claiming that one knows exactly what such a society looks like is another matter. In particular, the vast complexity of life suggests that a healthy dose of epistemic humility is in order. Given how complex life is, it seems impossible to design the best community. To the extent to which we have a conception of the best possible world or best possible society, this conception is significantly shaped by our experiences and is not simply the result of armchair theorizing. It is by reflecting on our experiences, as well as those of others, that we develop a conception of what the best society might look like. The impossibility of designing utopia from scratch then opens up room for instrumental arguments to the effect that having a diverse collection of associations

and the freedom to experiment allows us to overcome our epistemic limitations and identify the objectively best life. Instead of trying to design utopia, we need to rely on filter mechanisms that weed out inappropriate products from a large set of generated alternatives. This means that we require a plurality of associations and have to let people freely form associations and decide how to live their lives if we are to identify utopia, even if utopia itself should be unitary.[20]

10.9 THE MORE-THAN-MINIMAL STATE?

The appeal to epistemic considerations based on the superiority of filter-devices over design-devices suggests a third line of argument, namely to conceive of the framework argument as an instrumental argument. Rather than focusing on the inspiring nature of the framework or on the fact that it is the maximal institutional structure that can in principle be universally endorsed, instrumental arguments are based on the idea that the framework is the best means for approximating or realizing utopia. Such instrumental claims can be made both within the context of internal standards and within the context of external standards. The framework may have beneficial instrumental effects in terms of bringing about a situation in which everyone judges his or her association to be the best possible association, as well as in terms of bringing about a situation that corresponds to certain external standards that are taken to specify what utopia consists in.

Yet, all such instrumental arguments in favor of the minimal state that try to establish that such a state is a good means for achieving or approximating utopia (whether understood according to internal or external standards) are problematic since there might well be cases where the minimal state may be non-optimal and where either a less-than-minimal or more-than-minimal state may be superior. Accordingly, instrumental considerations will not uniquely and unconditionally support the minimal state and will thereby not establish the conclusion that Nozick intends to establish.

SUB-OPTIMAL EQUILIBRIA: As regards approximating utopia understood according to internal standards, we can see that there can be circumstances where this might be best achieved by means of non-minimal states. In particular, if the framework has the role of ruling out coercion given that coerced stability does not give rise to the utopian property, then it would seem that the framework should also have the role of avoiding other kinds of stable yet non-utopian situations. Such sub-optimal equilibria can, for instance, result from (1) transaction costs, (2) coordination failure, (3) faulty beliefs/reasoning, and (4) akrasia or practical irrationality.

1. As we saw above, stability that results from transaction costs does not give rise to the utopian property. If people remain in their associations for the reason that moving to a situation they would consider to be preferable is too costly, then such a stable situation fails to be utopian.

2. A sub-optimal equilibrium can arise if we have a situation that is stable, not because no improvements are possible, but because coordination problems prevent people from moving to an intrinsically better stable situation.

3. Given that a utopian association is understood not as the best possible association but as the best possible association believed to be stable, there seems to be room for epistemic mistakes (that do not rely on any value judgments). If someone judges an association to be the best possible stable association even though there is another association that that person judges to be better but mistakenly considers to be unstable, then one ends up with a sub-optimal equilibrium, that is, a stable yet non-utopian situation.

4. If someone remains in an association, not because that person judges this association to be the best possible association but because of weakness of will, then that association will be stable but not utopian.

In each of these cases, it seems to be an open question whether the minimal state is the best institutional structure for avoiding sub-optimal equilibria, or whether a less-than-minimal or more-than-minimal state may be better suited for that task. For instance, such non-minimal states might be required for reducing transaction costs in order to increase mobility which would allow us to avoid sub-optimal equilibria to a greater extent and hence get closer to utopia.[21]

Moreover, instrumental arguments based on internal standards face the problem of finding a principled way of weighing up the satisfaction of different people's preferences. When we are concerned with identifying the conditions that must be satisfied for the complete realization of utopia, "neutrality" between different people follows from the understanding of utopia since utopia is understood as being best for each of us, requiring that everyone counts equally in the sense of everyone's (self-regarding, first-order) preferences having to be fully satisfied if utopia is to be achieved. This, however, is not the case when it comes to instrumental arguments that aim at approximating utopia. When examining which option is best, one needs to weigh up and aggregate costs and benefits that accrue to different people. Yet, unless one brings in moral considerations it is not at all clear how to establish what weightings one should attach to different people's preferences. In the absence of such weightings, instrumental reasoning will not be able to aggregate and will not be able to always yield a determinate verdict as to which option is best supported by instrumental considerations.

Furthermore, if weightings can somehow be established, it might be possible to achieve a better approximation of utopia by compelling people to join or remain in certain associations, thereby making options available that otherwise would not have existed and that allow for optimizing the overall satisfaction of preferences. For instance, if association A would not be viable without x but x would prefer to be in A*, then it can be the case that forcing x to join or remain in A will lead to the result that a large number of people can be members of an association they consider to be utopian, namely association A, and x will be the only one who will be in a sub-optimal position. The option whereby x is forced, leading to a situation in which everyone other than x will be in an association they consider to be utopian, seems to be preferable from an instrumental point of view over the option whereby x is not forced but instead joins A* making it the case that x is in an association that x considers to be utopian, while everyone else who would otherwise have been in A will not be a member of an association that they consider to be the best possible association.

OPTIMAL RATE OF EXPERIMENTATION: As regards approximating utopia understood according to external standards, we can also see that there can be circumstances where this might be best achieved by means of non-minimal states. While Nozick makes a good case to the effect that the minimal state is commendable for allowing people to experiment and learn from each other, Nozick is aware of the fact that such an instrumental argument does not uniquely support the minimal state. To strengthen the epistemic argument, he notes that the framework has the distinctive advantages "of a filtering process incorporating mutually improving interaction between the filter and the surviving products of the generating process" (p. 317). Yet, this does not guarantee the superiority of the minimal state over alternative systems in all possible circumstances. It might well make the minimal state the best system on the whole, but this is compatible with there being particular exceptions. In particular, since the framework leaves room for experimentation but does not require it, it seems possible that there can be situations in which there is not enough experimentation, situations in which people are too reluctant to try out new things. Put differently, in some cases providing incentives for experimentation may allow us to achieve a more optimal rate of experimentation and the provision of such incentives is a role that might be fulfilled by a more-than-minimal state (see p. 329 fn.).[22]

While the minimal state may turn out to be optimal for overcoming our epistemic limitations as well as for dealing with sub-optimal equilibria, these claims require substantive argumentation. Whether such instrumental arguments uniquely support the minimal state cannot be established a priori but is an empirical question that may well vary from context to context. Whilst the minimal state might be optimal in a large number of cases, there could well be cases in which a different institutional structure would be optimal.

Additionally, since instrumental arguments are goal-directed, they cannot yield side constraints. As soon as optimization is at issue, trade-offs can become necessary to achieve the optimal way of approximating utopia, yet such trade-offs are precisely what side constraints are meant to exclude. This means that even if instrumental considerations should establish 'individual rights' corresponding to those that Nozick puts forward in Parts I and II, these rights would not have the status of side constraints but could be outweighed. Accordingly, clashes can arise insofar as instrumental considerations can recommend or require actions that are ruled out by the side constraints.

10.10 CONCLUSION

Nozick provides us with a fascinating investigation of the notion of utopia and clearly demonstrates the fruitfulness of utopian theorizing. Unfortunately, it is not entirely clear what he is arguing. We have identified three possible lines of argument in favor of the minimal state.

The first argument shows that the minimal state is a realization of Nozick's possible-worlds model and that it can consequently have the meta-utopian property. It then tries to argue on this basis that the minimal state can be considered to be inspiring. This argument is problematic since it is not at all clear in what sense such a framework is meant to be inspiring. Moreover, such considerations do not constitute an independent argument but at best provide support for a conception of the minimal state that has been established on independent grounds.

The second argument establishes that the minimal state can be considered to be the common ground of all possible utopian conceptions and can consequently be universally endorsed. This is because it is the maximal institutional structure that is in principle compatible with the complete satisfaction of the maximal non-arbitrary set of preferences that are in principle co-satisfiable. Moreover, we were able to extend this argument to show that at most the functions of the minimal state will be operative in utopia and that there should consequently be no in principle opposition to the minimal state. This argument also had some shortcomings. While it underwrites certain functions of the minimal state, such as ruling out coercing people against their will, it fails to rule out anti-akratic forcing and does not even generate a prohibition on killing. Additionally, there emerged conflicts with the understanding of the minimal state that Nozick developed in Part II of *ASU* due to the fact that Part II relies on a moralized conception of coercion, while a non-moralized conception is at play in the utopia argument. Finally, the argument can be circumvented by appealing to external standards.

The third argument attempts to establish that the minimal state is an optimal or at least a very good means for realizing or approximating utopia, independently of whether or not utopia is understood according to internal standards or external standards. The problem with this argument is that it makes advocacy of the minimal state contingent and dependent on empirical claims. In particular, significant additional arguments are required to establish the instrumental superiority of the minimal state over more-than-minimal as well as less-than-minimal states. Moreover, which institutional structure turns out to be best in promoting the realization of utopia may well differ from context to context, which implies that such instrumental considerations may well warrant a role for a more-than-minimal state, for instance in terms of reducing transaction costs. Finally, this argument does not establish restrictions that have the status of side constraints.

Thus, it seems most charitable to interpret Nozick's discussion in Part III of *ASU* not as an independent argument for the minimal state, but as an attempt to provide further support for the conception of the minimal state that has been developed in Parts I and II, by (1) showing in what ways the minimal state can be considered to be inspiring, by (2) highlighting the vast diversity of different utopian conceptions that can be accommodated by a minimal state, and by (3) specifying the instrumental benefits, in particular the epistemic benefits, that are likely to result when people are allowed to freely experiment and live their lives as they see fit. These supporting considerations derive from the fact that the minimal state does not specify a particular utopia that is to be achieved, but is instead a framework within which all possible non-coercive utopian conceptions can be realized. It is a system that allows people to create the communities they wish, to live their lives as they desire and to pursue their utopian dreams.

NOTES

For helpful discussions and comments, I should like to thank Asher Dresner, Alistair Isaac, and Jason Sorens. Thanks also to audiences at Oxford and at the 'Reappraising *Anarchy, State, and Utopia*' conference at King's College London.

1. Nozick imposes various restrictions on what can be imagined in order to avoid trivialising the model. In particular, we cannot (directly or indirectly) specify the preferences of the inhabitants of a world since we could otherwise specify that all inhabitants consider their world to be the best possible world which would ensure that the world would trivially be stable and that the model would accordingly be trivialized (see pp. 302–304). The model could be simplified by having populations

be randomly generated, since this would ensure that they could not be manipulated in a way that would trivialize the model.

2. Since the worlds that have to satisfy the condition of not being judged to be better than the utopian world are restricted to worlds that are believed to be stable, the characterization of stability is circular. Nozick is aware of this problem but sets it aside (see p. 305). We can note that this circularity is unproblematic since the conditions for stability of w will be disjunctive; that is, either there is no world w* that is judged to be better than w, or every world w** that is judged to be better than w is believed not to be stable, whereby the latter condition is cashed out as there being a world w*** that is better than w** and stable, whereby the conditions for w*** to be stable are again our original disjunctive conditions, i.e., either there is no world w**** that is judged to be better than w***, or every world w***** that is judged to be better than w*** is believed not to be stable, and so on, thereby making it the case that the stability conditions will not always be finitely statable.

3. There being stable worlds presupposes that the betterness ordering on worlds has an upper bound. Given the restriction (discussed later in this chapter) that worlds are only assessed with respect to institutional features, this does not seem implausible. Moreover, the arguments in favor of the minimal state can be restated in terms of utopian improvements. For instance, rather than arguing that the framework is compatible with utopia, one can argue that the framework is compatible with every possible utopian improvement. Similarly, rather than arguing that the framework is the best means for realizing utopia, one can argue that the framework is the best means for achieving utopian improvements.

4. It is worth noting that they do not even need to agree in terms of how they order sub-optimal options – all that is required is that they agree in terms of what they judge to be best. Agreement regarding sub-optimal options will only be relevant when dealing with utopian improvements and questions of approximating utopia.

5. It is important to keep in mind that assessments in the model are restricted to institutional features, which means that the model leaves room for improvements in utopia in terms of non-institutional features.

6. Nozick also considers the framework to be inspiring because of the conception of human nature that underlies it; that is, the framework treats people as autonomous beings who should be free to decide how to live their lives (see pp. 333–334). This basis for being inspiring also relies on a substantive conception of the good and cannot be brought

in at this stage given that the argument for utopia is meant to be independent of moral considerations.

7. See "It is what grows spontaneously from the individual choices of many people over a long period of time that will be worth speaking eloquently about" (p. 332).

8. This aspect of Nozick's argument has frequently been misinterpreted. In particular, Nozick's argument has often been misunderstood as having the consequence that imperialistic communities are excluded, that they are forbidden and outlawed by the framework (e.g. Lacey: 2001, p. 67 and Fowler: 1980, p. 552).

9. Since meta-associations are concerned with relations between individuals belonging to different associations and regulate interactions between different associations, including associations of which one is not a member, it follows that preferences regarding meta-associations are other-regarding preferences.

10. As long as people have different preferences regarding meta-associations, then the only situation in which no ideals are imposed is if there is no meta-association. While an anarchical situation will not involve the imposition of ideals, it will not satisfy preferences regarding meta-associations either (excepting those of anarchists since they prefer for there to not be a meta-association).

11. First-order preferences are here contrasted with preferences regarding meta-associations rather than with preferences concerning higher-order associations. The latter are self-regarding and in principle co-satisfiable, whereas the former are other-regarding and not in principle co-satisfiable.

12. See "you can't satisfy everybody; especially if there are those who will be dissatisfied unless not everybody is satisfied" (p. 320).

13. It should be noted that even the restriction on coercion is much more limited than that in place in Parts I and II, since the framework argument only rules out being coerced to belong to an association that one does not consider to be utopian. Yet, the absence of this type of coercion is compatible with other types of coercion that do not concern the issue of which association one is a member of. Put differently, it is possible that someone is in the association that he or she considers to be the best possible association despite the fact that this person is coerced to do things that he or she does not like.

14. This problem is closely related to what Nozick calls "moral avoidance" in *Philosophical Explanations* (see Nozick: 1981, pp. 460–462).

15. An analogous problem for Nozick's entitlement theory has been identified by Davis (see L. Davis: 1981). Whilst Davis's critique can be answered by appealing to Nozick's recursive characterization of justice

(see Bader: 2010, pp. 104–105), no analogous response is possible in the case of the framework argument since we do not have a recursive characterization of utopia in terms of procedures that must be satisfied to yield a utopian situation.

16. Here, again, it is important to keep in mind that the notion of utopia at issue is restricted insofar as only institutional features are being assessed, thereby making it the case that the objectionable character of brainwashing does not undermine the utopian nature of the resulting situation. While people are very likely to prefer being in a world in which they are not brainwashed, it is not the case that they would rather be members of different associations, and it is only the latter preference that is relevant for the notion of utopia that is at issue.

17. More precisely, the framework is not opposed to exit costs per se but only rules out those exit costs that prevent a utopian situation from arising and that keep us in sub-optimal equilibria.

18. A number of criticisms of the framework implicitly appeal to external standards. For instance, Singer's criticism that the framework does not pay sufficient consideration to the historical circumstances within which choices are made presupposes that there are external standards for evaluating preferences (see Singer: 1981, pp. 38–39). Such criticisms are ineffective against an operationalization based on internal standards since preferences constitute the standards by means of which we assess institutional structures, whilst they themselves are beyond criticism and evaluation.

19. At least, we can retain these results if we restrict our focus to first-order self-regarding preferences. Whether such a restriction can be justified in the context of external standards is not clear since it is questionable whether the justification we gave for the restriction to first-order self-regarding preferences in the context of the operationalization in terms of internal standards has an analogue in the context of external standards.

20. Care is required in interpreting the status of this argument. It has frequently been assumed that the epistemic argument is Nozick's main argument in Part III. This is incorrect. Nozick does not provide an instrumental argument for the framework on the basis of its beneficial epistemic effects, but instead appeals to instrumental considerations to respond to those who assume that there is one objectively best community, showing that even those who suppose that there is one best community should endorse the framework for instrumental reasons. This is clearly brought out by the disclaimer with which Nozick prefixes his discussion of filter mechanisms and design devices: "Suppose (falsely) ..." (p. 312).

21. To find out whether a more-than-minimal state would be required, one would have to look at how widespread such sub-optimal equilibria are, what the extent of their sub-optimality is and what the likely costs of removing them are.

22. Again, one would have to weigh up the likely costs and benefits of the provision of such incentives to see whether a more-than-minimal state might fill a useful role.

11 *E pluribus plurum*, or, How to fail to get to utopia in spite of really trying

11.1 INTRODUCTION

"The framework for utopia," Robert Nozick tells us at the beginning of the final section of Part III of *Anarchy, State, and Utopia* (*ASU*), "is equivalent to the minimal state" (p. 333). The rich and complex body of argumentation of Parts I and II had produced the conclusion that the minimal, and no more than a minimal, state was legitimate or morally justified. What Part III reveals is that the minimal state "is the one that best realizes the utopian aspirations of untold dreamers and visionaries" (p. 333). Although this happy convergence is surely no accident, neither, Nozick insists, is it contrived, for it is the conclusion reached by two independent lines of argument. If there is a framework for utopia – or, as I shall from now simply say, utopia – it is the minimal state.

The obvious question to ask, then, is whether Nozick is right that the minimal state gives us utopia – understanding utopia in the way that he would have us do. The thesis of this chapter is that Nozick does not succeed. What Part III offers is neither a plausible account of a utopian community nor the inspiring conception of a state that Nozick promises. The root of the problem lies in Nozick's initial rejection of anarchy, for the idea of utopia he wants to defend is one that is achievable outside the state but not within it. What he tries to do in Part III is to put back into his political philosophy that which was taken away in Part I, when the legitimacy of the minimal state's incorporation of ultra-minimal states was settled. It is within the framework of the minimal state "that one's nonimperialistic vision of the good society is to be propounded and realized" (p. 332). Indeed Nozick tells us that "[a]llowing us to do that is what the framework is *for*" (p. 332). The aim of this chapter is to show that the framework can do no such thing. In the end, the purpose of the state is to limit rather than enable people's pursuit of diverse ends. It is a way of making the many live as one. To the extent that those who do not wish to conform are compelled to do so, the state suppresses rather than enables the pursuit of diverse ideals. Of course, it may be that this is as much as is feasible in human society. But it may be too much to call this utopia.

This chapter is presented in five main sections. The first presents a critical account of Nozick's conception of utopia. The second then looks closely at Nozick's conception of the state (and his claim that both the legitimacy and justice arguments of Parts I and II and the utopia arguments of Part III lead to the minimal state). The third section argues that the minimal state cannot give us utopia. The fourth goes on to show that no state can give us utopia. The final section asks where this leaves Nozick's theory.

11.2 NOZICK'S CONCEPTION OF UTOPIA

Utopia is commonly understood to be an "imaginary place or situation of ideal perfection,"[1] although many dictionaries define it more narrowly as a place that has reached social and political perfection. For utopian theorists, from Thomas More to William Morris to B. F. Skinner, utopia has generally been presented as a place where people live as they should and in which they realize some important good. They imagine the best of all possible worlds. Nozick, however, begins his reflections on utopia by noting that the "best of all possible worlds for me will not be that for you" (p. 298). The world that I would most prefer to live in, he observes, will not be the one you would choose. "Utopia, though, must be, in some restricted sense, the best for all of us; the best world imaginable, for each of us" (p. 298). What Nozick suggests is crucial for any society to qualify as utopian is that it is a society whose members want to be there, or at least cannot imagine a place they would rather be. Utopia is not a place that's (objectively) *good* for human or rational beings to be, but a place that such beings would most *want* to be.

It is worth remarking how unusual this is in utopian thinking, which, as Nozick recognizes, generally gives a good deal of attention to the problem of how to bring the inhabitants of utopia to conform to its ideal. Utopians do not normally begin by accepting the diversity of human desires.[2] For Nozick this is crucial. This is not because he thinks that desires are fixed or unconditioned by circumstances or that people are incapable of being brought to new and better ideas of what ends are worth pursuing. Even desires can be discovered. But desires cannot and should not be discounted; and any good society must be one in which the inhabitants remain members willingly. Given the diversity of desires, or of views of what ends are generally worth pursuing, people are likely to hit upon different ideas of the ideal society; and while this is unlikely to issue in a world of societies of single individuals it will mean a world in which people settle voluntarily into a variety of communities of (like-minded) people. If utopia is to exist it cannot be in the form of a single society to which everyone belongs – unless people become very different than they are now, or at least all come to believe that the same particular society is the one for them. Utopia is better understood not as a single community of similar people but as a collectivity of different communities each made up of people who are drawn together because mutual association gives them the best life they can imagine.

It is highly unlikely, Nozick points out, that actual communities will be made up of people who are satisfied with every aspect of it. Even the best community anyone can imagine being a part of will, realistically, involve some compromise, since no one can expect to be a part of a community in which everyone else subordinates their interests to her. Why would anyone else join such a community? So every community, even the most utopian, will involve some compromise. Nonetheless, some communities will be more attractive to any particular person than will others. What will happen is that people will move into the communities they find the best of all possible – which is to say, available – communities. Of course, this means that some communities that are unable to attract members will wither away and die, or transform themselves into communities others truly want to join.

Utopia in Nozick's conception is not a final state, or a stage at the end of history, or an isolated world for which time has stood still. It is, rather, a changing condition that varies from person to person and place to place, as well as from time to time. For utopia to be achieved, however, what needs to remain constant is the framework that enables people to form communities, conduct experiments in living, move between societies, and discover what lives suit them.

Utopia is a framework for utopias, a place where people are at liberty to realize their own vision of the good life in the ideal community but where no one can *impose* his own utopian vision upon others. The utopian society is the society of utopianism ... utopia is meta-utopia: the environment in which utopian experiments may be tried out; the environment in which people are free to do their own thing; the environment which must, to a great extent, be realized first if more particular utopian visions are to be realized stably. (p. 312)

Although Nozick uses the term "utopia" in different ways, sometimes to refer to the "framework" that makes the pursuit of particular ideal communities or ways of life possible, and at other times to refer to the communities or ways of life themselves, the idea he is advancing is easy enough to grasp. There are many possible ways of living, and though it is unlikely that any one of them will be found fulfilling by each and everyone, the best we can hope for is a structure that makes it possible for us to find the society that best suits each of us, and that makes it possible to learn how to sustain and improve those that seem most successful. That structure, he thinks, is the state, albeit the minimal – and only the minimal – state.

11.3 NOZICK'S CONCEPTION OF THE STATE

In Part I of *ASU* Nozick sets out to refute the individualist anarchist contention that no state has legitimate authority by showing how the state can arise out of a (Lockean) state of nature without anyone's (Lockean) rights being violated. Whether or not Nozick's invisible-hand explanation (and justification) of the emergence of the state is successful has been hotly debated, and anarchists remain unconvinced. But if Nozick has justified the state (minimal or otherwise), what exactly is it that he has justified? After explaining that individuals' need in the state of nature to protect their rights would lead to the creation of protection agencies, which would ultimately be transformed into territorially bound, dominant protective associations, Nozick writes as follows:

[W]ithout claiming to possess any rights uniquely, a protective agency dominant in a territory will occupy a unique position. Though each person has a right to act correctly to prohibit others from violating rights (including the right not to be punished unless shown to deserve it), only the dominant protective association will be able, without sanction, to enforce correctness as it sees it. Its power makes it the arbiter of correctness; *it* determines what, for purposes of punishment, counts as a breach of correctness. Our explanation does not assume or claim that might makes right. But might does make enforced prohibitions, even if no one thinks the mighty have a *special* entitlement to have realized in the world their own view of which prohibitions are correctly enforced. (pp. 118–119)

The state, he goes on to say, is an institution that has the right to enforce rights, prohibit dangerous private enforcement of justice, pass upon such private procedures, and is effectively the sole wielder within a geographic territory of that right (see p. 119). This understanding of the state is a modified Weberian view, for it asserts that the state has a monopoly not on the use of violence but on making judgments on the permissibility of violence. It may exercise violence, particularly when it exercises the right to punish those who have exercised violence impermissibly, but so may others – if the state says it is permissible.

It is also important to note that for Nozick the state has no *special* rights. It has the right to enforce rights, and to prohibit the dangerous enforcement of justice, but it has no right to claim that all its actions are right. Neither the state nor its agents are immune from prosecution and punishment for the violation of others rights. The Nozickian state does not enjoy sovereign immunity.

Most importantly, no actual dominant protective agency or state has any entitlement to be the dominant agency or state. It might be perfectly legitimate for a king to rule over us, but this does not mean that any existing king is entitled to be king. The legitimacy of the state is necessary; but the legitimacy of any particular state is contingent.

There are a number of features of the Nozickian minimal state that ought to be noted. First, the minimal state is essentially a modified Dominant Protection Agency, so the great majority of people within it would be *clients* of the state. Thus, for the great majority of people within the territory the Nozickian minimal state does not differ from anarchy (since under anarchy people would still join protective agencies). Second, Nozick's argument is not only that a minimal state could emerge from a state of nature without violating rights but that people would find it to their advantage to establish a minimal state. The state is not the only institution that could arise without violating rights, and indeed some bad institutions could emerge without doing so. Nozick has sought to show not only that the state could arise without violating rights but also that this is to people's advantage. Third, the minimal state makes judgments about the permissibility of violence only when its own clients are involved. It has no right to dictate the procedures that other agencies may use against those who are not clients of the Dominant Protective Agency, unless those procedures adversely affect its own clients.

The account of the state Nozick offers is very much a normative one. His question is whether or not the state can be justified; and his answer is that it can be provided it is an entity of a certain kind: one whose underlying rationale is the upholding of a system for protecting individual rights. This account abstracts from actual historical states in two obvious respects. First, many, if not most, states have not acted as agencies dedicated to the upholding of a system of protecting individual rights – Lockean or otherwise. Second, even if we ignore the normative dimension, it is not clear that Nozick's concept of the state accounts for the various forms of political authority we find in the world. This is not merely because no modern states (and, arguably, no earlier ones either) can be described as minimal states. It is because the kinds of states we find in the world are so diverse it would be difficult for most theories to account for them all.

To begin with, if we think of the state as a kind of corporation, as many theorists have suggested,[3] there are many political corporations in the world, ranging from provinces, to nation states, to supra-national organizations such as the European Union, all with governments, the power to tax, and the capacity to control (to varying degrees) what goes on within their territories. The extent of control varies not only because some corporations are parts of some larger federal structure but also because some are condominiums (like Andorra) with limited control over their own affairs, while others are governments without statehood (like the Palestinian authority), while yet others are states without their own governments (like Somalia, Afghanistan, and Iraq at various stages of their recent histories).

The relationship between the state and its inhabitants or members also varies, with some exerting control over members beyond its territory and most exercising power over inhabitants within its borders. The extent of the state's authority varies quite considerably in part because of the traditions of a particular society, but also because membership of supra-national associations or of international regimes such as UN conventions conditions the powers of particular states.

The idea that the state arose out of a process of competition among contending protection agencies is not historically plausible, but it is unlikely Nozick ever thought so. Yet the idea that conceptually the state is a kind of protection agency with a client–service-provider relationship with its members is no more believable. The state as it exists now has a life, and interests, of its own. If one is to answer the question why anyone should obey the state or recognize the legitimacy of its authority, one must also supply an account of the state that makes sense of its character. Nozick's account cannot do this.

Of course it has to be asked whether a single answer to this question is even possible given the variety of entities that present themselves and are legally recognized as states. They come in all shapes and sizes, from the geographically largest (Russia, taking up more than 1.5 million square kilometers) to the smallest (Iceland, taking up barely 100,000 square kilometers); from the most populous (China, with 1.3 billion people, or 19.6 percent of the world's population) to the least populous (Nauru, with 10,000, or Vatican City, with 800, neither with as much as a ten–thousandth of a percent of the people of the world). They range in their forms of government from liberal democracy to authoritarian theocracy to communist monarchy (which is how one might characterize North Korea) to totalitarian dictatorship.

What Nozick offers in his account of the state is an idea that bears only a remote resemblance to any of the entities in the world today that we call states. It bears little resemblance to the entities that emerged with the development of systems of political authority, from principalities and kingdoms to self-governing towns, to city-states to republics to empires. All of this makes it difficult to see how he is going to be able to mount an argument to show that some kind of structure of power like a state can legitimately have authority over any one, or to show that some variant of this entity can bring us closer to utopia.

II.4 CAN A MINIMAL STATE BRING US TO UTOPIA?

What is it that a state might provide that can help us get (closer) to utopia? It seems unlikely that any of the particular features of actual states are what Nozick has in mind. But what Nozick seems to think states can offer in principle is something called "the framework." In the end, we do not live in states but in particular communities. "We *live* in particular communities" (p. 332), he says. "It is here that one's nonimperialistic vision of the ideal or good society is to be propounded and realized" (p. 332). So why do we need the framework? Because "[a]llowing us to do that is what the framework is *for*" (p. 332). According to Nozick, "[c]onjoined with many persons' particular visions, the framework enables us to get the best of all possible worlds" (p. 332). The problem is, it is not clear why we need a framework to get to utopia.

Nozick offers a number of arguments why, but none of them is convincing. The first argument is that the framework serves as a "filter device." While other utopian theorists have focused on the design question, trying to imagine or design the best society, Nozick suggests that what we need is a filter device that eliminates many designs from a large set of alternatives (see p. 314). When the alternatives are different kinds of societies, the framework supplies the appropriate filter device, allowing many different communities to flourish if they can. Within the framework, "some communities will be abandoned, others will struggle along, others will split, others will flourish, gain members, and be duplicated elsewhere" (p. 316). Design devices might generate specific communities to be lived in and tried out; but the filter device reveals to us which ones succeed, which ones need to be modified, and which ones need to be abandoned. Communities that are unattractive will be rejected by their inhabitants, other communities will adopt the best practices from communities people favor, and ideas for new communities often will improve as well (see p. 317).

What is obscure in this account, however, is how the framework – the minimal state – acts as a filter or generates knowledge of the best way to live. It seems plausible enough that people experimenting

with different forms of life will abandon them if they are unsatis-
fying, that successes will be imitated by people and communities
willing to change or adapt, and that people will come to know and
appreciate the greater worth of some ways of living by observing
the successes and failures of others. Yet, couldn't this outcome be
achieved just as well without any kind of state – without any kind of
framework? In the condition of anarchy people might form different
kinds of communities, some of which would prove more successful than others. It would seem fairly likely that the successful ones
would attract more adherents while the unsuccessful ones would be
abandoned.

If the argument is that the filter device is something like a competitive market economy it seems plausible enough to think that
different societies will, in effect, contend with one another for the
custom of potential members. The most attractive among them
will capture most of the population, although niche markets might
well develop for those with particular tastes if the communities
supplying the minority ways of life do in fact offer a product that
commands the interest and loyalty of a sufficiently large group. But
for this to happen there is no need for a framework for a filtering
process to operate. A market could operate perfectly well without
a structure that includes some communities and excludes others.
If this structure operates to restrict the size of the market it might
even limit the capacity of people to learn from the experiments of
others or to try out new products by moving from one community
to another. Yet if it imposes no restrictions of the mobility of people,
goods, and ideas, it is not clear in what way it is serving as a filter
device.

If the argument is that the filter device is something like a scientific community it again seems plausible enough to think that
the possibility of alternative hypotheses being proposed, examined
and tested can only enhance our understanding of what works and
what does not. Yet once again it is not clear how the framework of
the minimal state does anything to enhance or even facilitate scientific discovery. Is the state to act as an authority that decides what
counts as a valid scientific experiment? If so, it is embracing a view
of science we might criticize drawing on John Stuart Mill and Paul
Feyerabend, to argue that science knows no authority. Any effort to
close off of limit scientific inquiry or experimentation should not

be welcomed but regarded with suspicion. Yet if the filter device of the minimal state does no such thing, how does it contribute to scientific progress?

In his account of how the filter device does its work Nozick argues as follows:

> The operation of the framework for utopia we present here thus realizes the advantages of a filtering process incorporating mutually improving inter-action between the filter and the surviving products of the generating process, so that the quality of generated and nonrejected products improves. Furthermore, given people's historical memories and records, it has the feature that an already rejected alternative (or its slight modification) can be *retried*, perhaps because new or changed conditions make it now seem more promising or appropriate. (p. 317)

What he fails to explain, however, is what it is that the filter device, the minimal state, does to enable the 'nonrejected products' to improve. It also remains quite unclear how it is that the filter device here uniquely makes it possible for rejected alternatives to be retried. Why is it not possible for all of this to happen under anarchy – in a stateless society in which people live in different communities, learn from one another, imitate what they like, discard what they do not like, and abandon what they cannot improve? There are many examples of societies which have done just that. The Gauls in the century before Caesar's invasion, for example, had complex and sophisticated systems of trade that sustained a rich material and cultural life in a diverse array of communities. They had no state. Neither did the cities that made up the Hanseatic League have a state, even as they grew rich.

On the other hand, it seems quite plausible to think that the existence of a framework would prove an obstacle to experimentation and learning. For one thing, it would be very difficult for societies which did not produce a significant surplus to survive, even if their way of life was extremely congenial to their members, for such a surplus would be needed to pay even the minimal taxes any state would have to levy. Indeed, historically, the state has been the agency that has done significant damage to the diversity of human experiments in living because of its need to standardize the communities under its control in order to calculate the wealth of the people and to collect the taxes it sought to raise. If we have any examples of minimal states, perhaps the clearest ones are colonial regimes or empires that have tried to interfere only lightly in the societies under their control in order to disrupt their productive activities as little as possible and maximize the returns from taxation.[4] Yet even here, though to varying degrees, the result has not been a flourishing of experimentation but a growing conformity since administration inevitably requires a common metric by which to regulate diversity (see Scott: 1999).

Nonetheless, perhaps there are some things that a properly constituted minimal state might provide that help bring utopia a little nearer, even if it is true that, historically, states have not been very good at doing this. (After all, Nozick is, to be fair, offering a theory of the kind of state we should aspire to, and not defending the records of the states of the past.) One possibility is that the state brings us closer to utopia by bringing peace and the rule of law. The reason this matters from the perspective of the search for utopia is that for the process to work it must be possible for individuals to move between communities. If there is no mobility between communities, learning will be limited, unsuccessful models cannot be so readily abandoned, and the pressure on the less attractive communities to reform will diminish, to the detriment not only of their own members but of people more generally. A minimal state might play a useful role in facilitating or guaranteeing the freedom of people to exit the societies they no longer care to live in.

The state's playing such a role might well have some beneficial consequences. Certainly, a measure of mobility is important not only for individual wellbeing but also for the purpose of maintaining a sound social order. The obvious question, however, is how much mobility is desirable. The propensity to move from one community is not a natural fact but something conditioned by the complex set of circumstances an individual might face. The likelihood of anyone leaving anywhere is going to be profoundly shaped by the opportunity cost of exit. But if the state is to determine how easy exit is to be, how easy should it make it? Making exit very easy, say by subsidizing emigration, would make it easier for people to try new communities and ways of life, but may also make many people less likely to stick at ways which seems unrewarding at first. Many communities simply might not get going, or retain enough members to be viable. Some experiments would simply become harder to conduct. Even if the state simply guarantees to protect those who wish to leave their communities from being prevented or from reprisals from disgruntled community members there will be some important consequences for the way the community operates. It will increase the bargaining power of dissenters, who would be able to use the threat of leaving more effectively. This would not be a bad thing in itself, but would nonetheless transform the relations among people within the community. For one thing, with the state now a player in the game some people will now devote resources to cultivating the state. They now have to be in a position not only to leave but also to persuade the state that they have a case for protection. There is no doubt that in some communities the influence of the state would be a positive one as a consequence of all this, as it becomes harder for some societies to repress or restrict their members. But in other cases the consequence may be more destructive. The question is: what would be the overall impact of the state? It is hard to see why it must be a positive one overall. At best, we might conclude that the results will vary. That, however, is not enough to make the case for the usefulness of the framework as a filter device for getting us closer to utopia, either severally or collectively.

11.5 CAN ANY STATE BRING US TO UTOPIA?

Robert Nozick has tried to put the case for the value of the minimal state. He suggests that it is not only legitimate but also valuable because it brings us as close as we can get to achieving the best of all possible worlds. It may be that Nozick is right at least to the extent that the minimal state is the most likely kind of state to get us to utopia. In the minimal state, the framework is libertarian but the communities within it need not be. Yet even here, the case is not proven. If the question of what is the best kind of community is best settled by empirical testing, by experiments in living, the same might be true for the question of what is the best kind of state. Is there any reason to think, in advance of such experiments, that the minimal state is the best candidate compared with other more extensive states? (I leave aside the problem of how one would make the judgment when comparing states even if experiments could be conducted.)

The case for the minimal state looks even weaker, however, when we compare it with the alternative of not having a state – at least from the point of view of finding utopia. A world without states might in fact be one in which the greatest variety of experiments might be conducted. If we want people to participate in this process we might do better not to create states but to take them down (although, in the end, this may simply not be possible). States may turn out to be obstacles to the discovery process because states, like all institutions, once created, acquire lives and interests of their own. The state will never be merely a framework, though some states will be more minimal than others. The state will itself offer to people a way of life. The difference is that it will have the power to defend itself with force – to tax and restructure society in its own interests. With the growth of the state, the way of life that will become significantly more feasible and attractive will be the life of a cosmopolitan. Again, this may not be a bad thing in itself. But it is difficult to see the case for encouraging this from the perspective of the theory of utopia Nozick has tried to offer.

11.6 WHERE DOES THIS LEAVE NOZICK?

In spite of his best efforts to get us to a utopia that is a society of utopias, what Nozick takes us closer toward is the way of life that is life in the state. The source of this result, I think, is the initial aspiration of the theory. Nozick asks very explicitly in *ASU* whether the minimal state could ever be an inspiring ideal. Would people man the barricades in its defense? He then sets out to show that the minimal state is an ideal that can inspire – one that we might be prepared to fight for. But what he ends up arguing for, necessarily, is the state. He wants to show how the many can live as one. An appropriate motto for his state might be something like *E pluribus unum*. And of course it is hard to imagine any state taking for itself a motto like *E pluribus plurum*. Out of the many, well, *many*.

What Nozick has tried to do is show how we can leave anarchy, with its diverse people in different communities, and their diverse ways of life, and enter a structure which will not only preserve the diversity we find there but also enhance the benefits we might gain from having a world of diverse people. This, he says, would be utopia. In the end, I think Nozick fails to get us to utopia in spite of his best efforts. The problem, however, may lie not in the abilities of this most brilliant and imaginative of philosophers but in the aspiration itself. In Part I of *ASU* he tried to show why leaving the state of anarchy was morally legitimate; in Part III he tried to show why leaving it would be good. In neither enterprise has he been convincing.

NOTES

1. *Chambers Combined Dictionary Thesaurus* (1997).
2. For a libertarian utopia that does, see Heinlein: 1977.
3. See, for example, Van Creveld: 1999.
4. Nozick's minimal state does not levy taxes, since most people in its territory are clients who voluntarily pay for its services. The charges are not pure market prices, however, since the fees have to be adjusted to cover the below-cost or free services provided to those disadvantaged by the Dominant Protection Agency through its prohibition of risky decision procedures to its clients. (I thank David Gordon for making this clear to me.)

REFERENCES

Anderson, E. 1999. "What Is the Point of Equality?," *Ethics*, 109, pp. 287–337.

Arneson, R. 1982. "The Principle of Fairness and Free-Rider Problems," *Ethics*, 92, pp. 616–633.

2005a. "The Shape of Lockean Rights: Pareto, Fairness, and Consent," *Social Philosophy and Policy*, 22, pp. 255–285.

2005b. "Joel Feinberg and the Justification of Hard Paternalism," *Legal Theory*, 11, pp. 259–284.

2010. "Self-Ownership and World Ownership: Against Left-Libertarianism," *Social Philosophy and Policy*, 27, pp. 168–194.

Arthur, W. B. 1994. *Increasing Returns and Path Dependence in the Economy*. Ann Arbor: University of Michigan Press.

Attfield, R. 1987. *A Theory of Value and Obligation*. New York: Croom Helm.

Auyang, S. Y. 1998. *Foundations of Complex-systems Theories in Economics, Evolutionary Biology and Statistical Physics*. Cambridge: Cambridge University Press.

Bader, R. M. 2010. *Robert Nozick*. London: Continuum.

Bakunin, M. 1971. *Bakunin on Anarchy*. ed. S. Dolgoff. New York: Vintage Books.

Barnett, R. 1977. "Victim's Rights: Restitution or Vengeance," *Ethics*, 87, pp. 279–301.

1980. "The Justice of Restitution," *American Journal of Jurisprudence*, 25, pp. 117–132.

1998. *The Structure of Liberty: Justice and the Rule of Law*. Oxford: Clarendon Press.

Becker, L. 1982. "Against the Supposed Difference between Historical and End-State Theories," *Philosophical Studies*, 41, pp. 267–272.

Bogart, J. H. 1985. "Lockean Provisos and State of Nature Theories," *Ethics*, 95, pp. 828–836.

Brennan, J. 2007. "Rawls's Paradox," *Constitutional Political Economy*, 18, pp. 287–299.

Brink, D. 1989. *Moral Realism and the Foundations of Ethics*. Cambridge: Cambridge University Press.

Brook, R. 1991. "Agency and Morality," *The Journal of Philosophy*, 88, pp. 190–212.

Chambers Combined Dictionary Thesaurus. 1997. Edinburgh: Chambers Harrap.

Christiano, T. 2008. *The Constitution of Equality*. Oxford: Oxford University Press.

Christman, J. 1994. *The Myth of Property*. Oxford: Oxford University Press.

Coase, R. 1960. "The Problem of Social Cost," *Journal of Law and Economics*, 3, pp. 1–44.

Cohen, G. A. 1995. *Self-Ownership, Freedom, and Equality*. Cambridge: Cambridge University Press.

2000a. "Self-Ownership, World-Ownership, and Equality," in *Left-Libertarianism and Its Critics*, ed. P. Vallentyne and H. Steiner. New York: Palgrave, pp. 247–270.

2000b. "Self-Ownership, World-Ownership, and Equality, Part II," in *Left-Libertarianism and Its Critics*, ed. P. Vallentyne and H. Steiner. New York: Palgrave, pp. 271–289.

2000c. *If You're An Egalitarian, How Come You're So Rich?* Cambridge, MA: Harvard University Press.

2009. "Fairness and Legitimacy in Justice, And: Does Option Luck Ever Preserve Justice?" in *Hillel Steiner and the Anatomy of Justice*, ed. S. De Wijze, M. H. Kramer and I. Carter. London: Routledge, pp. 3–21.

Crisp, R. 2006. "Hedonism Reconsidered," *Philosophy and Phenomenological Research*, 73, pp. 619–645.

Davis, L. 1981. "Nozick's Entitlement Theory," in *Reading Nozick: Essays on Anarchy, State, and Utopia*, ed. J. Paul. Totowa, NJ: Rowman and Littlefield, pp. 344–354.

Davis, N. 1984. "The Doctrine of Double Effect: Problems of Interpretation," *Pacific Philosophical Quarterly*, 65, pp. 107–123.

De Brigard, F. 2010. "If You Like It, Does It Matter If It's Real?" *Philosophical Psychology*, 23(1), 43–57.

Driver, J. 2007. "Normative Ethics," in *The Oxford Handbook of Contemporary Philosophy*, ed. F. Jackson and M. Smith. Oxford: Oxford University Press, pp. 31–62.

Durlauf, S. N. in press. "Complexity, Economics, and Public Policy," *Politics, Philosophy and Economics*.

Epstein, R. 1995. *Simple Rules for a Complex World*. Cambridge, MA: Harvard University Press.

2003. *Skepticism and Freedom*. Chicago: University of Chicago Press.

Feinberg, J. 1986. *Harm to Self*. Oxford: Oxford University Press.

Feldman, F. 1997. *Utilitarianism, Hedonism, and Desert: Essays in Moral Philosophy*. Cambridge: Cambridge University Press.

2004. *Pleasure and the Good Life: Concerning the Nature, Varieties, and Plausibility of Hedonism*. Oxford: Oxford University Press.

Feser, E. 2004. *On Nozick*. Toronto: Wadsworth.

Fleurbaey, M. 2008. *Fairness, Responsibility and Welfare*. Oxford: Oxford University Press.

Foot, P. 1967. "The Problem of Abortion and the Doctrine of the Double Effect," *Oxford Review*, 5, pp. 5–15.

Fowler, M. 1980. "Stability and Utopia: a Critique of Nozick's Framework Argument," *Ethics*, 90, pp. 550–563.

Fried, B. 1995. "Wilt Chamberlain Revisited: Nozick's 'Justice in Transfer' and the Problem of Market-Based Distribution," *Philosophy and Public Affairs*, 24, pp. 226–245.

2003. "'If You Don't Like It, Leave It': the Construction of Exit Options in Social Contractarian Arguments," *Philosophy and Public Affairs*, 31, pp. 40–70.

2005. "Begging the Question with Style: Anarchy, State, and Utopia at Thirty Years," *Social Philosophy and Policy*, 22, pp. 221–254.

Gaffney, M. and Harrison, F. 1994. *The Corruption of Economics*. London: Shepheard-Walwyn.

Gaus, G. 2006. "Hayek on the Evolution of Mind and Society," in *The Cambridge Companion to Hayek*, ed. E. Feser. Cambridge: Cambridge University Press, pp. 332–358.

2009. "Recognized Rights as Devices of Public Reason," *Philosophical Perspectives: Ethics*, 23, pp. 111–136.

in press-a. "The Property Equilibrium in a Liberal Social Order," *Social Philosophy and Policy*.

in press-b. "Hobbes's Challenge to Public Reason Liberalism," in *Hobbes Today*, ed. S. A. Lloyd. Cambridge: Cambridge University Press.

Gauthier, D. 1986. *Morals by Agreement*. Oxford: Oxford University Press.

Glover, J. 1984. *What Sort of People Should There Be?* New York: Penguin.

Goldsworthy, J. 1992. "Wellbeing and Value," *Utilitas*, 4, pp. 1–26.

Griffin, J. 1988. *Wellbeing: Its Meaning, Measurement, and Moral Importance*. Oxford: Oxford University Press.

Hailwood, S. 1996. *Exploring Nozick: Beyond Anarchy, State, and Utopia*. Aldershot: Avebury.

Hare, R. M. 1981. *Moral Thinking: Its Levels, Method, and Point.* Oxford: Oxford University Press.

Haslett, D. W. 1990. "What Is Utility?" *Economics and Philosophy,* 6, pp. 65–94.

Hayek, F. A. 1976. *Law, Legislation and Liberty, Vol. II: The Mirage of Social Justice.* London: Routledge.

Heinlein, R. A. 1977. *The Moon is a Harsh Mistress.* London: New English Library.

Held, V. 1980. *Property, Profits, and Economic Justice.* Belmont, CA: Wadsworth.

Hobbes, T. 1994. *Leviathan,* ed. E. Curley. Indianapolis: Hackett.

Jollimore, T. 2004. "Meaningless Happiness and Meaningless Suffering," *Southern Journal of Philosophy,* 42, pp. 333–347.

Kagan, S. 1989. *The Limits of Morality.* Oxford: Oxford University Press.

  1991. "Replies to My Critics," *Philosophy and Phenomenological Research,* 51, pp. 919–928.

  1998. *Normative Ethics.* Boulder: Westview Press.

Kamm, F. M. 1996. *Morality, Mortality.* Vol. II. Oxford: Oxford University Press.

  2007. *Intricate Ethics.* Oxford: Oxford University Press.

Kawall, J. 1999. "The Experience Machine and Mental State Theories of Wellbeing," *The Journal of Value Inquiry,* 33, pp. 381–387.

Kramer, M. H., Simmonds, N. E. and Steiner, H. 1998. *A Debate over Rights.* Oxford: Oxford University Press.

Kukathas, C. 2003. "Responsibility for Past Injustice: How to Shift the Burden," *Politics, Philosophy, and Economics,* 2, pp. 165–190.

Lacey, A. R. 2001. *Robert Nozick.* Princeton: Princeton University Press.

Lemos, J. 2002. "Sober and Wilson and Nozick and the Experience Machine," *Philosophia,* 29, pp. 401–409.

  2004. "Psychological Hedonism, Evolutionary Biology, and the Experience Machine," *Philosophy of the Social Sciences,* 34, pp. 506–526.

Lemos, N. 1994. *Intrinsic Value: Concept and Warrant.* Cambridge: Cambridge University Press.

Lind, D. 1989. "The Failure of Nozick's Invisible-Hand Justification of the Political State," *Auslegung: A Journal of Philosophy,* 15, pp. 57–68.

Lippert-Rasmussen, K. 1996. "Moral Status and the Impermissibility of Minimizing Violations," *Philosophy and Public Affairs,* 25, pp. 333–351.

Locke, J. 1960. *Second Treatise of Government in Two Treatises of Government.* Cambridge: Cambridge University Press.

Lomasky, L. 2005. "Libertarianism at Twin Harvard," *Social Philosophy and Policy,* 22, pp. 178–199.

MacIntyre, A. 1985. *After Virtue.* Revised edn. London: Duckworth.

Mack, E. 1975. "Review of *Anarchy, State, and Utopia*," *Reason Magazine*, November, pp. 6–12.

1978. "Nozick's Anarchism," in *Anarchism*, ed. J. Chapman and J. Pennock. New York: New York University Press, pp. 43–62.

1981. "Nozick on Unproductivity: the Unintended Consequences," in *Reading Nozick: Essays on* Anarchy, State, and Utopia, ed. J. Paul. Totowa, NJ: Rowman and Littlefield, pp. 169–190.

1986. "The Ethics of Taxation: Rights versus Public Goods?" in *Taxation and the Deficit Economy*, ed. D. Lee. San Francisco: Pacific Research Institute, pp. 487–514.

1995. "The Self-Ownership Proviso: a New and Improved Lockean Proviso," *Social Philosophy and Policy*, 12, pp. 186–218.

2002. "Self-ownership, Marxism and Egalitarianism: Part 1: Challenges to Historical Entitlement," *Politics, Philosophy and Economics*, 1, pp. 75–108.

2006. "Hayek on Justice and the Order of Actions," in *The Cambridge Companion to Hayek*, ed. E. Feser. Cambridge: Cambridge University Press, pp. 259–286.

2010. "The Natural Right of Property," *Social Philosophy and Policy*, 27, pp. 53–78.

MacNiven, D. 1993. *Creative Morality: an Introduction to Theoretical and Practical Ethics*. London and New York: Routledge.

Meadowcroft, J. 2005. *The Ethics of the Market*. New York: Palgrave Macmillan.

Mill, J. S. 1867. *Utilitarianism*, 3rd edn. Longmans, Green, Reader, and Dyer.

2006. *A System of Logic, Ratiocinative and Inductive in The Collected Works of John Stuart Mill*, Vol. VII, ed. J. M. Robson. Indianapolis: Liberty Fund.

Miller, D. 1981. "Steiner on Rights and Powers," *Analysis*, 41, pp. 222–223.

2002. "The Justification of Political Authority," in *Robert Nozick*, ed. D. Schmidtz. Cambridge: Cambridge University Press, pp. 10–33.

Montmarquet, J. 1985. "Indexical Deontology," *Pacific Philosophical Quarterly*, 66, pp. 191–203.

Morris, C. W. 1998. *An Essay on the Modern State*. Cambridge: Cambridge University Press.

Nagel, T. 1981. "Libertarianism without Foundations," in *Reading Nozick: Essays on Anarchy, State, and Utopia*, ed. J. Paul. Totowa, NJ: Rowman and Littlefield, pp. 191–205.

1987. *The View from Nowhere*. Oxford: Oxford University Press.

1991. *Equality and Partiality*. Oxford: Oxford University Press.

Narveson, J. 1988. *The Libertarian Idea*. Philadelphia: Temple University Press.

　1999. "Original Appropriation and Lockean Provisos," *Public Affairs Quarterly*, 13, pp. 205–227.

Nas, T. F. 1996. *Cost-Benefit Analysis: Theory and Practice*. London: Sage.

Nozick, R. 1974. *Anarchy, State, and Utopia*. New York: Basic Books.

　1981. *Philosophical Explanations*. Cambridge, MA: Harvard University Press.

　1989. *The Examined Life*. New York: Simon and Schuster.

　1991. "Invisible-Hand Explanations," *The American Economic Review*, 84, pp. 314–318.

　1997. *Socratic Puzzles*. Cambridge, MA: Harvard University Press.

　2000. "The Pursuit of Happiness," *Forbes*, ASAP Supplement, 166, 9.

　2001. *Invariances: The Structure of the Objective World*. Cambridge, MA: Harvard University Press.

Olsaretti, S. 2004. *Liberty, Desert, and the Market*. Cambridge: Cambridge University Press.

O'Neill, O. 1981. "Nozick's Entitlements," in *Reading Nozick: Essays on Anarchy, State, and Utopia*, ed. J. Paul. Totowa, NJ: Rowman and Littlefield, pp. 305–322.

Otsuka, M. 1997. "Kamm on the Morality of Killing," *Ethics*, 108, pp. 197–207.

　2003. *Libertarianism without Inequality*. Oxford: Oxford University Press.

Parfit, D. 1984. *Reasons and Persons*. Oxford: Oxford University Press.

　2011. *On What Matters, Volume 1*. Oxford: Oxford University Press.

Pettit, P. 1996. *The Common Mind*. Oxford: Oxford University Press.

Quinn, W. 1989. "Actions, Intentions, and Consequences: the Doctrine of Doing and Allowing," *Philosophical Review*, 98, pp. 287–312.

Railton, P. 1984. "Alienation, Consequentialism, and the Demands of Morality," *Philosophy and Public Affairs*, 13, pp. 134–171.

Rawls, J. 1971. *A Theory of Justice*. Cambridge, MA: Harvard University Press.

　1996. *Political Liberalism*. New York: Columbia University Press.

　1999a. *A Theory of Justice*. Revised edn. Cambridge, MA: Harvard University Press.

　1999b. *Collected Papers*, ed. S. Freeman. Cambridge, MA: Harvard University Press.

　1999c. *Law of Peoples*. Cambridge, MA: Harvard University Press.

　2001. *Justice as Fairness: a Restatement*. Cambridge, MA: Harvard University Press.

Rivera-Lopez, E. 2007. "Are Mental State Welfarism and Our Concern for Non-Experiential Goals Incompatible?" *Pacific Philosophical Quarterly*, 88, pp. 74–91.

Roark, E. 2008. "Using and Coming to Own: a Left-Proprietarian Treatment of the Just Use and Appropriation of Common Resources." University of Missouri-Columbia dissertation.

Rothbard, M. 1978. *For a New Liberty: the Libertarian Manifesto*. Revised edn. New York: Libertarian Review Foundation.

   1982. *The Ethics of Liberty*. Atlantic Highlands, NJ: Humanities Press.

Ryan, C. C. 1981. "Yours, Mine, and Ours: Property Rights and Individual Liberty," in *Reading Nozick: Essays on Anarchy, State, and Utopia*, ed. J. Paul. Totowa, NJ: Rowman and Littlefield, pp. 323–343.

Sanders, J. T. 1987. "Justice and the Initial Acquisition of Private Property," *Harvard Journal of Law and Public Policy*, 10, pp. 367–399.

Sartorius, R. 1984. "Persons and Property," in *Utility and Rights*, ed. R. Frey. Minneapolis: University of Minnesota Press, pp. 196–214.

Scanlon, T. M. 1981. "Nozick on Rights, Liberty, and Property," in *Reading Nozick: Essays on Anarchy, State, and Utopia*, ed. J. Paul. Totowa, NJ: Rowman and Littlefield, 107–129.

   1998. *What We Owe to Each Other*. Cambridge, MA: Harvard University Press.

Scheffler, S. 1976. "Natural Rights, Equality, and the Minimal State," *Canadian Journal of Philosophy*, 6, pp. 59–76.

   1985. "Agent-Centred Restrictions, Rationality, and the Virtues," *Mind*, 94, pp. 409–419.

Schmidtz, D. 1990a. "Justifying the State," *Ethics*, 101, pp. 89–102.

   1990b. *The Limits of Government*. Boulder: Westward Press.

   1992. "Rationality within Reason," *Journal of Philosophy*, 89, pp. 445–466.

   1995. *Rational Choice and Moral Agency*. Princeton: Princeton University Press.

   2002a. "How to Deserve," *Political Theory*, 30, pp. 774–799.

   2002b. "Equal Respect and Equal Shares," *Social Philosophy and Policy*, 19, pp. 244–274.

   2006. *Elements of Justice*. New York: Cambridge University Press.

   2007. "When Justice Matters," *Ethics*, 117, pp. 433–459.

   2008. *Person, Polis, Planet*. Oxford: Oxford University Press.

Schmidtz, D. and Brennan, J. 2010. *A Brief History of Liberty*. Oxford: Blackwell.

Scott, J. C. 1999. *Seeing Like a State: How Certain Schemes to Improve the Human Condition Have Failed*. New Haven: Yale University Press.

Sen, A. 1982. "Rights and Agency," *Philosophy and Public Affairs*, 11, pp. 3–39.

Shaw, W. H. 1999. *Contemporary Ethics: Taking Account of Utilitarianism.* Oxford: Blackwell.

Silverstein, M. 2000. "In Defense of Happiness: a Response to the Experience Machine," *Social Theory and Practice*, 26, pp. 279–300.

Simmons, A. J. 1979. *Moral Principles and Political Obligation.* Princeton: Princeton University Press.

1992. *The Lockean Theory of Rights.* Princeton: Princeton University Press.

2001. *Justification and Legitimacy; Essays on Rights and Obligations.* Cambridge: Cambridge University Press.

Singer, P. 1981. "The Right to Be Rich or Poor," in *Reading Nozick: Essays on Anarchy, State, and Utopia*, ed. J. Paul. Totowa, NJ: Rowman and Littlefield, pp. 37–53.

Smart, J. J. C. 1961. *An Outline of a System of Utilitarian Ethics.* Carlton: Melbourne University Press.

Smart, J. J. C. and Williams, B. 1973. *Utilitarianism: For and Against.* Cambridge: Cambridge University Press.

Smith, P. 1998. *Explaining Chaos.* Cambridge: Cambridge University Press.

Sobel, D. 2002. "Varieties of Hedonism," *Journal of Social Philosophy*, 33, pp. 240–256.

Sober, E. 2000. "Psychological Egoism," in *The Blackwell Guide to Ethical Theory*, ed. H. LaFollette. Malden: Blackwell, pp. 129–148.

Sober, E. and Wilson, D. S. 1998. *Unto Others: the Evolution and Psychology of Unselfish Behavior.* Cambridge, MA: Harvard University Press.

2000. "Precis of Unto Others," in *Evolutionary Origins of Morality: Cross-Disciplinary Perspectives*, ed. L. D. Katz. Bowling Green, OH: Imprint Academic, pp. 185–206

Steiner, H. 1981. "Nozick on Hart on the Right to Enforce," *Analysis*, 41, p. 50.

1982. "Vanishing Powers – A Reply to Wilson and Miller," *Analysis*, 42, pp. 97–98.

1994. *An Essay on Rights.* Oxford: Blackwell.

Stringham, E. (ed.) 2007. *Anarchy and the Law.* Oakland, CA: Independent Institute.

Sumner, L. W. 1996. *Welfare, Happiness, and Ethics.* Oxford: Oxford University Press.

Tannsjo, T. 1998. *Hedonistic Utilitarianism.* Edinburgh: Edinburgh University Press.

2007. "Narrow Hedonism," *Journal of Happiness Studies*, 8, pp. 79–80.

Teichman, J. and Evans, K. C. 1999. *Philosophy: a Beginner's Guide*. Oxford: Blackwell.

Thomson, J. J. 1976. "Killing, Letting Die, and the Trolley Problem," *Monist*, 59, pp. 204–217.

1981. "Some Ruminations on Rights," in *Reading Nozick: Essays on Anarchy, State, and Utopia*, ed. J. Paul. Totowa, NJ: Rowman and Littlefield, pp. 130–147.

1985. "The Trolley Problem," *The Yale Law Journal*, 94, pp. 1395–1415.

1990. *The Realm of Rights*. Cambridge, MA: Harvard University Press.

Timmons, M. 2002. *Moral Theory: an Introduction*. Lanham, MD: Rowman & Littlefield.

Ullmann-Margalit, E. 1978. "Invisible-hand Explanations," *Synthese*, 39, pp. 263–291.

Vallentyne, P. 1998. "Critical Notice of G.A. Cohen's *Self-Ownership, Freedom, and Equality*," *Canadian Journal of Philosophy*, 28, pp. 609–626.

2000. "Left-Libertarianism: a Primer," in *Left Libertarianism and Its Critics: the Contemporary Debate*, ed. P. Vallentyne and H. Steiner. New York: Palgrave, pp. 1–20.

2006. "Robert Nozick: *Anarchy, State, and Utopia*," in *The Twentieth Century: Quine and After*, ed. J. Shand. Chesham: Acumen, pp. 86–103.

2007. "On Original Appropriation," in *Liberty, Games and Contracts: Jan Narveson and the Defence of Libertarianism*, ed. M. Murray. Aldershot: Ashgate Press, pp. 173–178.

2009. "Left-Libertarianism and Liberty," in *Debates in Political Philosophy*, eds. T. Christiano and J. Christman. Oxford: Blackwell Publishers, pp. 137–151.

Vallentyne, P. and Steiner, H. (eds.) 2000a. *The Origins of Left Libertarianism: an Anthology of Historical Writings*. New York: Palgrave.

2000b. *Left Libertarianism and Its Critics: the Contemporary Debate*. New York: Palgrave.

Vallentyne, P., Steiner, H. and Otsuka, M. 2005. "Why Left-Libertarianism Isn't Incoherent, Indeterminate, or Irrelevant: a Reply to Fried," *Philosophy and Public Affairs*, 33, pp. 201–215.

Van Creveld, M. 1999. *The Rise and Decline of the State*. Cambridge: Cambridge University Press.

Vaughn, K. I. 1994. *Austrian Economics in America: the Migration of a Tradition*. Cambridge: Cambridge University Press.

Vogel Carey, T. 1998. "The Invisible-hand of Natural Selection and Vice Versa," *Biology and Philosophy*, 13, pp. 427–442.

Voorhoeve, A. 2009. *Conversations on Ethics*. Oxford: Oxford University Press.

Waldron, J. 1976. "Enough and as Good Left for Others," *Philosophical Quarterly*, 29, pp. 319–328.

Weiss, C. H. 1998. *Evaluation*. Upper Saddle River, NJ: Prentice Hall.

Williams, B. 1973. "A Critique of Utilitarianism," in *Utilitarianism: For and Against*, ed. J. J. C. Smart and B. Williams. Cambridge: Cambridge University Press.

Wilson, P. 1981. "Steiner on Nozick on the Right to Enforce," *Analysis*, 41, pp. 219–221.

Wolff, J. 1991. *Robert Nozick*. Stanford, CA: Stanford University Press.

Zaitchik, A. 1977. "Trammel on Positive and Negative Duties," *Personalist*, 58, pp. 93–96.

Zwolinski, M. 2008. "The Separateness of Persons and Liberal Theory," *Journal of Value Inquiry*, 42, pp. 147–165.

INDEX